SNORRI KRISTJANSSON

# O. HENRY

Also by David Stuart

*Alan Watts*

# O. HENRY

### A Biography of
## William Sydney Porter

**DAVID STUART**

Scarborough House/Publishers

This book is dedicated to Helga Berliner, who sacrificed her personal copy of *Alan Watts* in a good cause.

Scarborough House/*Publishers*
Chelsea, MI 48118

FIRST PUBLISHED IN 1990

Text designed by Louis A. Ditizio

**Library of Congress Cataloging-in-Publication Data**

Stuart, David.
  O. Henry: a biography of William Sydney Porter.

  Bibliography: p.
  Includes index.
  1. Henry. O., 1862–1910—Biography.  2. Authors.
American—19th century—Biography.  I. Title.
PS2649.P5Z844    1990    813′.52  [B]        85-40242
ISBN 0-8128-3057-1

# Contents

# Photographs

# Preface

This book is a biography of O. Henry, not to be confused with a critical study of the man's works, which has seemed to be the preoccupation of virtually all who have written about him in the past. I have tried in these pages to stick to the man's life, and I have briefed his stories as little as possible. Even so, I know that some will believe I have, in at least one chapter, rather overdone the briefing. If so, it is because I felt it necessary to give at one place a feeling for what O. Henry was writing, and yet, as is the problem with writing about almost any author, the temptation is to fall into the critical mode.

In O. Henry's case, the temptation is even stronger, because his stories were so definitely autobiographical. As I have noted in the text and will not repeat here, several students have traced chapter and verse of story and fact.

There are marvelous stories that revolve around O. Henry, such as that of the making of the play *Alias Jimmy Valentine,* which had a long, successful, and financially rewarding run on Broadway. But O. Henry did not write the play; he tried, and failed, and sold his rights to the very successful short story to a Broadway producer for a pittance, and the story of the play from that point on has nothing to do with O. Henry. All that might be said about his relationship with it was that he went to see it, he liked it, and when someone suggested that he ought to be envious of its success since he was cut out of it, he said, "No, I am delighted that they were able to make it work." As I have tried to indicate in these pages, money meant nothing to him, except as he put it, "to purchase commodities offered in the marts." He gave money away by the thousands of dollars, and he died broke; at the end when he put his personal possessions down on the table in the hospital, he had twenty-three cents in his pockets.

The financial success of O. Henry, never enormous, was created after his death by Harry Peyton Steger of Doubleday, who was O. Henry's literary executor, and as such did the best he could with the properties in behalf of Margaret Porter, O. Henry's heir. Doubleday has ever remained faithful to O. Henry's memory, and in the 1980s continues to publish annually the O. Henry collection of best short stories and to give an O. Henry short story prize. They have also kept the O. Henry works, or most of them, in print. That, however, as one Doubleday executive told me, is not so much charitable as an indication that O. Henry still sells well. "Any book that doesn't sell a certain number of copies a year doesn't last long around here," the Doubleday executive told me. So somewhere O. Henry is still being read.

Harry Steger tried to do more. He went to enormous pains to track down letters and memorabilia, even old and long-forgotten copies of *The Rolling Stone,* O. Henry's short-lived newspaper. He was going to write O. Henry's biography, but he died before he could do more than amass much of the material. He did manage to put together fourteen volumes of O. Henry's letters and works, but the official biography was left to C. Alphonso Smith, a boyhood friend of O. Henry's who had become a college professor. Smith's biography was published by Doubleday, Page and Co. in 1916. It did not please the O. Henry heirs, largely because it virtually ignored the trial and imprisonment of the author, leaving the implication that he was guilty as charged. The material was all available. The court record must then have been extant (it has since disappeared), and many of the people involved were still alive. The reason for Professor Smith's attitude seems to be his sharing of O. Henry's feeling that any discussion of the matter could not but reflect badly on the author. Or, perhaps, Professor Smith secretly believed that O. Henry was guilty of the crime. What has emerged in recent years, however, is the indication that there was no crime insofar as O. Henry was concerned, but a technical violation of the banking laws, for which O. Henry was chosen by the bankers to take the rap because he was the teller at the time, and as such he was bonded and publicly liable.

I believe there was a crime, never revealed, which involved the officers of the bank, the violation of their fiduciary responsibility, and their manipulation of the bank's resources for their own selfish ends. It had nothing to do with an employee as low as O. Henry.

The case interested me enough to cause me to look into the records of the financial examinations of the First National Bank of Austin, as kept by the U.S. Office of the Controller of the Currency. What I discovered was that Vice President Frank Hamilton and others were playing fast and loose with the money of the First National Bank, and that for some time Hamilton and Cashier R. J. Brackenridge held highly illegal and immoral overdrafts of thousands of dollars, which they later converted to slightly less illegal loans, which they finally liquidated. Someone should have gone to jail for what was being done to the First National Bank of Austin, Texas, in 1894 and 1895, but it should not have been William Sydney Porter. He, stunned by the whole affair, learned for the first time that the world is a hard and selfish place. The knowledge changed the life of this naive and innocent young man. It caused him to create the surrogate character, the author known as O. Henry, who wrote so that William Sydney Porter could live in the shadows of New York, and slowly drink himself to death.

My conception of the duality of character is such that I have separated the man by the use of names. As a boy he was Will Porter, son of an alcoholic doctor who was the son of an alcoholic inventor and mechanic. The young man's love of liquor began in Texas and by the time of his imprisonment was notable enough that he was put down on the prison record as "intemperate in habits." He went into the Ohio federal penitentiary as William Sydney Porter, and there he lost his identity. He became Federal Prisoner No. 30664, and I have so called him in that section of the book. Federal Prisoner No. 30664 was left behind when the sentence ended, but the old William Sydney Porter did not come out of prison. Certainly the man who emerged was still known by that name to his daughter and her grandparents and to the few people with whom he kept contact after the Austin days. But the real character who emerged was the cynical, embittered author named O. Henry who would go through the rest of his life avoiding publicity and the limelight because he feared exposure as a jailbird. O. Henry was only forty-eight years old when he died and was at the peak of his success as a story writer. True, some critics had already tired of his insistence on writing in the colloquial dialects of the day. In fact, he was bedeviled by this criticism from the beginning, and it is true that now that the New York Irish have lost those broad accents from the old country, and radio and television and the motion pictures have more or less homogenized the American language, the reading of O. Henry is sometimes difficult. The New York stories are easiest, being written usually in more basic English than the tales of the American South, the West, and of Central America. But accent is not the basic reason for the general abandonment of O. Henry. Nobody reads Bret Harte these days, or Mark Twain, other than the Adventures of Tom Sawyer and Huckleberry Finn, reading which is finished by the high school level. Nobody reads de Maupassant, or Charles Dickens either, and these were two writers with whom O. Henry was constantly compared in his lifetime. As a writer for more than twenty-five years, I might almost venture to say that nobody reads, period. That is exaggeration, pardonable, I hope because of the nature of my profession.

For a time after his death, O. Henry enjoyed a renewed vogue. Although most people did not recognize it, a whole series of motion pictures was made about one of O. Henry's characters, the happy-go-lucky Mexican bandido, The Cisco Kid. Other biographers have called attention to *Alias Jimmy Valentine,* as the first of a whole series of stories, plays, and films built around a gentleman burglar. I think that is going a little far, but *Alias Jimmy Valentine* certainly did have its effect on theater and the literary arts.

That is about as far as I care to go in delineating the literary worth of O. Henry, that and saying as so many have before, that he wrote the best stories about New York City that have ever been written by anyone, and that his stories give a very good picture of life in the city in the period from 1900 to 1910, a picture that cannot be secured elsewhere.

Is that enough to create a permanent literary reputation? There is a lot more. Texans will tell you that his stories about the Southwest are "a danged sight better" than anything he wrote about New York. Students of Latin America will tell you that his picture of Americans in the banana republics of Central America is straight truth, much better than the descriptions drawn by Richard Harding Davis.

But I am falling into the trap I said I would avoid. This is the story of a gentle soul whose life was irremediably damaged by selfish "friends" and the machinations of an implacable government; it is also the story of his life in prison, and the emancipation of a writer.

"Someday," he told Editor Robert Davis, "I will tell you how I got the block of time that made it possible for me to become a fiction writer." He never did tell Davis that tale, but I have told it here. All the rest, the story of the stories, and the postmortem successes of O. Henry belong in another book along with the tales he told so well.

David Stuart

# 1

# The Blackest Day

It was a cold February day in Austin, Texas. The courtroom of Federal District Judge T. S. Maxey was silent. The court reporter yawned into his desk and fiddled with his pens. The clerk, sitting below the bench, shuffled papers. The bailiffs sat on their chairs at the entrances, arms folded, and tried to keep their eyes open.

At one table, U.S. District Attorney R. U. Culberson whispered to his assistant and left the courtroom. He was hoping that it would soon be over, for of all the prosecutions he had undertaken in his life, this one was among his most regretted. It was apparent that the root of it all was political. In fact, Culberson had not wanted to prosecute at all but had been forced into action by a series of letters written to the attorney general of the United States by a demon national bank examiner who was trying to make a reputation for himself at the expense of anyone at all.

That person was Federal Bank Examiner B. F. Gray, who had first recommended the prosecution of the accused more than a year before. When a federal grand jury had refused to indict the accused, Gray had raised holy hell in Washington, bringing accusations of malfeasance against the district attorney, R. U. Culberson, to the point that Culberson had written a series of letters to the attorney general defending himself. Oddly enough in the exchange, amid his charges ("I believe the U.S. District Attorney to be either incompetent or very indolent."[1]) Bank Examiner Gray had admitted his own peculiar role in this case from the empanelment of the first federal grand jury:

> After the Grand Jury was empaneled an officer of the court who was a friend of mine said to me that we had a good jury with the exception of one man, and, he added, "I am afraid that one man will spoil the whole jury."

The man referred to was J. W. Thornton, a nephew of the present cashier of the First National Bank of Austin, Dr. R. J. Brackenridge, and he was at one time years ago teller of the same bank. My informant stated that he was discharged from the bank because he, in connection with others, looted that institution of about $40,000. The former U.S. District Attorney was in possession of this knowledge but took no action because it was barred or about to be barred by the statute of limitations.[2]

Gray's friend had been right in one sense: Thornton had explained the manner of operation of the First National Bank of Austin to his fellow grand jurors, and they had agreed with him that the whole bank operation was so sloppy and sleazy that the teller certainly could not be held to account for it, and they had refused to indict.[3]

Thus, Bank Examiner Gray grew heated when he saw that no one was being prosecuted for the looting of the bank. Now, in 1898, he had a chance to make a glaring example of the First National Bank of Austin to show all banks in his Fort Worth district that they must adhere to the letter and the spirit of the banking laws. Small matter that the man they had chosen to prosecute had not been one of those looting the bank. He was "responsible" because he was the teller and the senior bonded employee of the bank, the one person easiest to prosecute for any apparent wrongdoing.

And so Gray had gone after this teller, hammer and tongs, and nothing had stood in his way until he forced the federal district attorney to seek a new grand jury. Gray also made sure that he was on hand to testify as an expert witness before the grand jury and that he was also engaged as an expert witness at the time of the trial.[4] In his testimony he had proved beyond doubt that there were irregularities at the bank. He had also conveniently said nothing about the fact that the bank had been looted steadily by its officers for nine years, the last few of those years under his own myopic view.[5] As the person with the formal responsibility, the teller would be held fully responsible; it was a simple as that, and the fact that everyone familiar with this bank knew who the real thieves were was unimportant to Examiner Gray. He might convict the teller, he was very doubtful of convicting the real criminals in an Austin court. He waited now, hopeful of his victory.

Also waiting, at the counsel's table were R. H. Ward and Ashby S. James, two prominent members of the bar of Austin, who had undertaken the defense of the accused for far less than their usual fees, because like nearly everyone else in Austin, they believed the accused to be a person of good character and morally incapable of theft of dishonesty.

Also in the court awaiting the verdict, was the accused himself, in his mid-thirties, well dressed, with a shock of unruly hair and a mustache. He would have been called handsome, save for the limpness of hair and mustache, the deep shadows beneath his eyes, and the sense of total resignation, of uncaring, on his face. For as the defense counsel knew only too well, the accused had believed from the moment this trial began that he would be convicted; the movers and shakers were all on the other side. He had refused to do anything to help his own defense, he would not even go over the bank papers with his attorneys.[6] For, he knew, he said, that all concerned would lie, and their reputations were great and his was small. From the beginning he had said that he had no chance of acquittal with the forces arrayed against him. Sure enough, the bank officials had come to testify against them, and some one—certainly not Bank Examiner Gray—had suggested that perhaps they were the malefactors and not the man on trial.

Just over an hour ago, the judge had given the case to the jury, instructed them in the law that covered the crime of embezzlement—for the accused was charged with embezzling about eight hundred dollars from the First National Bank of Austin on two occasions. Examiner Gray, seeking to tie up loose ends for all the missing funds at the bank, had first tried to get indictments covering more than $5,000 in embezzlement, but even his second grand jury had balked at that, and in the end, the case had come down to what was figuratively peanuts in terms of the $160,000 that had been written off by the First National Bank of Austin in the past nine years as "losses."[7]

So the young man waited, hopeless. But he did not wait long. The jury was out for scarcely an hour, when the foreman called the bailiffs and told them to inform Judge Maxey that they had a verdict.

The judge came out of his chambers in his black robes and settled himself on the bench. The little knot of spectators (the accused had specifically asked all his friends *not* to attend his trial), sat up and paid attention. One or two, who had lingered in the hall, came in the doors and a bailiff closed them. From the jury room, the jury filed out into the courtroom and took their places in the jury box. The foreman looked at the judge, who nodded, and the foreman then stood up.

"Have you reached a verdict?"

"Yes, your honor, we have."

The foreman paused. The judge looked quizzical. The foreman cleared his throat and spoke again.

"We find the defendant guilty of the indictments as charged."

Judge Maxey did not look happy and District Attorney Culberson, who had slipped into the room, looked wretched. The defense counsel looked miserable. The spectators looked sad, save one, who looked victorious. Only

17

the defendant seemed unaroused. He did not look as though he even heard, and if he had heard, that it mattered at all. He did not look as though he was in the same room as these people who were pronouncing his fate.

And thus, in that almost empty courtroom in Austin, Texas, on that February day, ended the life of a newspaper journalist, widower, and father, and thus began the ordeal of a man who would become one of America's greatest writers.

# 2

# Boy, Not Poet

In the English literary tradition of biography, from which American practice stemmed, and which was followed until the second half of the twentieth century, much was made of the ancestry of the subject. The quite proper English concept accepted that where a man came from, and particularly his family stock, indicated a good deal about his character and manner of thought. Moreover, that background would tell where he would probably end up, with his head impaling a coronet or a pike impaling his head. And thus begins this tale of intrigue, triumph, and tragedy but with the caveat that in the America of the late nineteenth century one class tradition had been cheerfully left behind and the new one had not yet developed. So the fact is that it was much more significant to the story of O. Henry—William Sydney Porter (born Sidney)—that he was born less than two weeks after the second Battle of Bull Run, and a week before the bloody battle of Antietam than that the more pretentious of the clan claimed relationship to the Royal Stuarts of Britain. The date was September 11, 1862. The place was the sleepy town of Greensboro in Guilford County, North Carolina; all of which meant that William Sydney Porter was a Civil War baby, and his boyhood was spent in the shadow of Black Reconstruction, which stamped his character and his writing much more firmly than any heritage he received from his ancestors, some of whom were, indeed, men and women of substance and intellect. His mother's father was William Swaim, editor of the Greensboro *Patriot,* and a southern gentleman of the old school, except that he detested slavery with the vim of a Hinton Rowan Helper, and he helped run a society for the gradual emancipation of the blacks.

O. Henry's grandmother, Mrs. Abia Shirley Swaim, created some confusion inside the family tree when Editor Swaim died, by marrying another man named Swaim, Lyndon Swaim this time. The confusion was furthered when Lyndon Swaim succeeded William Swaim as editor of the *Patriot.*

The Swaims were North Carolina gentry, although not universally beloved because of their stand on slavery. From this side of the family came southern respectability, which in the years after the Civil War was about all that most of the old southern families had to tie to. From the Porter side came other attributes: a love of strong drink and a curiosity and wanderlust that was to create the atmosphere for most of O. Henry's finest stories. The progenitor here was O. Henry's paternal grandfather, Sidney Porter, who wandered down to North Carolina from Bristol, Connecticut, in 1823, as agent for the Jerome Clock Company. Those Jeromes were the American ancestors of another great man, Winston Spencer Churchill. But the Jerome factor, whatever it was, did not rub off on their salesman. Sidney Porter was a big, jolly man with a prophet's whiskers, and some then hidden bad habits. He attracted the attention of a young lady named Mary Worth in nearby Center, North Carolina, a haven of Quakers, and passed the tests of his putative father-in-law as "a man of strictly upright character and worthy of his daughter's hand."

The Worths had reason for their pride: Mary's brother married a Daniel of Virginia and later became governor of North Carolina.

But, despite his connections, Sidney Porter did not prosper in the South, and ended up running a carriage and machinery repair shop in Greensboro. It was now, about the late 1830s, when Sidney was occasionally hailed into court for public drunkenness. The family was held together within the Greensboro establishment by his wife and her connections.

The feckless Sidney Porter fathered a number of children, among them Algernon Sidney, who decided he would become a doctor. There were two ways to become a doctor in the North Carolina at the time: one was to go to a prestigious medical school such as those in Boston or Baltimore. Another way, far more commonly pursued, was to learn materia medica from a doctor, a bit of chemistry and biology from books and lectures, and practical dosing from a druggist. That was Algernon Sidney Porter's route. He went to work in the drugstore of Dr. David P. Weir, the town physician who was also principal of the Edgeworth Female Seminary and the most celebrated figure in the town. Since Algernon Porter was a small fellow, never topping five feet six inches in height, he hastened to grow a beard to give him dignity, and it did. By the time the Civil War began he was proficient enough at the doctoring profession to work at the Confederate army hospital established at the Edgeworth Seminary, and saw off legs.[1]


MOST OF THIS history, of course, was ancient, occurring a score of years before the emergence of little Will Porter. In later years his compelling memory was of the Shirley branch of the family, which came from Virginia and produced Grandma Abia. Somewhere back in that line was the original Abia Shirley, O. Henry was pleased to recall, who had scandalized her whole House of Stuart by running off with a Catholic priest. Now, there, said the man who at the time was America's prime storyteller, there was a story for you. But as with so much of O. Henry that little anecdote is misleading, for there never was a man who put less stock in the fripperies of ancestry and more in the inevitabilities of character, American character, shaped by the warps and woofs and winds and waters of the American shore as was this boy of the postbellum South.

Among the family of Porters, Worths, Shirleys, and Swaims, by far the greatest influence on O. Henry was Grandma Ruth Worth Porter, wife of the former clock salesman and toper. When she was forty-three he died, leaving her with a mortgaged house and seven children. She opened a boarding house, and here Dr. Sidney Porter lived until 1858, when he married Mary Swaim. The young people then set up their own establishment, and three children were born: the first son being Shirley Worth Porter, the second William Sidney Porter, and the third David Weir Porter. In 1865, when Mary Swaim Porter died, the doctor and his three sons moved back into the boarding house with his mother and there they remained during the days of the boyhood of O. Henry, or Will Porter, as he was always to be known about town.

So it was Grandma Porter who shaped O. Henry's life as much as any female family can do. As for the doctor, he was an amiable and capable man in his profession. Many Greensboroites swore by him to the end, saying that "you got better as soon as he entered the room." And in the early years he was the epitome of the country doctor: "Honest, high-toned and generous, rain or shine, sick or well, he would visit the poorest family in the country."

Joe Reece, editor of the Greensboro *Daily Record,* recalled Dr. Porter with affection:

"Everybody in those days, when they got hurt, made for Doctor Porter's office as straight as a June shad in fly-time."

His best recollection was of a huge black man who had been drinking more than he ought to have, who had been cut badly down the back in a street fight.

21

"He passed me making straight for Doctor Porter's office and yelling like a steam piano.

"When I got to the little office, I'll be john squizzled if Alge Porter didn't have that darky down on the floor. He was sitting on him and sewing him up and lecturing to him about the evils of intemperance all at the same time.

"He lectured sort o' unsteadily on that theme, but nobody could beat his sewing."[2]

What Editor Reece implied was true: Doctor Porter was given to a little drink now and then, and as with his father before him, the habit grew as time passed. Dr. Porter also had an innate dislike for money and its problems. He did not send bills. It was understood, as with many country doctors, that the bills should be paid when the patients had "a little extra," but in the 1870s there was little extra in North Carolina. Very little money stuck to Dr. Porter's fingers, and what came in was largely at the insistence of Grandma Porter. Those who could settle up were reminded at the end of the year by Grandma Porter, and those who could but would not sometimes became the objects of her wrath. But as for the doctor, he remained benign. In this age when industrialization was reshaping America, Dr. Porter took an interest in inventing. He began work on a perpetual motion machine, claimed he had solved the problem, and built a water wheel that almost—but not quite— worked. It was, he said, just a matter of a few adjustments. He started work on a flying machine and on a horseless carriage that would be driven by steam. He said that one of his inventions would soon solve all the family financial problems. He kept his inventions under the bed for several years, until Grandma Porter lugged them out to the barn as a commentary. So the barn became the doctor's haven during clement weather.

It was also said that as the years went by Dr. Porter spent more time in the barn, with perpetual motion and the bottle, and Grandma Porter actually presided over the fading medical practice. Finally the doctor's failings became so noticeable that another doctor, James K. Hall, was persuaded to settle in Greensboro and soon absorbed most of the practice, leaving Dr. Porter happily undisturbed. Unfortunately none of the inventions revolutionized American science or industry.

Grandma Porter and Aunt Lina managed to hold the family together with their relentless energies, spent in sewing, managing the boarding house, and teaching.

As for education, postwar Greensboro did not offer much. The family, particularly the Swaim side, had been well educated, by and large, and so were the Worths. But the poverty of the South in the years of Reconstruction precluded much thought about education outside the community. Given the time, and the conditions, O. Henry was lucky to have in Evalina Porter an aunt who was highly educated. She had attended the Edgeworth Female Seminary, an advanced institution for the teaching of young women, established in the happy antebellum years but, like so much else, lost in the war. When the Porter children came into the boarding house to live, Grandma Porter and Aunt Evalina Maria Porter took them in charge. Five-year-old brother Shirley, whom everyone called Shelly, showed himself virtually impervious to book learning. Three-year-old O. Henry—Will—showed himself to be quite the opposite, and as soon as Miss Lina, as Aunt Evalina was universally known, could cram the alphabet into him he was ready to begin the reading that would be his education. Miss Lina opened a one-room schoolhouse for what remained of the white gentry of Greensboro, and here O. Henry was educated until he was fifteen years old. By that time he had the foundation in English literature and languages (at which he was very good) that would seem to show up full-blown in his prose a quarter of a century later.

Later, long after Will Porter had cast the dust of Greensboro off his shoes and had become O. Henry, he confided to a friend that his childhood years were not very happy, at least within the household. Miss Lina was a hard taskmistress at school, and at home she showed little preference for her nephew over other scholars. Although she told others of her fondness for Will, he did not get that impression. Grandma Porter was too busy running her boarding house, sewing factory, and the doctor's medical affairs to pay much attention to the children. O. Henry said he never got along at all with elder brother Shelly, and his younger brother, David, died before O. Henry had much to remember him by.

That is not to say, however, that Will Porter was a lonely or a moody boy. Quite to the contrary.

Will was three years old when the Civil War ended and the carpetbaggers and scalawags took over the government of North Carolina. What the boy learned of politics he learned from listening to the casual conversations of his elders and the mutual reports exchanged with his contemporaries. The bete noir of the Greensboro of O. Henry's youth was Albion Winegar Tourgee, a well-meaning carpetbagger elected judge by manipulated black votes. The judge finally tired of the charade and exposed Black Reconstruction as "A Fool's Errand" in a novel that was quite popular in North and South in the 1880s. That was after the "deal" done in Washington in the election of 1876 had given the presidency to Republican Rutherford B. Hayes and control of the South's political and economic life back to the whites. Ol' Judge Tourgee lived in a big house sheltered almost as a fortress by immense trees, set back

23

from the dirt road, and popularly believed by the seven-year-old set to be haunted by Indians, dead soldiers, and horrendous spirits. O. Henry scarcely ever set eyes on the judge, but he believed him to be the epitome of evil, as was the judgment of his elders. There were many other haunted houses in the district, big, white frame places abandoned by the once wealthy planters who could no longer afford to live in them. These and the woods and streams that lay just outside the limits of the town were the playgrounds of the boys of Greensboro. There was virtually no organized amusement in this town of 3,000 people, but there was also very little supervision of lazy afternoons, and much time for fishing and nibbling on the sweet stems of long grass, and idle reading in the shade.[3]

One of his friends was Tom Tate, who later recalled:

"My first remembrance was of a small freckled boy of five or six, the freckles down to his feet. Our first meeting was on one of those warm days in early spring. In straw hat and rolled up Holland breeches he was wading barefoot in a cool, willow-shaded little stream in front of our house. I stood on the bank watching him envious to my toes . . . my mother had warned me it was too early to go barefoot."

Tate and young Will Porter started school as desk mates and were soon boon companions.

The heroes of Will Porter and his chums were the Ku Klux Klansmen, who met in those days (or nights, to be specific) at the old Presbyterian High School. From there they often started out on wild rides across the night countryside to burn crosses and terrify the blacks who had been told by the Northerners that they were to be the equal of the whites in the South. Will and his friends dressed up in sheets and paper conical hat and masks cut for them by one of the approving mothers and charged out of the shadows to frighten black townspeople, most of whom reacted with suitable "fright" to delight their wicked little hearts. But playing Ku Klux Klan had its limitations. A more soul-satisfying game was Indians. Tom Tate's father owned a large flock of turkeys and a "fine passel" of hogs. The turkeys supplied feathers for the young Indians' war bonnets and the shafts of their arrows. The heads of the arrows were real, culled from local battlegrounds and Indian burial places. There were so many Indian arrowheads available that any boy who did not have a big collection was either lazy or blind. Tom Tate and Will Porter and their chums went into the woods to cut hickory sticks for bows and arrows and bound the feathers and the arrowheads to the weapons. From the berries on the edges of the farm fields they made dyes and painted themselves up as proper warriors. Then the boys seized their weapons and took out after the "deer" and the "grizzly bears" who ran away squealing most satisfactorily to

24

provide moving targets for the brave bowmen. Occasionally one of the homemade arrows would stick in the side of a Poland China or a Berkshire, and then there would be a furious chase, to catch the hog and pull out the arrow lest it be discovered by Tom Tate's father, whose attitude toward the hunt can be imagined.[4]

On the right sort of days, sunny but not hot and perhaps with a pleasant breeze, Will liked to go to the top of the piney hill overlooking old Caldwell's Pond, and lie down with a book. Best of all, of course, was a dime novel, if he could get his hands on a new one. Between them, Will Porter and Tom Tate boasted the biggest private collection of dime novels in town. Only the hotel cigar stand had more. *Red Rover, The Wood Demon, The Miller and His Men,* and *Three-fingered Jack* all passed through their hands, along with scores of unremembered heroes. By the time the young O. Henry was ten years old he had imbibed so deeply of this heady stuff that he could concoct his own tales of the genre. The boys gathered round the pond in the afternoons sometimes and made up stories. Will's were always the best.

On Friday nights Miss Lina held "story telling" at the Porter house. Will loved to tell stories about knights in shining armor.[5]

Out of this came a game invented by Will Porter and Tom Tate. Their school friends were divided into two societies, the Brickbats and the Union Jacks (after a story Will had read in an English boys' magazine). Each club built up an armory of wooden swords, shields, spears, battleaxes, and other knightly appurtenances. These were secreted against parental seizure in a disused shed of the old Edgeworth seminary (which had burned down in 1872). On Friday nights the knights emerged, to roam the edges of the town, lurking in the shadows of the great trees, careful not to penetrate too far into the haunted corners, and seek adventure and derring-do, calling lustily to each other:

"Hark ye, Sir Mordred."

and

"Zounds, what sound betrayeth yon poltroon, Sir Val?"

and other most satisfying exclamations of feudal fervor that delighted boyish souls.

All went well until some ghost stirred in the shadows. It might be a fox, or a town dog, or even a pair of lovers hiding away in the deep of the wood, but a ghost was a ghost was a ghost, and many a wooden sword and buckler was discarded beneath a shady oak tree in the hasty departure of the heroes bent on finding safety, light, and familiar faces.[6]

The hi-jinks of youth were never ending. One day when school was over and the boys were playing follow the leader, J. D. Smith followed his leader in a jump out the classroom window, to fall and dislocate his ankle. Will and his brother Shelly carried Smith to Grandma Porter's house, and Dr. Porter was summoned from his contemplation of perpetual motion in the barn to reset the joint. Shelly held J. D. down and Will grabbed the affected leg, and the doctor began twisting the foot. J. D. began to yell, and to cover it up Will began to sing a song he had learned from a dime magazine story:

> If you don't stop fooling with my Lula
> I'll tell you what I'll do;
> I'll feel around your heart with a razor
> And I'll cut your liver out too.[7]

It was the first time J. D. had heard Will Porter sing, and he was impressed enough to remember it and also to stop yelling. In a moment the joint was back in place.

Perhaps because he felt so little tied to home, Will Porter was a fearless boy. When he was about twelve he and J. D. used to hang around the house of the town dentist, whose son was the most fascinating character they knew. He had run away to sea, joined a New England whaler, and come home after a long voyage to tell lies about his adventures in catching whales in the dangerous but romantic Pacific Ocean. So impressed were J. D. and Will that they decided they, too, would go to sea, and pooling their available funds, one morning before dawn they caught a ride with an eastbound drayman, and set out for the Carolina shore. Their money gave out at Raleigh after they had bought a twenty-five-cent meal. Suddenly life on the open wave lost its attractions, and the thought of a good home-cooked dinner gained new ones.

But how to get home with no money?

At the train depot, they saw a conductor at whom they had waved a thousand times when he came through Greensboro, and he told them they could ride on top of the caboose and work the brakes, which were controlled by a wheel attached to a long rod that ran down to the wheel carriage. One toot meant put the brakes on. Two toots meant take them off.

Did they understand?

Sure, said Will.

So they climbed up on top of the last car, and the train began to move. It was a lengthy train, and it was not very long in time before the engine disappeared around a bend. The train seemed to pick up speed. The boxcars rattled and the scenery sped by at an awesome rate, the cars bucking and clanking and threatening, as far as the boys could see, to jump the rails at any moment and head into the forest. Both boys became petrified with fright. Will lay down on the top of the car and began to say his prayers:

26

Now I lay me down to sleep
I pray the Lord my soul to keep . . .

J. D. closed his eyes and waited for the end—when their boxcar would head off into the woods and smack into a tree. But the train just kept going, and the clickety clack assumed a steady rhythm, and the boys looked up, saw they were still alive, and grinned at each other.

"If you don't stop fooling with my Lula . . ." sang Will Porter, with bravado,

"I'll tell you what I'll do . . ."

Home again for supper, not even missed by a busy household, it was time to plot new adventures for the morrow.[8]

The early adventures were often prompted by the dime novel, as noted, but as Will Porter grew older, his reading became more eclectic, guided by Miss Lina. Ghost Stories were favorites for a time. Then came Alexander Dumas and Victor Hugo. He devoured the gaudy *Arabian Nights.* From there he went to the novels of Sir Walter Scott, William Makepeace Thackeray, Bulwer Lytton, Willie Collins, He was anything but the casual reader, picking up an author, devouring his work, and then abandoning it to go on to another. He read Charles Dickens and paused to try to put together his own ending to *The Mystery of Edwin Drood,* Dickens's unfinished tale. He was fascinated by Charles Reade's *The Cloister and the Hearth,* in which even as a beardless youth he saw material for dozens of short stories. For already O. Henry was writing stories (which he discarded almost immediately), and he knew that it was the short story that he wished to attack above all literary forms.

In Miss Lina's attempt to bring more than the Three R's to the pupils of her one-room schoolhouse, she offered instruction in drawing, which she had learned at Edgeworth. Will Porter was an apt student, so apt that by the time he was twelve he had surpassed his instructor in skill.[9]

One of Will's relatives was Tom Worth, a cartoonist for *Harper's Weekly.* There was inspiration! Soon Will became quite adapt at rude cartooning, and his caricatures were faithful enough to evoke guffaws from his audience, although somewhat "busy" in attention to detail. In the evenings the boys of the neighborhood would assemble on the porch of one of the young women of the town, and sit, whittling, telling stories and cracking jokes as the moon came up. Later, the favorite place was "Miss Sally's" porch. Miss Sally was really Sara Lindsay Coleman, who lived in Weaverville, near Asheville, but came to visit her mother's relatives during the summers of Will Porter's adolescence, and he was smitten with her. She had a guitar and could sing. When the boys came it was seldom long before the guitar was out and the chorus had begun.

Will Porter would sit on the steps and sometimes he would sketch. He drew a sketch of the burning of the Edgeworth seminary, which he had witnessed. He drew a sketch of Judge Tourgee with his carpetbag flying north again after the compromise of 1876 had restored white supremacy to the South. Family and friends admired his caricatures and predicted great things for him. But what he needed, Grandma Porter and Aunt Lina knew, was education.

"I would have given my eyes for a college education," O. Henry said later, and at the time Miss Lina and his grandmother talked about the possibility of college for this bookish youth. But it was not in his stars; there simply was not enough money in the family to afford it, and such rich men as Colonel Carr, of Durham, the founder of the Bull Durham tobacco company and educational philanthropist, were all too few in the impoverished southland.[10]

Instead, when Will Porter was fifteen, he went to work in the drugstore of his uncle, Clark Porter, opposite the old Benbow Hotel on Elm Street. Will Porter was general handyman and clerk, with an eye to learning the pharmaceutical business. Thus had his father, Dr. Algernon, begun his career. Will dutifully swept out the store mornings and evenings, ran errands, tended the counter, and learned to mix simple compounds under the eye of his uncle.

The sketching earned Will Porter a reputation as a local wag. It also earned him an educational opportunity. Colonel Robert Bingham, a relative of the Porters by marriage, was superintendent of the Bingham School at Mebane, North Carolina. He heard about Will's abilities as a cartoonist and offered a scholarship, board and room, if Will would in turn be the school artist. But so poor were the Porters in the late 1870s that they could not afford the uniforms, books, and travel expenses to send Will away, so the offer was rejected.[11] By 1881, when Will was nineteen years old, "The grind in the drugstore was agony to me." Everything was predictable. The sign painter who kept his shop behind the drugstore came in with a jug and liquid refreshment to head to the back room for ice and glasses. Doctor Hall came in several times each day to pick up prescriptions for his patients. In the mornings the mayor and the other dignitaries assembled in the drugstore to talk over the morning paper and the gossip of the day. It was almost always the same, people, places, things. A dog fight on Elm Street was enough to create conversation for two days.

By 1881 Will Porter was thoroughly despondent. Part of the reason was his health. He was a small young man, no taller than his father, and underweight. He had a bad cough, and suspected, as did Dr. Hall, that he had consumption (tuberculosis) and that it would kill him as it had killed his mother and was killing his grandmother. If anyone had asked him what the future held, or "what's around the corner?" as he liked to put it, he would have told them nothing, nothing at all.

# 3

# Ranch Hand

It was not long before the young drug clerk knew virtually everyone in town by name. Once in a while someone came in whom he did not know. One day a stranger to Will Porter came in and said he wanted to pay his bill. He left seven dollars on the counter and went away. When Will's Uncle Clark came back he asked who had left the money. Will said he did not know the man's name, but he drew a quick sketch and his uncle recognized the identity of the bill payer.

He learned fast. By 1881 he was a registered pharmacist and a member of the state pharmaceutical association. It looked as though he was going to stay on in Greensboro, and one day take over the store.

Will now blossomed. His money went on clothes, and he soon had a reputation as a "fashion plate."

Occasionally, life at Porter's drugstore was livened by some unusual event, often manufactured by Will Porter, who began manifesting a flair for practical jokes. The Porter drugstore had prospered and another clerk, Ed Michaux, had been added to the team.

In spring, summer, fall, and winter the young men's fancies turned toward romance. Along with a handful of other young bucks, Will and Ed Michaux formed a serenading choir. Will played the guitar a little and that was their tuning fork. They moved around town in the evenings, serenading the girls. Among these still was Sara Lindsay Coleman, who, after some absence, in the summer of 1881 again came to visit her relatives. One day, running errands for her grandmother, Sara came into the Porter drugstore, and Will Porter was again smitten. Night after night the boys came to serenade at her house.

29

One night Will and Tom Tate walked six miles out of town to pick magnolia blossoms from a grove Sara had admired, and delivered them. Sara let down string from her bedroom window, and the lovesick one tied his offering to it, and then she drew it up to the applause of the serenaders. But summer waned, and Sara went home to Weaverville, and young love was forgotten.[1] That fall of 1881, Will Porter and Ed Michaux were lordly young men, no longer coming in early and sweeping up and building fires and opening the shop. This manual labor was now done by an old roustabout named Pink Lindsay.

Pink Lindsay also cleaned out the cellar and moved the boxes of supplies into the shop from the wagons that brought them up the street. Now Pink Lindsay had a fine taste for bourbon whiskey, which was dispensed in Porter's drugstore to fill prescriptions from time to time. A barrel of very good whiskey was kept in the cellar. Since whiskey was prescribed quite frequently, a large bottle was also kept back of the counter. When the bottle needed refilling one of the clerks would take it down to the cellar and tap the cask with a rubber tube; he would then bring the bottle and siphon back upstairs, knowing Pink Lindsay's proclivities. This task was something of a nuisance since the cellar was reached from the outside of the store, by lifting the iron doors and descending a flight of steps, then lighting a kerosene lamp, filling the bottle, blowing out the lamp, closing the doors and coming back up. No one wanted to go down any more often than necessary.

That winter of 1881 the whiskey kept evaporating faster than Clark Porter thought it ought to, and for a time some consideration was given to the habits of his clerks. But in those days Will Porter had no taste for alcohol, and neither, apparently, did Clerk Michaux. Both were removed from suspicion and the proprietor took them into his confidence about the rapid evaporation problem.

One day while down in the cellar on other business, Will discovered the secret: two long reed straws hidden in the cellar wall near the whiskey barrel.

The straws and Will's knowledge of the habits of Pink Lindsay stirred the budding cartoonist's imagination. He took them upstairs to the pharmacy and there he loaded both straws with what he, as a practicing pharmacist, called capsicum, or *c. annuum,* but what lesser citizens called red pepper.

The next morning, when Pink Lindsay had finished sweeping out the store, and business was beginning to stir, Will found a pretext to send the handyman down to the cellar on an errand. He called this gesture to the attention of his uncle and his fellow clerk and all else who were in the store.

They waited. A few moments went by and then from the depths of the cellar came a terrible shriek, followed by the crashing of the cellar doors, and a body went hurtling up the stairway and down to the town pump a half a block along Elm Street.

"Poisoned! I've been poisoned" were the words that trailed along behind the speeding figure.

Will hastened to the pump, his admirers in his train, and he pumped and he pumped and he pumped as Pink Lindsay crouched beneath the pump mouth inhaling water and spitting. Finally the fire was put out, and then Will Porter pumped the truth out of Pink Lindsay.

How, demanded the roustabout, had he been poisoned? Without cracking a smile, Will invented a cock-and-bull story about the effects of whiskey on reed straws, and Pink Lindsay believed. He never did learn that he had been flummoxed.[2]

On another occasion, Will took pity on an eccentric old black named Charlie Hill, who wandered up and down the streets talking about his troubles and claiming he had snakes in his legs. The whites of the town smiled and went on, but the young blacks took to ridiculing and taunting Old Charlie. Will Porter did not think much of that, so he decided to do something about it. He found a small snake one day, and put it in a pharmaceutical bottle, poured in alcohol, and pickled it. Then he put the snake in the drugstore window with a little placard that said this was one of the snakes taken from Charlie Hill's leg. The young blacks drifted by, saw the snake, incontrovertibly a snake, done up in "scientific fashion" in the window of the drugstore. It must be true, then, they said—Charlie Hill did have snakes in his legs. And thereafter they left the old man alone as he wandered up and down telling the story of his snakes.[3]

BUT SUCH MOMENTS of levity were not frequent in the dusty streets of Greensboro. Further, in the early months of 1882 Will Porter's cough became so serious and the pinched look on his face so obvious that Dr. Hall took a hand in the young man's affairs. Two of Dr. Hall's sons had gone to Texas after the Civil War seeking opportunity. They were managing a ranch in La Salle County, down by the Rio Grande. The spread belonged to a Pennsylvania capitalist named Dull. The elder Hall brother, Lee, was also a celebrated gunfighter and Texas Ranger whose exploits were already known to the drugstore crowd of Greensboro. "He did more to rid Texas of desperadoes," said a Texas admirer, "than any officer Texas ever had." So when Dr. Hall announced that he and his wife were going to Texas in March and he wanted Will to go along and stay awhile at the ranch in behalf of his health, there were plenty of attractions.

They caught the train at Raleigh for New Orleans. O. Henry had his first sight of that lusty, beckoning city of the South that is quite unlike any other in its vieux carre and soft Frenchified accents. Then it was west to Houston and southwest to Cotulla in La Salle County, where they left the railroad and traveled by buckboard south a hundred miles to the Nueces strip. There was the ranch surrounded by assorted badmen who lived around the fringes.[4]

It was a typical south Texas livestock ranch, extending for miles and miles and miles. In 1882 the ranch covered about 250,000 acres. Later it was extended to be more than 400,000 acres. The livestock were about 12,000 Texas longhorn cattle, about 12,000 sheep, and uncounted native mustangs, which were rounded up from time to time for the cowboys or to sell to the army. Most of the ranch was in La Salle County, but it also went north into Frio County and east into McMullen County as far as the juncture of the Frio and Nueces rivers. The compound was built at the top of a rise for safety's sake. All around lay the Texas prairie, chaparral plain they called it locally, a land of thin, tough grass surrounded by stunted oak and the brush known as greasewood, cactus, and tough little twisted pine trees.

Will Porter arrived at the ranch at an exciting time. Captain Hall, as Lee Hall was then known (and sometimes also as Red) was engaged in a battle against a gang of rustlers who were operating in La Salle County. A number of forays were made along the fences against these desperadoes and there was some shooting. Finally that year, 1882, Captain Hall campaigned successfully for the election of former Texas Ranger Charles McKinney as sheriff of La Salle County and that helped settle the strip down somewhat. Will was in residence during most of this excitement.

The ranch to which the young Porter came was not precisely a hacienda. Captain Hall and his wife lived in a log and adobe house thirty-five feet long and twelve feet wide, surrounded by a twenty-foot-wide gallery where the family spent much of its time in the open air. Will Porter went to stay with the captain's younger brother Dick and his wife. They lived in the first shelter that had been built on the ranch, a one-room frame house, eight feet wide and twelve feet long. The Dick Halls took in Willie Porter, as he was always known to them. He was treated as one of the family and fell easily into their ways although he was a shy boy, the senior Mrs. Hall said.[5]

What a life for an impressionable young man! At the height of the war against the rustlers, Captain Hall was threatened constantly. In the mail came rude sketches of the captain, with his neck encased in a rope "necktie." Around the perimeters of the ranch appeared skulls and crossbones. When the captain traveled it was usually by night, and with loaded guns at hand. Here was a West that was indeed wild and woolly, and Will Porter drank it all in. The cowboys had all the experience of the West at their fingertips. The foreman had been a ranger with Captain Hall. Two of the hands had been members of the posse sent to capture that dangerous bandit Sam Bass at Round Rock. Around the bunkhouse campfire in the evenings they told their tales, with a wee bit of embroidery, perhaps, and young Porter took them all in and stored them away in his mental filing system.

No one asked him to work, but he felt he wanted to learn and to earn his keep, so he set out to become a cowboy, and learned to ride and rope calves, to brand and to fix fences, to dip sheep and to lamb. He learned to shoot and became an excellent marksman with rifle and pistol. In the two years on the ranch he spent as a hand, most of it in the lonely job of shepherd, he learned the ways of the Texas West.

He wrote long letters home, describing, in as humorous a way as he knew how, his adventures. "On the south side of a bush," he began one such in 1884, which meant he was out on the flat herding sheep.

In one letter written in 1884 as a Christmas and New Year's greeting, the young sheepherder gave predictive evidence about the future story writer:

Christmas, my dear friends, is a time of great joviality and of wonderful deeds. Sometimes the charitable and beneficent actions that are performed at this season amount almost to miracles. For example. A rich Banker or Merchant steps down his marble doorsteps, buttoning his warm, fur-lined overcoat with his gloved and shapely hand; and as he goes off down the street toward his warm and comfortable office, he meets a poor bricklayer whom he knows as a most deserving man, although poor, and at this season of the year, out of work. With the generous and warm hearted spirit of the day impelling him, the Banker runs his hands down into his pockets—to keep them warm—and gives the poor bricklayer a Smile, a Nod, and a Cheery Good Morning, and moves on, happy with the consciousness of having done a good deed. Now is where the great wonder and Miracle comes in. The poor bricklayer, with his heart glowing with pleasure and thankfulness goes home—and he can take that Smile, you know, and buy a turkey and truck [sic] to make a plum pudding with it and have a royal Christmas dinner. And he can take that Nod and his wife can cut out lots of nice, comfortable clothes for the children and have enough to pay off the rent on the house; and with that Cheery Good Morning he can buy a pig and some chickens, and a new coat and a pair of suspenders and some panes of glass to put in his windows and a nice large bottle of medicine for the sick baby, and a barrel of flour, and he can buy his old mother a warm shawl and get her another pair of spectacles to read the Bible with, which she had not been able to do since hers were broken, and lots of other things that will bring comfort and a little pleasure into his family, if not save a life or two. Such power and blessing cheerful greetings do bring at this season. And the kind Banker will surely meet with his reward.[6]

The long letter was full of words unusual for letter writers (compendium, habitants), an indication of O. Henry's interests. That lonely work as sheepherder gave the young O. Henry time to read. Now it was history, biography, and every magazine that could be begged or borrowed. He rode once a week to Fort Ewell, fifteen miles from the ranch, to pick up the mail. One time he was caught in a thunderstorm and sought shelter in a cave. There he found he was not alone: half a dozen local outlaws had holed up there, too. But like wild animals taking shelter from nature, the predators were on their good behavior, and the youngster emerged with no more damage than an enlargement of his vocabulary that would not be appreciated by mesdames Hall.

About once a month the cowboys of the ranch rode to Cotulla, which was forty miles away on the International and Great Northern Railroad. They picked up supplies at the station, stopped at the saloon for a little liquid refreshment, and spent the night at "the house down by the railroad tracks" where lived a group of accommodating senoritas. Occasionally someone had to go to Austin (the capital), or San Antonio (the market center), which boasted the Buckhorn Saloon on Dolorosa Street—it was the most famous building in the city after the Alamo. Part of their assigned task was to bring back any books they could round up there.

As important as Will Porter's study of the English language was at this time, it was matched by his study of other languages. Dick Hall had attended Guilford College, the Quaker school near Greensboro, and he knew some French and Spanish. On the ranch were some Germans, who had come down from the German community around New Braunfels. So Will had teachers for French and German and all around him others for Spanish. In a few months O. Henry spoke border Spanish as well as anyone on the ranch, but that was not good enough for him. He bought a Spanish grammar and studied Castilian, too.[7]

IT WAS NOT long before Will Porter was a proficient rider, and he knew his job as a ranch hand. He was "elevated" to the bunkhouse, then, to join the odd assortment of former soldiers, Germans, Mexican political refugees, and drifters and outlaws who lived their lives mostly in the open air and worked the ranch. One night he was hazed in a ceremony that ended with his being beaten across the backside with a pair of leather chaps. Then he was declared to be a real hand—one of them—and taken into the brotherhood of cowboys, and on the wild monthly treks into Cotulla.

Will wrote home to Greensboro, mostly to Dr. Hall's wife, about his life on the ranch. The sheep business was prospering. Dick Hall had just built onto the little house and had hired a black cook with such airs that Will suspected (he said) that she was a countess in disguise. Cotulla had grown in a year to a settlement of forty houses. The Halls were busy building fence, with some seventy men setting posts and stringing wire. A fellow Greensboro boy named Ed Brockman had come out to join the Hall work force, and had taken charge of the supply tent at the range camp. When Brockman had to go to San Antonio for supplies, Captain Hall asked Will to take over the commissary tent in Brockman's absence, so Will saddled his horse and rode seven miles south from the main ranch compound to the line camp where the fence building was in progress.

> On arriving I counted at the commissary tent nine niggers, sixteen Mexicans, seven hounds, twenty-one sixshooters, four desperadoes, three shotguns and a barrel of molasses. Inside there were a good many sacks of corn, flour, meal, sugar, beans, coffee, and potatoes, a big box of bacon, some boots, shoes, clothes, saddles, rifles, tobacco and some more hounds.*
>
> The work was to issue the stores to the contractors as they sent for them, and was light and easy to do. Out at the rear of the tent they had started a graveyard of men who had either kicked one of the hounds, or prophesied a norther [the vicious shivering wind that brought rain in sheets]. When night came, the gentleman who had the good fortune to be dispensing the stores gathered up his saddle-blankets, four old corn sacks, an oil coat and a sheepskin, made all the room in the tent he could by shifting and arranging the bacon, meal, etc., gave a sad look at the dogs that immediately filled the vacuum and went and slept outdoors. The few days I was there I was treated more as a guest than one doomed to labour. Had an offer to gamble from the nigger cook, and was allowed an especial favour to drive up the nice, pretty horses and give them some corn. And the kind of accomodating old tramps and cowboys that constitute the outfit would drop in and board, and sleep and smoke, and cuss and gamble, and lie and brag, and do everything in their power to make the time pass pleasantly, and profitably—to themselves. I enjoyed the thing very much and one evening when I saw Brockman roll up to the camp I was very sorry, and went off very early the next morning in order to escape the heartbreaking sorrow of parting and leavetaking with the layout.[8]

EXCEPT FOR THE gentlewomen of the ranch, during these two years Will encountered few but Mexican girls. There, was, however, one girl, with the odd name of Clarence Crozier, who came to visit her uncle, M. P. Kerr, who

---

*The word nigger as used by O. Henry in this letter and in his writings generally was not deliberately pejorative. O. Henry was a boy and man of his times—Black Reconstruction— and the white people of the South of his times referred to blacks as niggers. Rather than bowdlerize O. Henry, and at the risk of offending, I have left his words as they were written in the interest of authenticity.

ran the store and post office in Fort Ewell. She was, recalled O. Henry, "a regular old gum chewing, ice cream destroying, opera ticket vortex, ivory-clawing girl" of a sort he had almost forgotten about. She caught Will Porter's fancy and apparently the compliment was returned for there were extra trips to Fort Ewell that season. Too many extra trips, in fact, for the feeling of well-being of Mrs. Kerr, who felt the responsibility of managing the welfare of a pretty teenaged guest in a frontier village. Will Porter took to riding in for the mail twice a week, and then he began showing up in the evenings. He would arrive, the dust of the prairie thick on his boots, just about supper time. He would refuse to eat with the family but after dinner he would join them in the parlor where the Kerrs had an organ. There were long evenings of singing around the organ, with Will Porter holding up his end, Clarence playing "I Stood on the Bridge at Midnight" and "Gathering up the Shells at the Sea Shore," as beside her sat fourteen-year-old cousin Mary Nett Kerr, singing away as well. Aunty Kitty and Uncle Monroe sat in their chairs and tried to appear interested. After the singing, the three youngsters would play casino, under the frown of Aunt Kitty, who believed in the devil, and the evenings lasted sometimes until ten o'clock. Then, the young cowboy would leave the house, get on his horse, and ride the fifteen miles back to the ranch, to snatch a little sleep and be awake at dawn to start another day.

He began coming on Sundays, and Aunt Kitty frowned when he took Clarence off on long horseback rides. Her worries grew by the week, until one Sunday she found Clarence's autograph book, and an inscription.

> Thy looks, thy words, each well remembered smile of light,
> Like precious gems, or jeweled caskets rare;
> In memory's vault are hid from human sight,
> And oft she counts them o'er from year to year;
> As misers count their golden coins at night
> Or pale sweet nuns their rosaries in prayer.
>
> Truly your friend<br>W. S. Porter.[9]

Now there was nothing in this bit of pirated verse that could be pointed at by Aunt Kitty as indication of goings on between the young people, but there was something very disconcerting about the intimacy of it. It was not as if the young man was a Hall, heir to the ranch or anything as respectable as that; he was a mere ranch hand; no matter his highly respectable North Carolina background, the Boot Hills of Texas were filled with the bones of respectable-backgrounded southern youngsters.

The acquaintanceship had been worrisome for Aunt Kitty all the while. So Clarence Crozier was suddenly taken down to the station. The steam engine roared up with the cars behind it and the whole train screeched to a metallic stop. Aunt Kitty hustled her charge toward her Pullman car, and at the step, she kissed her and offered her last advice:

"Go aback to your folks at Brenham. And when you get there think no more about him, and do not write. That's a good little lady."[10]

Brenham was about a hundred and twenty-five miles northwest of Houston, which might have been across the Sahara Desert as far as availability was concerned. And there at home, Clarence Crozier swiftly forgot all about the blondish, short, young swain from the Dull ranch in La Salle County. Her organ playing now was transferred to the church, and there, within a matter of months she was engaged to a young man named Stuckert, whom she later married, never knowing what she had missed until forty years later, when Will Porter was unmasked to her as the real O. Henry.

So, gone was the regular old gum-chewing girl, which Will discovered sadly on his next ride over to Fort Ewell. The reason, of course, was plain for him to see on Aunt Kitty's triumphant countenance. So Will picked up the mail and tarried not a moment in Fort Ewell. "She has vamoosed," he wrote a friend, "and my ideas on the subject are again growing dim."

WILL TOOK TO poetry, and Tennyson became his favorite. He also began reading *Webster's Unabridged Dictionary,* to improve his precision in the usage of words. "I carried Webster's 'Unabridged dictionary' around with me for two years while herding sheep for Dick Hall," he said.[11]

There was a certain amount of contact with people from the towns, many of whom came down to the ranch to see Captain Hall. One visitor was John Maddox, an Austin businessman who dealt in real estate and traveled around the countryside looking for business. One of Maddox's Austin friends was an old, grizzled mining prospector from Colorado named Joe Dixon. Maddox had persuaded Dixon to write a book about his experiences in the gold camps and Dixon was looking for someone to illustrate it with sketches. Through John Maddox, Dixon learned about the young North Carolinian who was staying on the Dull ranch and he rode over to see for himself.

"I found Porter to be a young silent fellow, with deep, brooding blue eyes, cynical for his years and with a facile pen . . ."[12]

By that time Will Porter had taken to writing stories about the Southwest, and occasionally he showed them to Mrs. Dick Hall. She, who was a fan of the writings of H. Rider Haggard, said they were every bit as good as any of her hero's tales, but she couldn't prove it, because Will would read her the stories, and then tear them up and throw them away.

There was plenty of time on the ranch. In the daytime Joe Dixon would discuss the book with Will Porter while they rode out to see to Wills's chores, and in the evening when the sheep had been watered and were settled down for the night, they would sit around the fire and Will would draw the pictures. In all, he drew forty illustrations for the book. They were like his Greensboro work: ". . . while crude, they were all good and true to the life they depicted." For three weeks they worked on the illustrations. By the end of the three weeks, Joe Dixon had gained Wills's confidence to the point that the younger man showed him some of his stories. He pronounced them excellent.

"Will," he said, "why don't you try your hand at writing for the magazines?"

But the man who would be O. Henry just looked at him with his cynical smile and gave a little hiss through his pursed lips, which he did when he was amused, and said no more, but continued to tear up his stories.

Joe Dixon was a critic by nature, obviously. After the illustrations were finished he went back to Austin, and when all was ready with his manuscript, he reread it, snorted, and tossed the whole into the Colorado River.[13]

Will Porter was beginning to feel the same way about ranch life.

After two years on the ranch the livestock no longer looked interesting. His major task was the sheep:

"I'd drive 'em to the corral and pen 'em every evening, and then cook my cornbread and mutton and coffee and lie down in a tent the size of a tablecloth, and listen to the coyotes and the whip-poor-wills singing around the camp."[14]

It was a lonely existence for a twenty-one-year-old youth, now recovering in the dry Texas air from his lung ailment, and fresh-reminded of the world of men and women in the towns not so far away. That year, 1884, brought a crisis to the Dull ranch that decided Will Porter's immediate future. The "wild frontier" was wild no more; fences crisscrossed the great prairie country. Buffalo Bill had given up trying to make a living on the open range and organized his Wild West Show in 1883 to bring a taste of what used to be to the city dwellers.

Civilization, lawyers, and fence ranching sucked the guts out of the profits of the old cattle-driving ranchers. In earlier years they had turned their beasts out into those thousands of acres along the waterways and let them roam and let nature take its course, just once or twice a year organizing a drive to round up the cattle and push them into Cotulla for shipment over the railroad. Captain Hall sold off his cattle and began to think about going into politics.

Dick Hall bought a ranch of his own in Williamson County, northeast of Austin, and prepared to move his sheep operations there. Will Porter had options: he could go home to Greensboro, which meant back to the drudgery of the drugstore; he could go to work for Dick Hall on the sheep ranch, or he could go to Austin and make his way in the city of 10,000 people. That option was made possible because the Joe Harrell's Greensboro people, who were friends of the Dick Halls, lived in Austin with their four sons, Harvey, Dave, Joe, and Clarence, and after some contact through the Dick Halls, they invited Will to come and stay with them. He had no difficulty in making up his mind which option to pursue. He was ready for city life.

# 4

# Oh, That Rolling Stone . . .

One day in the spring of 1884, Cowboy Porter rode over to Fort Ewell for the last time and gave his dun-colored pony to Mary Nett Kerr, the cousin of his now half-forgotten inamorata. The Dick Halls were all packed up and so was Will Porter; they, to start a new life on their sheep ranch up north, and he to beard the big city of Austin. Will went to Austin in the spring of 1884 as the guest of the Harrell family, in the big, shady house at 1008 Lavaca Street. After a few weeks he felt impelled to find some sort of work to pay his way. For the past two years he had been practicing animal husbandry, which did not have much future in a city like Austin, so Will Porter reverted to the experience of the Greensboro years and looked for a job in a pharmacy. He wrote back to Greensboro for recommendations, and two months later received two. One letter was signed by all the physicians of Greensboro (four), recommending him as "druggist and citizen." The other was signed by the clerk of the North Carolina Supreme Court and endorsed by the register of deeds of Guilford County and the Greensboro postmaster. This imposing document declared him to be "undoubtedly a young man of good moral character, an A No. 1 druggist and a very popular man among his many friends."

Armed with these recommendations, Will got a job as drug clerk at the Morley Drug Store in Austin, and almost immediately realized that he was repeating the Greensboro life and detesting it every bit as much. He disliked the long hours and cramped quarters even more, in fact, spoiled by the two years on the open range. He resigned, knowing, at least, that whatever he did in the future he did not want to be a druggist again. The final straw was added

41

when the owner told him one of his duties as druggist was to "jerk sodas." He quit.[1]

JOE HARRELL OWNED a tobacco shop, and while Will looked around for something more compatible he clerked at the store. Here he got into book-keeping, because of the need of the Harrells, and he did a careful job of taking care of the store accounts, although he had no experience except as clerk in his uncle's store.

The next job came through John Maddox, who knew of Will Porter because of the illustrations for Joe Dixon's ill-fated autobiography. Maddox Brothers and Anderson was the name of the real estate firm. They offered Will a job keeping the books and he accepted. Part of his pay was board and room at the Anderson house, which was fine because Anderson's son Will was one of Will's friends. "He learned how to keep books faster than anyone I ever knew," said Mr. Anderson.

Will Porter stayed with the real estate firm for the next two years, sometimes living with the Harrells, sometimes with the Andersons, and sometimes "batching" with Will Anderson and Ed McLean in rooms downtown. One such bachelor place was at 110 East Ninth Street.

For a young bachelor without family, it was important to show a figure of respectability. Will achieved this first by singing in the Methodist Church choir, St. David's Episcopal Church choir, the First Baptist Church choir, and the Southern Presbyterian Church choir.

Before long, Will Porter, Howard Long, R. H. Edmondson, and C. E. Hillyer formed the Hill City Quartet. They began the group as a sort of a lark, but their voices were good enough and their arrangements of music solid enough that soon they were much in demand to sing at church festivals, picnics, and weddings. All the while, however, the real interest of the Hill City Quartet was more romantic, and involved the loading of a small foot-operated organ on a hack and serenading the current light of love of one of the four. As O. Henry put it later, they "made an assault upon the quiet air of midnight that made the atmosphere turn pale."

When a group of amateur actors decided to stage a show called *The Black Mantles* at Miller's Opera House, the Hill City Quartet was eager to join in. Will Porter played the role of Sampson. "That performance took me two years to live down," said O. Henry later. But it could not have been that bad; the quartet was soon asked to sing in other towns, even outside the county, which meant more than local allegiances were at work. And in the next year or so, the young men appeared in the chorus of *The Bohemian Girl, The Mikado,* and *The Chimes.* Light opera was to Austin of the 1880s what television would be to the Texas capital a century later, and soon Porter and his friends had established reputations as young men on the go.[2]

Will continued to draw but only for the amusement of his friends. The Harrells and the Andersons agreed that he had a good talent, and they offered to send him to New York to art school. So did John Maddox. But Will was not really interested. The offers were not declined, but nothing ever came of them.

In 1886 the Halls had prospered and no longer needed to spend all their time on the ranch. Dick Hall had built a big, red-brick house above Barton Springs, a suburb of Austin. He was elected Texas state land commissioner, a post that was prominent enough to become a springboard to political power. Dick Hall's star seemed to be rising, and Will Porter hooked back on, asking for, and securing, a job as assistant compiling draftsman for the land office. He had to spend three months working to qualify for the post, but he did, and for the next four years he held the job with a salary of a hundred dollars a month. Five and a half days a week he spent in the state office building on the hill, across from the state capitol, that building where "when you enter you lower your voice and time turns backwards for you, for the atmosphere which you breathe is cold with the exudations of buried generations. The building is stone with a coating of concrete; the walls are immensely thick; it is cold in the summer and warm in the winter; it is isolated and sombre; standing apart from the other state buildings, sullen and decaying, brooding on the past."[3]

Despite Will's chilly assessment of his office surroundings, these were happy years. Theatricals and music were not all of young Porter's amusement these days. He joined the Austin Grays, the local militia company that was as much a social club as a military organization, and he worked his way up from private to lieutenant. He loved to wear the uniform on parade, and he waxed his mustache, very much the young blade in the gray uniform. He also joined the Texas Rifles, a National Guard unit, in which he rose only to become corporal, but here again the aim was more social than military.

It was still a life of adventure, although he worked in town. One day a charcoal burner who lived in the hills west of Austin came into the land office with an old document signed by Jim Prescott, who claimed to have found the Lost Bowie Silver Mine back in 1859. The piece of paper on which the document was written checked out, it had an 1854 watermark on it. So Will Porter and one of his pals grew excited by the tale. Getting leave from the state government they set out on a search for the buried treasure. They hired an old hillman named Charlie Hogue and his team of mules, put together a camping outfit and surveying instruments, and hit the trail. They passed through Pleasant Valley, Dripping Springs, Johnson City, Fredericksburg, Noxville, and Menardville. They reached the site of the old San Saba Mission, which, they had been told, would be the point of departure. Then they looked at Jim Prescott's directions:

> Begin at the old San Saba Mission and go south, at the 21 or 22 mile you will cross a river, to the right are two saddle shaped mountains covered with cedar, on the right one of them, the mine is located. I been to it once and got silver. I am an old man now but I want my children to find this mine and have it.
>
> Signed<br>Jim Prescott.

But thirty years had passed. Jim Prescott was long dead and his children were scattered, so there was no moral problem involved, but there were all sorts of physical problems, not assumed by the mapmaker when he drew his sketch. The roads were not the same. Timber can do a lot in thirty years, and so can forest fires. River beds shift with flooding and other obstacles spring up.

Had Jim Prescott meant true north or magnetic north? That was the sort of decision over which the prospectors had to puzzle. Figuring Jim Prescott to be more miner than scientist, they went for magnetic north, where the compass points.

When they got into the mountains they noticed that nearly every hill had a saddle back. There were several pairs of saddle back hills well within the limitations of the map. If Jim Prescott said twenty-one or twenty-two miles, it might as easily be twenty or twenty-three miles. Now, face to face with these problems, the confidence of the treasure hunters was easily dissipated. They searched, and searched, and were rewarded with sunburn and a grand appetite, and, although Will Porter did not know it, a knowledge of the Texas hill country that would be worth much in the future. Finally their time ran out, and they had to return to the workaday world of Austin, rueful and without apparent treasure.[4]

At least they were pleased to be back among their cronies and told their tales during the long evenings in the watering holes of Austin. Their friends were the young business and professional men of the town, in their late twenties and early thirties, most of them bachelors still: Walter Wilcox, Dave and Joe Harrell, Bert Randolph, Joe Cavalier, Sherm Drake, Ed Byrnes, Joe McCarty . . .

"The old burg was filled with cowmen, slush of money, rearing to spend it on gambling, booze, and the women of the night. We trailed and piked along with this bunch of high rollers. We were cronies of Bud and Tobe Driscoll, Miel and Alf Mienel, Alex Casparis, Billy Searight, and other topnotch night rounders. We played Faro, Chuckaluck, Keno, stud poker, and roulette at Ben Marshall's or Bill Perkins."[5]

They acquired a big boat, suitable for river and lake fishing.

"We made many happy excursions for hunting and fishing. On one of our trips, Ed Struber, while we were splitting a keg of beer, hit upon the happy expedient of naming our boat after some prominent citizen and collecting $50 for the honor. It worked fine for a time. Our noble craft bore in succession the names of Major Wheatley, Major Burke, then Charles Hicks, and then finally of A. P. Wooldridge."

These were also the young beaux of Austin. "We danced at the old Turner Hall until our collars wilted. At times we had Germans which called for evening clothes. As for inaugural balls, they were all night revels . . ."[6]

OCCASIONALLY, HOWEVER, THE young men were reminded that all life was not short beer and free lunch. If nothing else, the purpose of the Texas Rifles was serious. During a railroad strike the Austin company was ordered to Fort Worth to guard the train depot. The "soldiers" regarded the outing as something of a lark, and Will Porter wired a girl he was chasing, who was visiting in Waco, that he would be coming through. She came down to the Waco station, and there, sure enough, sitting on the cowcatcher of the train bearing the guardsmen was Corporal Porter waving and showing off his waxed mustache.

He was a very busy bachelor. He went to an encampment of the Austin Grays at Lampassas. It was supposed to be hard work, but there was a dance at the Park Hotel, and Lieutenant Porter and the other three members of the quartet were given leave to attend, provided they return to camp by midnight.

Midnight came, and the quartet was still on the dance floor. A few minutes later someone saw a corporal's guard marching determinedly up the street toward the hotel, and Lieutenant Porter knew what for. Their commanding officer was not amused. How to escape?

When the guard arrived, one of the dancers went to the door of the hotel and asked the soldiers to stack arms outside so they would not frighten the innocent ladies. That seemed reasonable, and the soldiers stacked their arms. As they were doing so their quarry were escaping out the back door of the hotel, turning around the corner, seizing the stacked rifles, and hastening back to camp as though they were the military police. Will, pretending to be the officer of the guard, marched his men into camp, cocky and assured, and saluted the sentries as he came. By the time the searching party returned, the miscreants were all tucked in their bedrolls, there was no record of any misdeeds, and nothing could be proved.[7]

WILL PORTER COURTED several girls, and one of them very seriously. She was Lollie Cave, the daughter of a Houston family he had met on his trip west with Dr. and Mrs. Hall. She came to Austin to visit relatives in 1886 and Will was a frequent caller. The family had a cat named Henry, which Will swore would come only if you called it O. Henry, and that is where the young man from Greensboro seems to have gotten the idea of using that particular pen name. In Lollie Cave's autograph album he signed himself O. Henry. He also wrote a composition, "A Soliloquy by the Cat," to which he signed the name O. Henry. He proposed marriage to Lollie Cave, but she rejected him. He was handsome and debonair and enormously amusing, but he was, after all, just a draftsman in the land office, and not really a very good catch for the daughter of a prominent family.

The Austin Grays marched at the laying of the cornerstone for the new Texas state capitol, and at the dance that followed the ceremonies, Will Porter met Athol Estes, the daughter of Mrs. P. G. Roach, who was just nineteen years old. She was, as far as Will was concerned, the belle of the ball. He began calling at the Roach house. There were long afternoons on the porch, long drives in the countryside when he could afford to rent a buggy, and complicated discussions of life and literature. There were too often too many young men on that porch, but at least they could all sing together, and Will Porter had an edge because he could draw pictures that amused Athol. He had the edge with Athol, that is, but not with Athol's mama, who did not believe this slender, short, young man was a sufficiently serious person to have her daughter's hand, and Mr. Roach looked askance at the Porter prospects.

Now there was another suitor on that porch, a young man named Lee Zimplemann, who came from a highly respectable family of wealthy German burghers who lived in the New Braunfels area. Zimplemann's prospects were excellent, with a ranch in the background, and so Zimplemann was encouraged while Will Porter was given fewer and fewer parental smiles.

Zimplemann had the inside track all the way. He and Athol had "an understanding" when Will entered the scene, and it was sealed with a locket and an opal friendship ring. But as Will Porter saw immediately that was not quite the same thing as a real engagement with a date for marriage all settled.

Will began to court Athol with all his might. His moustache was never more highly waxed. His drolleries on the porch were never more droll. His drawings were never more chic. The Hill City Quartet was brought to the street outside the house time and again to help Will press his suit. They threatened to become a nuisance to the neighborhood. They were a nuisance to mama, who reminded Athol of her previous commitment to Zimplemann. Papa reminded her of Zimplemann's superior prospects.

Athol's girl friends, however, pressed Will Porter's case, for he was, at twenty-five, what they considered "simply adorable." And, with Athol, adorable won out over substantive. Will Porter assured her that someday he would be somebody. Athol swore that she believed and she fretted over her mother's constant furtherance of the Zimplemann cause. One day at the end of June, Athol confided her fears and the doubts of her mother and stepfather to Will, and he saw immediately that he was about to lose this game, too, and that something drastic must be done.

His only advantage was the slowness of his rival. On July 1 he went to the house to propose that they elope, but could not find Athol. She had gone off on an errand for her mother. He discovered where she had gone and made chase. He found her and she was embarrassed because she was not expecting him and was wearing an old, torn dress.

He proposed the elopement.

Athol fingered her dress and objected. She did not say, "What will mama think?" or "what will Mr. Roach think?" but only "oh, my dress!"

Will Porter then understood that he had won, and brushing aside all objection, he hustled her off to the license office, and then to the house of her minister, Rev. R. K. Smoot. He left her there and hurried to the Anderson house, where he secured the services of the Andersons as witnesses. They all came back and the marriage was performed that afternoon. The newlyweds then went to the Anderson house, where they stayed until Mr. Anderson could inform the Roaches and secure ex post facto approval.

They were with the Andersons for six months, proving the worst of Mr. Roach's fears about Will Porter's solvency. Finally, however, all was forgiven and at about the same time the young couple moved to a cottage on East Fourth Street. A few months later they found a more suitable place on East Eleventh Street, near the land office.[8]

With his marriage, for the first time Will felt the need to earn extra money. He began doing what Joe Dixon had suggested years earlier: writing notes and stories for newspapers. The *Detroit Free Press* was one of the first and from August 1887 he wrote for them regularly. He also sent sketches of Texas life to *Truth* in New York City.

Two years went by, undoubtedly the two happiest years of Will Porter's life. His wife, Athol, supported his literary activity and encouraged him to write more. They furnished their little house on the easy payment plan, with Will bringing in ever more money by writing for a string of newspapers around America. The prose sketch was still his métier, and newspapers welcomed his little set pieces about life in the Southwest. The newspapers did not pay much—*Truth* paid him $6 for "The Final Triumph"—but since several of his sketches were accepted each month, the income was real if not munificent. The young people suffered an emotional setback in the spring of 1888: William Sidney Porter, Jr., was born on May 6 but died that same day. On September 30, 1889, daughter Margaret Worth Porter was born.

The happiness of the young couple was even greater, except that the birth of the second child confirmed one unhappy suspicion: Athol was not well. In fact, she had tuberculosis, the great killer disease of America in the nineteenth century.

In 1882 when O. Henry went to Texas, he and Dr. Hall suspected that he had the disease. No cure was known. Treatment consisted of rest, cleanliness, and a diet high in raw eggs, milk products, and vegetables.

That same year, in Germany, Professor Robert Koch announced the discovery of the tubercle bacillus. At least by 1889 the scientists knew what they faced, but they still had no cure.

In Athol's case, the birth of little Margaret in September brought about a virtual collapse, and the young couple had to close their house, because she could not manage it. They moved in with Athol's parents. In the summer of 1890 Athol and Margaret went to Nashville with Mrs. Roach to visit relatives. They also went to Greensboro to visit Grandma Porter, who was also ailing with tuberculosis, and Aunt Lina. Will Porter joined them there for a short time. The same trips were made the next year. That summer of 1891 marked the last time Will would see grandmother or aunt, the last visit he would pay to North Carolina for twenty years.[9]

Since Will Porter always needed money these days, he was usually drawn ahead on his government salary, but that was not enough. He continued to write the newspaper sketches, and he illustrated a book, J. W. Wilberger's *Indian Depradations in Texas,* published by the Henry Hutchings Printing House of Austin. It was the sort of book a dime novel aficionado would love, and Will's twenty-six sketches were replete with scalpings and murder scenes, such as "A Comanche Warrior Dragging to Death Mrs. Plummer's Child."

In the absence of his wife and daughter in North Carolina, Will moved into a house on East Fourth Street; it had a barn where he could store his books. He collected about a thousand books in the next few years and stored them in his study in the barn.

In 1891 Dick Hall gave up the land commission and ran for governor; he was defeated by James Hogg. That meant the end of Will Porter's life under political patronage. He resigned from the land office. Charles Anderson, who had instructed Will in bookkeeping, suggested that there was a job at the First National Bank of Austin as a paying and receiving teller, and he convinced Will that he could handle it. He also persuaded the bank officials that Will

Porter was the man for the job. Neither persuasion was very difficult; Will really wanted a sinecure that would allow him to continue his outside work, and he was happy enough to take this job at the same salary he had earned at the land office, $100 a month. The bank officers were easygoing men; the First National Bank of Austin operated as a country bank, although it had gained enormously in deposits and had become a national bank, subject to the federal government's laws and examination. Until recently it had been run by one family, with some close friends let into the company. A few months earlier most of the stock had been purchased by members of a private investment bank in Austin, but this meant nothing to Will Porter; he was not on that level of business and finance.

He went to work for the bank as teller, which meant he was solely responsible for the cash of the bank, and had to take a $10,000 fidelity bond. He had an assistant, Byrne the bookkeeper, who was bonded at $5,000.

Being new to banks, Will Porter was not surprised at the easy way of the bankers; they covered overdrafts without question, and if the officers needed a bit of cash, they wrote a check and dropped it into the cash drawer, almost like an IOU. Or sometimes they just took the money with a remark that they would make all the adjustments later.[10]

In the summers of 1892 and 1893 the Porters lived in the Dick Hall house across the Colorado River from Barton Springs, while the Halls were on their ranch. Will continued his writing although he worked every weekday at the bank. In the summer of 1893 he wanted Athol to have another change of scene (this was part of the mystique of consumption) and he suggested that she take a trip to the Chicago World's Fair. But Athol said she would be too lonesome, and, instead, she spent the money on new furnishings for the Fourth Street house.

Marriage and illness changed Athol and unfortunately not for the better: the romantic, spoiled young lady of 1887 became a shrew. The Lord knew she had reasons: Will Porter continued to enjoy the companionship of his old friends of bachelorhood and liked to stop off at a saloon for a glass of beer after work. But when he came home late, he found Athol up in arms. Sometimes she lay on the floor and screamed at him. When they went out in public, she might begin a quarrel to embarrass him. By Will's lights, she was a spoiled, possessive woman. By those of another generation she might have just been regarded as a woman who wanted her rights.[11]

"In all matters of the heart the word ownership should be expunged," said O. Henry later. "Friends of mine, who have forced confidence upon me, are a unit in the conclusion that romance is a form of proprietorship, that is to say a gent supposedly living a free and unencumbered existence casts a languishing eye upon a fair woman, lets a few kind words slip from his conversation, allows her hand to repose in his for a split second and then finds himself on a par with the leading character in Uncle Tom's Cabin."

Obviously, sometimes Will Porter felt repressed, there was no question about it. But sometimes he was the perfect husband and father, writing sketches to please daughter Margaret and other children of the neighborhood, telling the children stories, and drawing freehand sketches for them. For all the rest of his life, he doted on his daughter, as much as his emotional nature would allow.

IN THE WINTER of 1893–94 Will Porter saw an opportunity to further his literary ambitions, without severing his lifeline to the bank. A radical intellectual named W. C. Brann had started a newspaper in Austin called the *Iconoclast*. Given the Texas intellectual climate of the period a seer might have noted without much fear that Editor Brann was doomed to failure. And so it was, after two years of trying to raise the blood pressure of Austin to many social wrongs, Brann decided to throw in the towel. He received an offer to become an editorial writer on the *San Antonio Express,* a post which would give him plenty of room to fulminate without having to worry about paying the bills. He wanted to go, fast. He let it be known that the physical equipment of the *Iconoclast* was up for sale, lock, stock, and barrel, for $250.[12]

Will Porter heard of the offer and was intrigued. But, as usual, he did not have $250. Nor was he a printer. He was encouraged by a pair of businessman friends, Will Booth and Herman Pressler, who offered to cosign his note. There was still the problem of the printer.

At this same time, a tramp printer named Dixie Daniels had rolled into Austin and had gotten a job at the state printing house. He heard about the *Iconoclast,* and Will Porter's interest, and the pair got together. Will's friends signed the note, and he was a newspaper editor. Two copies of the *Iconoclast* were brought out, but that was largely a matter of making use of type already set. Will and Dick Daniels wanted another sort of publication, to deal with local events in a humorous fashion, with lots of sketches, drawings, and verse, to appeal to Texans who really didn't care a lot for world issues.

Will Porter did all the editorial work, after banking hours. He drew all the cartoons and wrote the original reading matter. Some was "boilerplate"— picked up from other publications in time-honored fashion. Athol helped out with the copy, and Mr. Roach took care of business matters. The paper was a weekly publication, eight pages, slightly larger than modern tabloid size, five columns wide.

So Will Porter began a new sort of life as a newspaper editor—or was it really a return to the old, now protected from Athol's wrath by a good excuse?

"Night after night," said Dixie Daniels," after we would shut up shop he would call to me to come along and 'go bumming'. . . . We would wander through streets and alleys, meeting with some of the worst specimens of down-and-outers it has ever been my privilege to see at close range. . . . He never cared for the so called 'higher classes' but watched the people on the streets and in the shops and cafes, getting his ideas from them night after night."[13]

*The Rolling Stone,* as the new publication was called, seemed to be destined for success. Bill Nye, the nationally famous writer, sent them a letter of encouragement. Later they ran his syndicated column. The offices were moved to the second floor of the Brueggerhoff Building at Tenth Street and Congress Avenue.

Austin and the surrounding area liked the paper. Will Porter was full of bright ideas; when he wanted to promote circulation he wrote an advertisement offering a special premium.

The price of the paper was $1.50 per year. Anyone who brought two dollars to the office would get a fifty cent "premium." Nobody was fooled, but a lot of people came in with their two dollars to get their fifty cents.

Will promoted the paper with considerable skill, but he was seldom satisfied, and he was a very difficult employer. He was constantly making staff changes. On May 12, 1894, the paper announced that S. W. Teagarden was manager, but he did not last. Business managers and circulation directors came and went as they failed to meet the demands made by the editor in view of the apparent success of the paper.

The first two issues of *The Rolling Stone* were printed in thousand-copy batches. For the third issue, O. Henry ordered six thousand copies, most of which were distributed free to impress the Austin business community.

WEEKLY COUNTRY NEWSPAPERS were heavy on local social notes, with a country correspondent serving every hamlet and faithfully describing the marriages, births, parties, and visits from far-flung relatives. O. Henry invented a burlesque of this "forks of the creek" kind of weekly. One page of *The Rolling Stone* was called "The Plunkville Patriot," as edited by Colonel Aristotle Jordan. Colonel Jordan's spoofery began with the issue of October 27, 1894, and was immediately acclaimed by Will's growing readership.

Obviously "The Plunkville Patriot" was the only paper in the world that gave a damn about Plunkville. And Colonel Jordan considered himself the leading light of the town. So, when opportunity knocked, he was ready:

"Our worthy mayor, Colonel Henry Stutty, died this morning after an illness of about five minutes, brought on by carrying a bouquet to Mrs. Eli Watts just as Eli got in from a fishing trip. Ten minutes later we had dodgers out announcing our candidacy for the office. We have lived in Plunkville going on five years and have never been elected to anything yet. We understand the mayor business thoroughly . . ."

But Colonel Jordan failed to receive the support expected, from such as the proprietor of the Elite Saloon, which he had frequented so often he had rubbed his own niche into the bar. As a matter of public service, the Colonel then noted "there is a dangerous hole in the front steps of the Elite Saloon."

Another time, Colonel Jordan sought the postmastership of Plunkville, and when he did not get the job, he spent three paragraphs in a roaring denunciation of the federal administration in Washington.

The Plunkville page had its own advertisements (fake) and when Adams and Company, Grocers, "discontinued" their two-dollar ad, the colonel took revenge:

"No less than three children have been poisoned by eating their canned vegetables, and J. O. Adams, the senior member of the firm, was run out of Kansas City for adulterating codfish balls. It pays to advertise."

So Will Porter went along, having his fun, poking at the foibles of newspaper editors, businessmen, and politicians.

Colonel Jordan was only one of many running jokes. Gilmore's Band was the most popular musical organization in Austin, and *The Rolling Stone* had accumulated a number of "cuts" of bandmaster Gilmore. So, no matter the important figure who was subject of a leading article, a picture of Gilmore was run, perhaps captioned "Governor Hogg," or "William Jennings Bryan." Always it was Bandmaster Gilmore in the picture.[14]

Governor Hogg had a daughter named Ima, who later became celebrated in American song and story. Somewhere along the line she acquired an imaginary twin sister named Ura. Listing the names of the Hogg daughters became a typical Texas joke of the sort Will Porter was perpetrating weekly.

Typographical errors—very carefully conceived—were an integral part of the paper. Even when the paper grew and extra help had been brought in, Dixie Daniels used to get out his stick and compose those paragraphs himself, to make sure there were no mistakes in the mistakes.

One of Editor Porter's favorite characters was Congressman Sockless Jerry Simpson, a leader of the growing Populist movement from Kansas. The adventures, real and imaginary, of this very real political character appeared week after week in *The Rolling Stone*.

The detective story was beginning to come into fashion in the United

States, following Edgar Allan Poe's writings and the reading public's discovery of A. Conan Doyle's Sherlock Holmes. A prominent literary detective just then was a Frenchman named Lecocq. *The Rolling Stone* had its own supersleuth, Tictocq, who became deeply involved with Sockless Jerry Simpson. In one spoof, Tictocq created a national scandal when he discovered a pair of clean socks in Sockless Jerry's luggage.

After only six months of publication, Will was encouraged by the success of *The Rolling Stone*. He had brought it up from nothing to a paid circulation of 1,500, and he could see how that figure could be tripled at least, without extending his resources beyond the county.

# 5

# The End of *The Rolling Stone*

In the fall of 1894, Will Porter and partner Dixie Daniels were riding high. Not that *The Rolling Stone* was a superb financial success, but they were enjoying themselves, and the newspaper gave signs of growth that exceeded its performance.

Daniels was a real genius with type. For effect, as noted, he could purposely manufacture with ease the sort of typographical errors that have plagued country newspapers from time immemorial:

### PERSONALS

Miss Hattie Green of Paris, Ill, is Steel- riveted steam or water powor automatic oiling thoroughly tested visiting her sister Mrs. G.W. Grubes Little Giant Engines at Adams & Co. Also Sachet powders McCormick Reapers and oysters.

# THe
# PLunkViLle PaTriOt,

o o Published nEarlʃ evᵕry Friday. o o

## COL. ARISTOⱢLE JORDAN,
Editor & Excandidate for **COUNTY JUDGE·** — ⁓

---

O&ce next door to the colored ɥap-graʌeyarp, over $mith !s Tin shop.

---

.Sub$cription per >‾ear  •  $1.oo
"  ,' 6 moS  •  ;  .2oo

---

writeUp for candipates 5c per lineE.
Obituary poetry  1oc  "

---

R. R. timetable.
N. bound arr. Plunɥville´ 7.15  AM
"  leaves  "  7.15$\frac{1}{16}$  "

---

O. Henry was a genius with words, as the readers of *The Rolling Stone* learned when they read his "sketch of Plunkville," his legendary town.

56

VIEW OF BELL MEᵥDF AVENUE
looking South.

PLUNKVILLE'S
PROGRESS

The Garden City Grows In
GRANDUER

Follows Fastin the Wake
Of Chicago and New York

A Brief Description of Her Mammoth
Emporiums, Business, Enterprises,
Educational Institutions, factories,
Mills, and Special Features.

A Literary Center, and the Biggest
Hide and Bone Market in the County.

Every Advantage Offered to Persons
Coming to Stay Over Night.

A Sketch of Plunkville as it is Today.

When in 1857 Silas Q. Plunk laid out the then little town of Plunkville little did he think it would be the city it is today. If he had he would have kicked himself down Avenue C, torn up his plans and saved trouble. General Plunk came to Texas in 1427 about one mile in advance of the sheriff of Sangareee Co., Ohio. He and the sheriff made friends and laid out the town of Plunkville. Some difficulty arising about corner lots, the sheriff laid out Colonel Plunk.

## OTR. PROMINENT BUILDINGS

There are many magnificent buildings in Plunkville. The Court House, Judge perkins's barn McCrackin's Slaughter House, the Blue Mass canning factory, widow Pogram's residence and Hefflinger's faro rooms are all model's of modern architecture.

We present below a half tone cut of the 2nd Nat'l Bank.

Second Nat'l Bank of Plunkville.

Today Plunkville has nineteen stores, 21 saloons, 8 undertakers, one school, 1 proposed opera house, one insane asylum, one Y.M.C.A., and 2 establishments for throwing rings over knives.

## COLONEL MOSES MORDECAI,
### President of the 2nd Nat'l Bank.

The 2nd Nat'l Bank

This bank was established by Moses Mordecai in 1880. Col. Mordecai, now the president of the bank, whose portrait we present in this issue, is one of our sterling citizens. He is conscientious to a degree in his management of the bank. We left the door of his private office open one day last winter and allowed a draft to enter. He protested it and charged our account with four $, making an overdraft of 11 instead of $7 . . .

59

**Widow Pogram's Residence**

The residence of Mrs. Pogram is between Belle Meade Avenue and the Fresh Air Fund Soap Factory. The Widow is a daisy. Major Pogram died in 1890 of heart failure while trying to play the joker as a side card with four aces against five jacks. Mrs. Pogram takes a few boarders as a relief from ennui. Her home is a model of neatness and luxury. We have boarded there three years and know whereof we speak. We owe the widow 97 $ which we have never been pressed for. Stop at the Pogram House.[1]

SO, THE NEWSPAPERMEN were doing very nicely, as Daniels said, "getting the paper out every Saturday—approximately—and blowing the gross receipts every night."

Not far from the offices of *The Rolling Stone* was the Bismarck Cafe, which became Will Porter's usual place of recreation. "One of his favorite amusements," said printer Daniels, "was lounging about the cafe, eating caviar sandwiches and throwing dice for beers."

The beer came in huge seidels—at least Will Porter's did—and "he could drink half a gallon without taking the vessel from his mouth."

He liked the Germans, he liked German food, and the atmosphere, with its portraits of Prince von Bismarck and Kaiser Wilhelm I. He liked *The Rolling Stone,* because it gave him an excuse to stay away from the house several nights a week. There were poker games in the office, and Athol sometimes came down to try to break them up, only to face a locked door. Sometimes Will came home in a highly liquified condition, much to the embarrassment and irritation of his spouse. These proclivities were also reduced by the author to the written word, as in a parody of Thomas Hood's "The Bridge of Sighs," which appeared in *The Rolling Stone*:

> "One more unfortunate,
> Weary of breath,
> Chewing cloves hastily,
> Scared half to death.
> O it was pitiful
> He left the city full
> Quarter past one.
>
> Prop him up tenderly
> By the hall stair,
> On a big bender, he,
> Needs some fresh air.
> Now run! His wife's got her
> Hands in his hair.[2]

If that sort of behavior did not make for the best of family relationships, it did indicate a certain split personality not uncommon to writers; the joyous lover of the good life whose passion it was to look too long upon the wine in good fellowship, struggling with the husband and the father. Will Porter did drink too much a great deal of the time. In other matters he was a good father and a good husband. His excuse for staying out late was that it was part of the job; he was doing his best to provide for his family, whom he loved with all his heart. There were two distinct views of *The Rolling Stone,* depending on the characters involved. Friends of the family and of the Roaches long remembered that it was a family effort, with everyone but little Margaret participating. But Will Porter's men friends of the day recalled the hi-jinks and the drinking parties and the laughter of putting out a paper that no one took so very seriously. The real *Rolling Stone* was a bit of both, obviously, started in seriousness, carried on in good humor, and then, once again, reverting to a certain seriousness.

# THE ROLLING STONE

VOL. II. NO. 3.  AUSTIN AND SAN ANTONIO, TEXAS, SATURDAY, FEBRUARY 2, 1895.  PRICE FIVE CENTS.

DEPARTMENT CLERK . "Mr. Legislator, if you want to save money for the State, why don't you stop that leak instead of cutting down my salary?"

## ARISTOCRACY VS. HASH.

THE snake reporter of the ROLLING STONE was wandering up the avenue last night on his way home from the Y M C A rooms when he was approached by a gaunt, hungry-looking man with sad eyes and disheveled hair he accosted the reporter in a hollow weak voice

"Can you tell me, sir, where I can find in this town a family of scrubs?"

"I don't understand exactly."

"Let me tell you how it is," said the stranger, inserting his fore finger in the reporter's button hole and badly damaging his chrysanthemum. "I am a Representative from Somptuous county, and I and my family are houseless, homeless and shelterless. We have not tasted food for over a week. I brought my family with me, as I have indigestion and could not get around much with the boys. Some days ago I started out to find a boarding house, as I cannot afford to put up at a hotel. I found a nice aristocratic-looking place that suited me, and went in and asked for the proprietress. A very stately lady with a Roman nose came in the room. She had one hand laid across her nose—across her waist, and the other held a lace handkerchief. I told her I wanted board for myself and family, and she condescended to take me. I asked for her terms, and she said $300 per week.

"I had two dollars in my pocket and I gave her that for a fine teapot that I broke when I fell over the table when she spoke."

"You appear surprised, says she. You will please remember that I am the widow of Governor Riddle of Georgia, my family is very highly connected, I give you board as a favah, I do not consider money any equivalent for the advantage of my society, I—

"Well, I got out of there, and I went to some other place. The next lady was a cousin of General Mahone of Virginia, we wasted four dollars an hour for a back room with a pink mould and a Buront granite bed to it. The next one was an aunt of Davy Crockett, and asked eight dollars a day for a room furnished in imitation of the Alamo, with prunes for breakfast and one hour's conversation with her for dinner. Another one said she was descended of Benedict Arnold on her father's side and Captain Kidd on the other.

"She took more after Captain Kidd."

"She only had one meal and prayers a day, and counted her money worth $10 a week

"I found nine widows of Supreme Judges, twelve relicts of governors and generals and twenty-two ruins left by various happy colonels, professors and majors, who valued their aristocratic society worth from $90 to $500 per week, with weak-kneed hash and dried apples on the side. I admire people of fine descent but my stomach yearns for pork and beans instead of culture. Am I not right?"

"Your words," said the reporter, "convince me that you have altered meat you have said."

"I mean. You see how it is. I am not wealthy, I have only $3 per diem and my per quisites, and I cannot afford to pay for

high lineage and moldy ancestors. A little corned-beef goes farther with me than a coronet, and when I am cold a coat-of-arms does not warm me."

"I greatly fear," said the reporter, with a playful hiccough, "that you have run against a high-toned town. Most all the first class boarding houses here are run by ladies who do not do so to make a living they want to put the kibosh on Hoity Green."

"I am now desperate," said the Representative, as he chewed a tack awhile, thinking it was a clove. "I want to find a boarding house where the proprietress was an orphan found in a livery stable, whose father was a dago from East Austin, and whose grandfather was never placed on the map. I want a scrubby, ornery, low-down, snuff-dipping back woodsy, puebald gang, who never heard of finger-bowls or Ward McAllister, but who can get up a mess of hot cornbread and Irish stew at regular market quotations

"Is there such a place in Austin?"

The snake reporter sadly shook his head. "I do not know," he said, "but I will shake you for the beer"

Ten minutes later the slate in the Blue Ruin Saloon bore two additional characters

## 10.

### HAD THE DROP ON HIM.

Last night about 8 o'clock, a man was seen standing on the walk in front of the Capitol with both hands raised high above his head. A ROLLING STONE reporter happened to see him and went over to investigate. The gentleman proved to be a member of the House from one of the western counties.

"What's the matter?" asked the reporter

"Gen'l man gorver drop on me. Look out, m free, you'll get shot in minute Bester hol' up your hands.

"I don't see anyone," said the reporter

"I see 'm. Called 'm a liar las night 's a poker game. Said he'd 'try f' me to-day Gozzer gun's big as er cannon. Gon' ter boos 'i minute. Bezzer run. See 'm up in window?"

"Yo' might as well put your hands down," said the reporter The 'fello.' with a gun is a bronze figure on the Alamo monument."

"s t so. You don't know how mush you've relieved me. Been standing 'here half hour Mush 'bligo', stranger, you're shaved m' life t 'ou' home now G' bye."

The released representative took a zig zag course northward and the reporter felt in his vest pocket unsuccessfully for a moment, and also turned his face homeward.

### AND IN A HURRY, TOO.

"What time did Mr Spooner leave last night?" asked Mrs Tompkins at the breakfast table.

"He was close upon eleven," said the old man, gazing proudly at his boot, which was one number larger than a

## A LUNAR EPISODE.

THE scene was one of supernatural weirdness. Tall, fantastic mountains reared their seamed peaks over a dreary waste of igneous rocks and burned out lava beds. Deep lakes of black water stood motionless as glass under frowning, honey-combed crags, from which ever and anon dropped crumbled masses with a sullen plunge. Vegetation there was none. Bitter cold reigned, and ridges of black and shapeless rocks cut the horizon on all sides. An extinct volcano loomed against a purple sky, black as night and as old as the world

The firmament was studded with immense stars that shone with a wan and spectral light. Orion's belt hung high above.

Aldebaran faintly shone many millions of miles away, and the earth glowed like a new risen moon with a lurid, blood-like glow

On a lofty mountain that hung toppling above an ink black sea stood a dwelling built of stone. From its solitary window came a bright light that gleamed upon the misshapen rocks.

The door opened, and two men emerged, locked in a deadly struggle.

They swayed and twisted upon the edge of a precipice, now one gaining the advantage, and now another

Strong men they were, and stones rolled from their feet into the valley as each strove to overcome the other

At le igth one prevailed. He seized his opponent, and raising him high above his head, hurled him into space

The vanquished combatant shot through the air like a stone from a catapult in the direction of the luminous earth.

"That's three of 'em this week," said the Man in the Moon, as he lit a cigarette and turned back into the house. "Those New York World interviewers are going to wear me out tired if they keep this thing up much longer "

### THE RIGHT MAN

Biggs— "I see they have a new scavenger on our street. Wonder what has become of the old one?"

Griggs— "Oh, he's been selected by Hopper & Co to write the society novel in their Black and Blue series."

### CHICAGO FORESIGHT

Miss Links— "How could you be so unwise as to reject Mr Wiener's suit? He is regarded as one of the biggest catches in the west."

Miss Porque— Yes, but he only pays $21000 weekly.

### THE ROLLING STONE One
Year and half a dozen of Hill's best
Cabinet Photographs for $2 00! Do you
want photos of your wife, baby, broth'r.
sister, or yourself, free?    not. le' th
cook have some taken

## SPECIMEN PAGE OF "THE ROLLING STONE"

WHEN WILL PORTER resigned from the bank in the fall of 1894 and decided to devote himself entirely to the newspaper, the prospects seemed quite bright. He was covering Austin quite well considering everything. The county remained, and then the surrounding counties should be good for a little bit of circulation. He had a big plus in the Texas University community in Austin. With good effort, he could hope for a circulation of perhaps 5,000, which would enable his business agents to sell advertising with some success. All this could come slowly. There was no real need to break with the bank, but Teller Porter had recently heard some unpleasant rumblings about changes that included at least one that would affect him negatively. National Bank Examiner Jonathan J. Gannon had come into the First National Bank of Austin on July 31, and, after completing his examination, complained about the sloppy management of the institution. He was told that there was soon to be a major shakeup in the bank. Jonathan H. Raymond and Company, an investment firm, owned most of the capital stock of the First National, and the examiner was told that that outfit would soon take charge of the bank and bring in new people. President Brackenridge was going to retire, and J. R.

Johnson, a big stockholder and member of the firm of Jonathan H. Raymond and Co., was going to succeed him. Frank Hamilton, vice president of the First National, was also going to leave the bank and return to full-time work at the Raymond company. The rumor was that an experienced teller would be brought over to be placed above Will Porter and M. F. Byrne, the book-keeper. Even at the same salary it would not be the same for Will Porter, his position demeaned. So, just after December Will wrote a friend who had gone to Chicago: "I quit the bank a day or two ago. I found out that the change was going to be made, so I concluded to stop and go to work on the paper."[3]

Of course he would try to make something of *The Rolling Stone.* But he was not so blind as to expect that it would satisfy either his literary ambition or provide security for his family.

"Are you still in Chicago and what are the prospects? I tell you what I want to do. I want to get up in that country somewhere on some kind of newspaper. Can't you work up something for us to go at there? If you can I will come up there any time at one day's notice. I can worry along here and about live, but it is not the place for one to get ahead in."

Still, having quit the bank, *The Rolling Stone* was all Will Porter had, and he worked at trying to expand its horizons.

December 20 found Porter in San Antonio, where he hoped to begin that expansion by bringing out a simultaneous San Antonio edition of *The Rolling Stone,* with a San Antonio page leading, replacing the Austin page of the northern edition. While in San Antonio he conferred with Henry Ryder-Taylor, an Englishman with a cultivated Mayfair accent, double-barreled name, and a diamond ring on his finger "big as a two bit piece and shinin' like granulated sugar." Ryder-Taylor had written Will Porter about a job.

It must have been the accent that persuaded Will Porter; he had a real respect for English letters. So he swallowed Henry Ryder-Taylor's claim that he had been Charles Dickens's secretary, and also an editor of the London *Telegraph,* two tales that would hold about as much whiskey as a lace mantilla. Ryder-Taylor also indicated that if Editor Porter-Henry would set him up, he, Ryder-Taylor would make an international success of *The Rolling Stone.* So, on January 26, 1895, *The Rolling Stone*'s front page announced that thereafter it would be published in San Antonio simultaneously. It was, for several issues. But then Will Porter fell ill (whether from alcoholism or another ailment does not seem to have been determined), and there was no one else who could produce all that editorial matter. *The Rolling Stone* was out of publication for several weeks.

If initially Dame Fortune had looked with favor upon the proprietors of *The Rolling Stone,* then she seemed to have a change of heart. The first evidence of difficulty was a result of one of Will Porter's little jokes. One weekly feature of the newspaper was a humorous cartoon with caption to match, done by Will Porter. One week he drew a cartoon of a fat gentleman leading an orchestra, beating the air with his baton. It was drawn from the rear to emphasize the enormous backside of the maestro. And beneath ran this verse:

> With his baton the professor beats the bars,
> 'Tis also said, beats them when he treats.
> But it made that German gentleman see stars
> When the bouncer got the cue to bar the beats.[4]

From a point of nearly ninety years this bit of humor loses virtually all its snap. But consider it thus: There has been a minor scandal running around among the town's saloons concerning a certain large gentleman of German extraction whose unwillingness to pay his bar bill after setting up drinks for the house has caused him to be ejected from one of the watering holes.

Now consider this situation, true, false, or halfway in between, in terms of a minority (the Germans of the Austin area, who tended to be very serious people and very sensitive to ethnic remarks). Then the reader can begin to understand why that particular issue of *The Rolling Stone* created a sensation in Austin.

There was even more to it. In fall and spring the German community of Texas celebrated the old country's famous holidays; in fall was Oktoberfest and in the spring came the Saengerfest, the season of bock beer and bock sausages. In the spring of 1894 *The Rolling Stone* had reported, ostensibly from Houston:

> Yesterday was the first day of the Saengerfest, and today is universally acknowledged to be the second. Tomorrow if the beer holds out, will be the third . . .

Although that seems pretty tame, still some of the German community had taken umbrage at this pleasantry, another indication of the serious nature of Texas Germans. Since Will Porter poked fun at Mexicans and cowboys and Eastern capitalists too, it got by, particularly after the editor apologized in print for causing any unhappiness, took his "Houston correspondent" to task for his wickedness, and assured all his readers it had been written purely in the spirit of fun. But the editor could not leave the matter alone. A few weeks after the controversy died down he had published an indignant reply from his "Houston correspondent" to the editorial chidings:

> I not de half of it you told. It was der krandest wunderschoen, most peautiful, high-doned and boetical dime efer seen in dis country. We trink tree hundert kegs peer. De music vas schveet und knocked most all der blastering from der valls in der opera house.[5]

This foray caused more complaint. Then, in the midst of the search for "detective stories," Will had invented a German detective, Hans von Pretzel, a companion to the French Monsieur Tictocq. Detective von Pretzel was assigned to a case that involved a notorious diamond thief who was said to have taken refuge aboard a schooner. The great detective then sought his quarry in a beergarden.

All this had brought tight lips to some of the German community. But the depiction of the fat German musician who did not pay his bar bill was the final straw, and the Germans of central Texas declared war on *The Rolling Stone.* Advertisers suddenly withdrew their ads. Circulation in the German community suddenly evaporated. The contretemps tended to take some of the fun out of the enterprise, and it certainly took the steam out of *The Rolling Stone*'s forward progress.

Despite the dismay brought on by punishment of error, Editor Porter did not lose heart. The end of December 1894, found him in San Antonio talking to Ryder-Taylor about the future.

Soon *The Rolling Stone* was being printed in San Antonio, too, with all its features and a special San Antonio front page, partially edited by Will Porter, but unfortunately not enough to keep Ryder-Taylor from getting them into even worse trouble.

APPARENTLY MR. RYDER-TAYLOR believed that he could score a victory for the paper by helping win a political campaign, and he backed the wrong horse with considerable vigor. When the other man won, the campaign committee did not forget, and the circulation and advertising of *The Rolling Stone* in San Antonio fell to zero. It was on April 27, 1895, only four months after Will Porter's initial decision to expand, that *The Rolling Stone* closed its doors.[6] The retired editor then began to support himself by writing short pieces for a larger number of newspapers, including the *Cleveland Plain Dealer,* and putting out lines elsewhere for a newspaper job. There was nothing for him in Austin.

But while Will Porter was waiting, the long shadow of fate was stalking him, in a manner he had never expected. As noted, like the 2nd National Bank of Plunkville, the First National Bank of Austin was a casual institution, where the president and other officials thought nothing of drawing money out of the till with a simple signature or sometimes not even that, but a notation "cash withdrawn." This practice tended to drive some bank workers wild. Will Porter's predecessor as teller had been persuaded to take early retirement because of it. But Will, the most genial of men, went along with the tide while he was at the bank, and he allowed all to draw funds from the till with no more formal notice than a scrawl. As biographer C. Alphonso Smith put it:

> It was notorious that by Washington officialdom's standards, the bank was wretchedly managed in the "old boy" fashion. President Brackenridge and Cashier Brackenridge thought nothing of authorizing loans on a moment's notice, and producing the cash, often without collateral. The bank patrons, following an old custom, used to enter, go behind the counter, take out one hundred or two hundred dollars, and say a week later: ". . . I took out two hundred dollars last week. See if I left a memorandum of it. I meant to."[7]

ON FEBRUARY 23, 1895, Federal Bank Examiner Jonathan J. Gannon made another examination of the First National Bank of Austin. In those days the examiners came three or four times a year to banks they considered "troublesome" and the First National Bank of Austin was certainly one of these. He was disappointed to see that virtually none of the promised changes had been made. The bank was still making loans without meetings of the directors. No directors' meeting had been held since August. It soon became apparent that Vice President Hamilton, not President Brackenridge, was running the bank, but that said nothing either for the efficiency of the management or for the condition of the bank. Indeed, new questions now emerged, the sort of questions that would raise eyebrows in Washington.

In less than a year Vice President Hamilton's overdrafts had jumped from $2,300 to $13,500. Cashier Brackenridge's overdraft had risen from $2,000 to $10,300. What did that mean? It could mean that Hamilton and Brackenridge had been dipping into the till and had now regularized their withdrawals in the form of overdrafts against their personal accounts.

But—they were honorable men, "of good reputation in the community" and well-to-do. The overdrafts, while improper, were adjudged by the bank examiner to be safe as far as the bank was concerned.[8]

THE PRINCIPAL SHAREHOLDERS of the First National Bank of Austin were Vice President Hamilton and Director J. R. Johnson, both members of the private investment firm of Jonathan Raymond and Co. Of the total 1,000 shares of bank stock outstanding, members of the private investment firm owned 800 shares. Director and Vice President Hamilton owned 266 2/3 shares and Director Johnson owned a similar amount. J. T. Brackenridge, the president of the bank, owned only 10 shares, and his son, R. J. Brackenridge, the cashier, owned 18¾ shares. J. S. Myrick, another director, owned 36¼ shares. The other shares were owned by Austin businessmen.

One of the examiner's objections to the management of the First National Bank was its sloppiness. Apparently, the president and the cashier had been making all the immediate decisions, and this was supposed to have changed. They were "of good reputation but they are *not* [examiner's italics] considered either *competent* or *efficient* bank managers."9

The only change was that President Brackenridge had been pushed into the background, and now Vice President Hamilton and Cashier Brackenridge made the decisions, without board meetings. The bankers tried to argue that directors Hamilton and Johnson were taking more active roles, but the minutes of the board meetings—or lack of them—was further proof of the unacceptable state of affairs. The only major change was that of teller. William Sydney Porter had left and H. Pfuefflin had been employed—for $1,500 per year, $300 more than Will Porter had been getting. Will's intuition had been sound; the management had planned to put someone in over his head. Had they been promoting from within, Bookkeeper Byrne would have been promoted to teller. The management had also added two clerks and an assistant bookkeeper to do the detail work that Will Porter and Byrne had done before all alone.

What did not show on the First National Bank's ledgers was the fact that "the banking firm of Jonathan H. Raymond and Company virtually *owns and controls* the management. Directors Hamilton and Johnson are members of the firm of Raymond and Co." So, also, was Director Myrick, which gave the Raymond firm members control of the board of directors.

The bank was really a satellite of the Raymond firm and had been since the reorganization several years before. No effort was made to get new business; the whole impetus was to take care of the Raymond Company.

"There does not appear to be much of a future in store for them while it remains under its present management," said the bank examiner in concluding his report.10

The Brackenridges were high among the first families of Austin, above reproach, one might say. They served on boards of directors and their wives ran the city's charities. They were movers and shakers.

For the purposes of the bank and its customers, the system seemed to work well enough. The federal bank examiners certainly did not approve, however. In 1894 the examiners had begun to crack down on banking practices in view of the hard times the country was going through and complaints of the hard-money people that the country was turning to Populism.

Then, in his remarks to the comptroller of the currency, Examiner F. B. Gray gave the First National Bank of Austin the kiss of death: "In my opinion the bank is not in good condition," he wrote in the conclusion of his report.

IN THIS FLURRY of criticism, President Brackenridge resigned. Apparently his son took over the management.

Examiner Gannon was back in July 1895, and he complained that the directors still had not held a meeting, not even one to elect officers! The bank had no president. R. J. Brackenridge, cashier, was listed as chief operating officer.

The real management of the bank, said Examiner Gannon, was totally in the hands of Vice President Hamilton, although to the outside world it seemed that Cashier Brackenridge was in charge.

The affairs of the bank were even a worse mess than before. There was not a bonded employee in the bank!

The Hamilton loans were still on the books. Further, Mr. Gannon this time found a new wrinkle: over the past six years the bank had charged off $189,000 to "losses." Its balance sheet showed only $384,000 in assets and liabilities. Its capitalization was $100,000. It had not paid a dividend on its stock in ten years. The bank existed as the creature of the private banking firm, a source of ready cash that could be manipulated and milked.

There were so many irregularities in the affairs of the First National Bank of Austin that a closer investigation was ordered.[11]

The bankers really became frightened at this point and began scurrying around to protect themselves.

By December 1895, when Examiner Gannon returned to the bank, Frank Hamilton had resigned as director and had paid off all but $6,000 of his overdrafts. Cashier Brackenridge's overdrafts had now been formalized into loans, but still stood at $10,000. For what purpose was, of course, unsaid by the bank examiner.

Whatever the problem, during all the fuss, the bank officials adjusted the records, and no one, depositor or draft-casher at the bank lost a penny. But the affairs of the bank were in such a morass that year that the examiners demanded that a "federal case" be made of the matter.

Gannon went away reporting, "It looks as though the proper person had at last taken hold of the management of the bank, and the indications are that they will now be able to do both a safe and profitable business."[12]

Meanwhile, however, the furor over the past irregularities had brought about the investigation, and the investigation had shown that several thousand dollars had been mishandled, lost, in fact, and that this loss had been made up by the directors. In other words, the money had flown out of the bank, and then had miraculously reappeared.

Questions: Mr. Hamilton's overdrafts? Cashier Brackenridge's loans?

Nobody asked those questions.

Someone, said the federal authorities, had to be in trouble. But who? As teller, Will Porter was the responsible party. Aha! But, the grand jury found no evidence on which to indict him or anyone else, and it dropped the matter.

Skulduggery, said someone in Washington. The teller was being protected. He was the logical miscreant. Let the investigation be renewed and come to the right conclusion this time.

At the end of 1895, the bank had indeed come under new management. James R. J. Johnson, of the Jonathan H. Raymond Company had become president; Hamilton had retired, J. S. Myrick had become vice president. R. J. Brackenridge had remained as cashier, but H. Pfuefflin had not only become teller, but had been promoted to assistant cashier and held ten shares of stock! There was no one in the bank management except young Brackenridge who had been there during Will Porter's tenure.[13]

AMONG THE NEW officials, money began to talk as it always does, and the bankers fell out among themselves about the money that was missing, which was somewhere in excess of $4,000.

Former Vice President Hamilton was called to account by President Johnson. He repaid $3,000 to the bank, but he also came to Will Porter, pointing out that as teller he was responsible for everything that happened during his tenure, and thus he should share Hamilton's losses. Will felt the responsibility, naive as he was, and agreed to put up $1,500. Thus he violated the first rule of self-protection: when trouble starts, no matter how friendly anyone seems, the wise man admits nothing and does nothing.

Will said he would accept "responsibility." He did not have the $1,500 demanded by Hamilton. To "save his son-in-law's good name"—which was all that seemed to be at stake—P. G. Roach agreed to advance the money, which Will would repay. Thus Hamilton was in the position of having had his cake and now eating part of it. Then, he had a better idea. Why should not the surety company, which had bonded Porter for $10,000, make up the entire loss? The question of criminality—the lack of it—had been settled by the grand jury's refusal to indict anyone. As teller, everyone agreed that Will Porter was responsible for the cash. But the surety company representative, Carr Lucy, said there was no evidence of wrongdoing by Porter, and therefore no reason for the company to pay.[14]

The argument grew somewhat heated, particularly when the bank examiners suggested that if Will Porter hadn't stolen the money, someone else had, and indicated that a new investigation might be undertaken. This was the last move the bankers wanted. Frank Hamilton said again that he did not think the teller had stolen any money, but this time his tones were not convincing. To the federal investigators Will's agreement to share Hamilton's losses meant an admission of guilt by the former teller of the bank. The investigation was renewed, focused on Will Porter's activities. And so, out of the mare's nest that Frank Hamilton and his associates of the Jonathan H. Raymond investment firm had made of the First National Bank of Austin, with the assistance of Cashier Brackenridge, now came real trouble, exacerbated by Hamilton's greed. Someone had to take the rap. Indictment was sought of the one man involved in handling these funds who was no longer connected with the bank, Will Porter. The investigators took all evidence of all funds awry to Federal District Attorney R. U. Culberson. He was accused officially in letters in Washington of having yielded to political pressures in failing to prosecute vigorously enough to achieve an indictment. This time, National Bank Examiner Gray would be the government's primary "expert witness." The jury investigated, was led along as the bank examiners now wanted, and various officers of the bank testified. This time their testimony was different, not nearly so convincing about the innocence of the bank's former teller. Good Old Frank Hamilton, the big stockholder, and vice president, no longer gave Will Porter a character reference. He didn't say anything about his own practices, about loans that suddenly appeared on the bank's books, and nobody asked him. They were looking for a fish. He didn't have to be a big fish, just a fish.[15]

WHILE ALL THE financial maneuvering was in process, in the summer of 1895 Will Porter was offered a newspaper job in Washington, and the matter went far enough that he and Athol sold off their furniture. They did not have to worry about the house because they had never amassed enough capital to buy one. But just as they were about to set out for the Potomac Athol came down with a high fever, and this time the doctors diagnosed her case definitely as consumption. It was as though they had signed a death warrant.

Her condition was so acute that there was no question of her traveling to Washington, and Will refused to leave her. So they moved in with the

Roaches, and Will increased his output of sketches and cartoons and humorous articles, and somehow they survived.

In the interim, various friends had been using their influence to help Will. His crony Ed McLean had some connection with Colonel R. M. Johnston, then the editor of the *Houston Post.* He sent a copy of *The Rolling Stone* to Houston, and Johnston liked what he read. He agreed to give Will a try as a special writer for the *Post* at $15 a week. It was quite a comedown, but the Porter straits were such that summer that he had to take it. There was no question of Athol moving, so in October 1895, Will took himself down to Houston and Athol and little Margaret stayed with the Roaches.[16]

Will Porter made his reputation very quickly in Houston. He was given a column, "Tales of the Town," which allowed him to roam around and examine the subjects he liked. He spent many an afternoon and evening at the Hutchins House, the central hotel of Houston, and at the Grand Central Railroad Depot, watching people.

He told all sorts of tales.

"Speaking of the $140,000,000 paid out yearly by the government in pensions," said a prominent member of Hood's brigade to the *Post*'s representative, "I am told that a man in Indiana applied for a pension last month on account of a surgical operation he had performed on him during the war. And what do you suppose that surgical operation was?

"Haven't the least idea."

"He had his retreat cut off at the battle of Gettysburg."[17]

A young lady in Houston became engaged last summer to one of the famous shortstops of the Texas baseball league. Last week he broke the engagement. This is the reason why:

He had a birthday last Tuesday and she sent him a beautiful bound and illustrated edition of Coleridge's famous poem, "The Rhyme of the Ancient Mariner."

The hero of the diamond opened the book with a puzzled look.

"What's dis bloomin stuff bout anyway?"

He read the first two lines.

"It is the Ancient Mariner,
And he stoppeth one of three . . ."

The famous shortstop threw the book out of the window, stuck out his chin, and said, "No Texas sis can gimme de umpire face like dat. I swipes nine daisy cutters outer ten dat comes in my garden, dat's what."

The *Post*'s readers also liked what they read and Will Porter's scope grew broader. He had another column called "Postscripts." "The man who pens Postscripts for the Houston Post is a weird, wildeyed genius and ought to be captured and put on exhibition," wrote another editor. Editor Johnston soon learned that his new writer could draw, too, and he was assigned to do political cartoons. He got a raise to $80 a month, and the lavish praise of Editor Johnston, who announced that his new writer was a real comer and ought to eventually graduate to the big leagues of New York or Chicago and make as much as $50 a week. At the moment, Will was earning his money. One week he had to do twenty-nine drawings for the Sunday paper.[18]

Feeling more settled than he had been in a long time, Will moved Athol and Margaret to Houston. Lollie Cave, now married to a rancher named Wilson, lived just outside the city, and the Porter family went out to the Wilson place frequently. Life looked bright until January 1896. Then Will had a new series of shocks. His father-in-law, P.G. Roach, wanted to know how he was going to be paid back the $1,500 he had put up for Porter's good name?

On January 19, 1896, Will Porter tried to deal with this new problem:

I believe I wrote you that my salary is now $80 per month. I have no objection of course to sending you monthly or weekly a portion of same. If you will say how much you think of that amount I ought to pay. I will send it to you each month. I expect another raise soon, as the management express themselves frequently as much pleased with my work. I am commencing to send out matter to other papers. Have had a couple of columns printed in the New York *World* a week or two ago. They have not remitted yet although I have written them. I ought within a month to be making from five to ten dollars a week extra. I have no money on hand. Have used what little was over from the $60* for the first two months in buying coal and necessities. We are not spending a cent unnecessarily and are not going to."[19]

Will did have a raise again very quickly, to $100 per month, but it did not really help, for the situation in Austin had grown far more serious. Mr. Gray, the demon bank examiner, insisted that wrongdoers must be prosecuted. In Washington tempers had been aroused, and the comptroller of the currency threatened Federal District Attorney Musgrave. And so because of cupidity,

---

*Roach had apparently lent his son-in-law $60 when Athol came down to Houston to join him.

irritation, ambition, and self-protection, the case against Porter was dug up and dusted off and reversed although the facts had not changed.

This time Porter's banker friends were his enemies. At least one of them was prepared to tell a pack of lies. Banker Hamilton assuaged his conscience by telling everyone that he had said all along that Will Porter was guilty only of a series of mistakes, and that he ought not to be prosecuted. But he did not try to stop it. The case was resubmitted to the grand jury on February 10, 1896. No one spoke up for the accused this time, and Will Porter was indicted on four counts of embezzlement, totalling $4,702.94, a total which represented every inexplicable "error" made by every bank employee for several years past. On February 14, 1896, Porter had his valentine from the government: arrest by the federal marshal at Houston. He was put on the train that day with the marshal and taken back to Austin.[20]

Ed McLean met him at the depot, and found a Will Porter he had not known before, sullen and disconsolate. He refused to discuss the matter except to say that he was innocent of the charge. "I made a mistake of five hundred dollars in paying out money." To whom or how, he would not say, and he never did. The only real statement he made on the subject was to his old friend Lollie Cave Wilson:

> The guilty man, if charged, would take the stand and call me a liar. He is not, as I thought, a man of honor, or he would have kept his word to me and straightened the matter out when I left Austin and the bank.
>
> Therefore when he is caught in a trap he will take the crook's viewpoint and clear his own skirts. His word will be taken against mine, because my word is the only thing that accuses him—the books, those silent accusers, are pointing fingers of guilt at me. You know those men at the bank are too close together to give an outsider a chance. . . .
>
> I was not cut out for that kind of work. But I took the job and held a position of trust. I failed that trust when I permitted such an outrageous thing to happen. Since I did not report the shortages as they occurred, I can legally be held as an accessory to the fact."[21]

And who might the guilty party have been? Neither then, nor later, would Will Porter name the man, but he had given all the clues. Who was his contemporary among the bank's officers, who had access to his teller's cage almost every day, a man who had suddenly taken out a $10,000 personal loan when the bank examiners began prying?

And who was really running the bank all these years when Will Porter was working there, and had suddenly taken out more $13,000 in loans when the bank examiners began prying?

If the sleuths had looked into the finances of Vice President Frank Hamilton and R. J. Brackenridge, cashier of the bank, they might have learned the real truth of the bank defalcations. Will Porter never knew it either, but before the end of 1896 Cashier Brackenridge's salary at the bank had been reduced from $2,400 a year to $1,500, certainly no sign of approval by his superiors. It would have been interesting to learn what Bank President Johnson had to say about that.

# 6

# Honduran Interlude

Will Porter faced the court proceedings gloomily, recognizing that if the deck could be stacked against him by the bank, it would be in the interests of the tight little group who controlled the institution. It was so well known that the bank was run shoddily that Will had made a wisecrack to that effect when he left the bank's employment. It was predictable that his old acquaintances would throw him to the federal wolves if they could, now that the government was trying to crack down on the lamentable practice of country and small town bankers of treating customers' money as if it were their own. They were obviously trembling in their boots lest they, too, be indicted.

In the late winter, the *Houston Post* moved into a new building. The editorial staff was housed on the second floor in small cubicles, which made it much easier to work. Will Porter was beginning to feel like a fixture, and more so when Editor Johnston came into his cubicle one day and announced that he had instructed the business office to raise Will's pay again. More important, he told Will not to worry about the difficulty in Austin, the paper would stand behind him and pay all his expenses.[1]

But in February came those indictments, and the need to raise bond or go to jail.

Ed McLean, now secretary of the Railroad Commission of Texas, did what he could to help his old friend. P. G. Roach, Will's father-in-law, and Herman Pressler, one of the cronies from the land office, put up $4,000 as bond to guarantee Will's return to court. The bond posted, the federal district court allowed O. Henry to return to Houston to continue his work.[2] But, in fact, it was hard for him to continue his creative efforts because the world was suddenly coming down on his shoulders. Athol's tuberculosis had reached the acute stage in which she would be seized by a fever of perhaps 105 degrees, and would collapse.

In March, Will enlisted the help of officials of the *Post* to secure a continuance in the case. Dick Hall, who happened to be in Houston, went back to Austin on the same mission in behalf of Will Porter. District Attorney Culberson, always uncomfortable with this affair, agreed readily, but had to secure the permission of Examiner Gray, the moving force in the prosecution. The column suffered. There were not so many bits of fun—such as the long poem about the Mexican gentleman who avenged Santa Anna and the defeat of Mexico by selling indigestible tamales to the wicked Texans. But Editor Johnston of the *Post* was very generous; he continued Will's salary even though the columns were few and spare, and he advanced him additional money.

On March 16, Will Porter was back in Austin again where he was supposed to enter a plea to the charges against him. But, he said, so difficult had been his life since the indictment was returned that he had not been able even to engage counsel, and was completely unready for any court action. Since he had been gone from the bank for more than six months, memory would not serve, and to prepare a defense against the charges he would have to have access to the records of the bank for the period of his employment. This would take some time and would demand a continuance of the case.[3]

He did secure counsel, R. H. Ward and Ashby S. James. They began the laborious processes of securing evidence. Their client was very little help. "I never had so non-communicative a client," said Attorney Ward.

Will Porter went back to Houston to try to put his life back together again, but it was almost a hopeless task. Athol's tuberculosis was progressing very rapidly, and she was wasting away before his very eyes.

From some "prominent source"—probably his friend Judge Hill in San Antonio, who took the view all along that this was all politics and thus could be disposed of behind the scenes—Will got the intimation that the whole matter could be "arranged" in Washington. So he told several friends. There was no question of "nolle prossing" the case; but what all concerned knew was that the zeal with which the case would be pressed was primarily dependent on the demand of the comptroller of the currency that these Southwestern banks clean up their sloppy practices.[4] It was indeed a political matter.

A month later Will Porter was feeling very comfortable about this and other matters. He had decided that the *Houston Post* would be his cocoon from this point on. Editor Johnston had predicted to a friend that it would not be long before Porter was making $100 a week. All seemed serene. In a letter to Herman Pressler, Will stopped to take dictation from daughter Margaret for a letter of her own about a pair of rabbits Pressler had sent her. Will obliged by drawing a picture of the rabbits. The one dark spot in the happy domestic scene concerned Athol. She had been very sick again for three days, with high fever. Then, as is the way with tuberculosis, the fever subsided and she seemed well once more.[5]

In June, Will prepared to go to Austin to stand trial. Athol was to remain in Houston. They were suffering from money troubles, but they were so used to that situation that it did not seem to bother them overmuch. On June 16, Porter was waiting only for the return of Editor Johnston from a trip so he could draw the money necessary for his expenses for the next few weeks. On March 16, Will wrote Herman Pressler that "my capital is just $1.40 today." He was prepared to go to Austin immediately, and was only waiting for the money. Porter had again been assured that the matter would be arranged in Washington, outside court.

But a week later Will Porter's troubles began to mount. Athol was extremely sick and unable to travel. On the night of June 20 he was up with her all night long. Mrs. Roach came down to help.

It was not long before Mrs. Roach said she could not cope in a strange city, and it was agreed that Athol and Margaret would go back to the Roach house in Austin. Several Austin friends, including Dick Hall and Frank Maddox, urged him to come up immediately.

When Athol got away from steamy Houston she had one of those remissions that are so kind and yet so cruel, for it convinced all the hopeful family that her health was improving. Will Porter was told and he grew more cheerful.

The trial had been set for the summer term of 1896 in Austin, and on June 22, Porter delivered his last column to the *Houston Post.* Editor Johnston gave him some extra money for his expenses, and assurances of more support to get him through the trial. Obviously, he did not believe Porter was guilty of theft. No one who knew Will believed he was dishonest.

Other newspapermen gave him a royal and very liquid departure, and he boarded the Houston & Texas Central Railroad's evening train. The line led to the town of Hempstead, some sixty miles to the northwest, where the Austin branch broke off. During the two hours of the trip, Will Porter mulled over his future. He had no confidence in his ability or that of his lawyers to sort out the dreadful mess of the bank's books. Yet, as teller, he had been principal bookkeeper and was responsible for their condition, even if he had neither brought the books to that condition nor added to their confusion. It was as simple as that and as deadly. Will also knew that he had been betrayed by Frank Hamilton, who had promised to return money he took from Will's till and had not done so. Will knew how, when, and why. So at least one indictment was going to stand up; he would have to choose whether to get into a mudfight with Hamilton or not. He had no confidence that he could win such a fight, for Hamilton would have the support of Cashier Brackenridge, Brackenridge would have the support of his father, the former bank president, the other officers, and the "moral support" of the pillars of the community.

As far as Will Porter was concerned the deck was stacked and it had to be a losing game. The news from Austin had been good; Athol was better. So why go back? Would it not be simpler to stay away from Austin altogether, move about or to some foreign clime until the three-year statute of limitations ran out, and he could return to Austin a free man? Or perhaps he would never go back, but find a new place and bring Athol and Margaret there to start a new life.

To a man of William Sydney Porter's temperament, hating confrontation and difficulty, the temptation to chuck it all was overwhelming, and when he came to Hempstead, instead of catching the northbound train on the Austin line, he turned about and bought a ticket for New Orleans, retraced his steps through Houston on the main line, and a few hours later arrived in New Orleans.

For a journeyman reporter it was not too hard a task to secure a temporary job or assignments from newspapers, and Will was reportedly associated in one way or another with several of them in the next few months. One tale says that under the name Shirley Worth he worked for the *New Orleans Delta* and later the *Picayune.* Perhaps he did. Another tale has it that he joined a cooperative down in Frenchtown, where they employed one of the finest cooks in all the city, and spent much of his time in the Tobacco Plant Saloon. This sounds believable, for Will Porter was a great eater and an even greater drinker, with a love not just for the gross matter, but for all the trimmings. At this time the infernal Sazerac cocktail became his favorite drink. He would sit for half an hour culling a bowl of fresh strawberries to perfection, and he would spend many minutes making a mint julep in a silver cup, with his sprigs of mint and his ice packed just so. He was ever the lover of the good life, and in the last half of the next century he would have been labeled "gourmet" and would have objected, as he did to all excess and phony verbiage.

WHILE IN NEW Orleans, Will informed Athol of his decision, which was needless since he was now a bailjumper, and of his reasoning. Whatever she thought of that, she kept to herself and destroyed his letters. Their go-betweens were Mrs. Lollie Cave Wilson in Houston and one or two people in Austin. They needed go-betweens, because Will Porter had become a fugitive from federal justice. He dare not tarry overlong in any American city. What he had to do was find a hole and head for it, someplace south of the border that did not have a treaty of extradition with the United States. There he would be safe.

Will considered settling down in Honduras for the three years, and perhaps for longer. His Spanish was completely in working order. He had polished up his style of sketches and was beginning to make stories out of them. As a newspaperman, he might expect to write enough tales to survive, if he were lucky. The life of the free lance was not an easy one, as he already knew from his experiences in Austin after the collapse of *The Rolling Stone.*

What was to be done now was to begin work, raise the money to send for Athol and Margaret, put the child into a good English-language school, and settle down. He stayed on in New Orleans as long as he dared, until shortly before Christmas. Athol, meanwhile, seemed to be growing better, or so her letters testified. She entered a business college in Austin, perhaps to prepare herself for a business career in the new land. Will continued to work on the New Orleans newspaper and to dream. When he had replenished his financial coffers, Will took ship as a passenger for Trujillo, in the banana republic of Honduras, which had no treaty of extradition with the United States and was consequently a haven. Here, Will met several other desperadoes, including Al Jennings, a train robber on the lam, and in their drinking sessions in the open-air cafes he heard enough lies and tall tales to fill a book of stories.[6]

He did not know, and Athol did not tell him, that she had reached the critical stage of her disease. More and more often she was confined to bed with bouts of fever. Yet with the Christmas season approaching, and no money, she found a way to give a gift to her husband. With enormous effort, she made a point-lace handkerchief, which sympathetic friends auctioned off. She got $25 for it and spent the money on presents for her husband's lonely Christmas. Off in Honduras, Will Porter was eating lotus, still creating visions of the new life away from all the trouble.

But it all came to nought. For in the excitement of the Christmas season of 1896, Athol came down with a burning fever and this time it did not go away. She was put to bed, but after a month the Roaches had to get in touch with Will and tell him that his wife was dying.

So the best-made plan had ganged agley for Will Porter. His world was falling into shards, and what happened to him no longer seemed to be of much importance.[7] His first task was to get back to Austin and Athol, and this is what he did. He reached New Orleans once again, found himself without funds, and telegraphed P. G. Roach for $25. He arrived unannounced in the Texas capital on February 5, 1897, and a week later appeared before Judge Aleck Boardman in federal court. It is an indication of the feeling in Austin about the whole embezzlement case that Will Porter, although technically he had been a fugitive for months, was released once again on a new bond, and no attempt was made to collect the previous bond, although Will was definitely in default.[8]

For the next five months the court left Will Porter completely alone. The only person eager for a trial was National Bank Examiner Gray and he was not in town, but on his circuit. The doughty executives of the First National Bank were running scared and keeping mum. The federal prosecutor had already made his views known by dropping the case once. So the dignity of the law was well served for all in Austin by letting the accused and his dying wife enjoy as much time together as nature would allow.

Mostly they went driving. Will would bring up the phaeton. Athol would come out of the Roach house all bundled up. He would tuck a rug around her and then leap into the cab and cluck at the horse. Away they would go, over the hills or down the road toward San Antonio, for an afternoon's outing. They visited many of the scenes of their past together. As the weeks went on, Athol grew weaker, and could not easily get in and out of the buggy. But on Sundays they sat outside the Southern Presbyterian Church and listened to the familiar hymns, which they had sung together—it seemed like yesterday. Spring turned to summer, but by then Athol was too weak to leave the house, and she was propped up on a couch in the parlor when old friends came to call. And then it was too much even to make that effort, and she was confined to their bedroom. Suddenly, in the third week of July, she seemed to improve remarkably. The flush left her cheek, the dreadful bloody cough waned, and, wonder of wonders, she had no fever. It was nature's way of preparation. She was vivacious and insisted on staying up all day and into the evenings, until Sunday, July 25, when she admitted that she had been doing too much, and stayed in bed all day. That night she died. She was twenty-nine years old.[9]

FOR MONTHS, WILL Porter had devoted every hour to his wife and daughter. Now he had other matters to consider, primarily the settlement of the criminal case, about which he never had any real doubt, and secondarily the establishment of a way of life for the future and some stability for the life of his daughter Margaret.

The Roaches operated a store on Sixth Street and let Porter take over the room on the second floor above the store. Here, after Athol's funeral, he began to write furiously in a new genre, the short story, aimed at the newspaper syndicates and new magazines that were coming into existence to fill the needs of a growing population with more time, more money, and the education to read for pleasure.

His first sale of a short story was of "An Afternoon Miracle," which was purchased by the S. S. McClure Syndicate in the fall of 1897. It was a story set along the Tex-Mex border, a story from Will's ranching youth. Lieutenant Bob Buckley, the leader of the Texas Rangers, was drawn from his old friend and benefactor Captain Lee Hall, "a man who would allow no man of them the privilege of investigating a row when he himself might go."

"Peculiarness of Bob is he hain't had proper training," said one of his men. "He never learned how to get skeered."

The reader of the 1980s who investigates O. Henry's stories will have to get used to his regionalisms for they abound throughout the dialogue: if it is a Mexican who speaks, he talks like a Mexican speaking English; if it is a Texan, he talks like a Texan, and the same with the Irishman of the city and the Jewish peddler and the Heathen Chinee. Among all the apparent deficiencies that time has cast upon the O. Henry mold of prose, his use of the vernacular is by far the most disconcerting, particularly to a society whose police investigations are often impeded because authority considers a fugitive's rights to be violated if a cop says whether the miscreant is black, yellow, red, or white, and in which claims are *taken seriously* for the establishment of multiple official languages. The fault is scarcely O. Henry's, but as he learned in 1898, being right is no excuse, and so the American reader of O. Henry is often at a greater disadvantage than the reader of his prose translated into some forty other languages, because regional dialogue in America has gone out of style in the American written language in the attempt to homogenize the spoken tongue.

And, of course, there may be those who would take umbrage at the following from this first O. Henry story, as the hero encountered the villain who had made untoward advances at the fair young maiden:

> The Mexican, suddenly stirring, ventilated his attitude of apathetic waiting by conjuring swiftly from his bootlet a long knife. Buckley cast aside his hat, and laughed once aloud, like a happy schoolboy at a frolic. Then, empty handed, he sprang nimbly, and Garcia met him without default.*
>
> So soon was the engagement ended that disappointment imposed upon the ranger's war like ecstasy. Instead of dealing the traditional downward stroke,

---

*That sentence, itself without an iota of regionalism, is indicative of one of the great strengths of O. Henry as a writer of American prose—the absolute mastery of the dictionary tongue as well as of the spoken tongue. It is his mixture of the two that elevated him far above the writing crowd of his own day; that, of course, plus half a dozen other small items such as plot mastery and superb characterization.

the Mexican lunged straight with his knife. Buckley took the precarious chance and caught his wrist, fair and firm. Then he delivered the good Saxon knockout blow—always so pathetically disastrous to the fistless Latin races—and Garcia was down and out, with his head under a clump of prickly pears . . .

Yes, the American reader of O. Henry's priceless stories must these days be warned, *autres temps, autres moeurs.* And if he doesn't know what that means, then he ought to find another author.

# 7

# Hard Times

The announcement from S. S. McClure Syndicate that they wanted to buy Will Porter's first story was accompanied by a request from the editor for any more of the same sort that the author might have in mind. So the career of the writer was begun. But immediately it had to be melded into a most difficult life and for much of the time suspended. Will Porter was not the newspaper writer of the sort who could sit behind a pillar in a city room and turn out "deathless prose" by clacking away on a typewriter while a dozen others were doing the same. He required silence, loneliness, and total concentration in order to work. Very little time of this sort was granted him in the last few weeks of 1897 and the early weeks of 1898. His attorneys wanted to make a case for him, and, much as he detested the entire process, he had to cooperate to the best of his ability.[1]

When the trial began, on February 15, 1898, it was an enormous emotional shock to the defendant. All the evidence presented by the prosecution was circumstantial and technical. It had to be, for what the accusation leveled down to was: William Sydney Porter was responsible for the bank's cash. Certain sums disappeared. They were his responsibility. How slight the case was altogether was indicated by changes in the indictments brought forth on the day the trial began. Two were dismissed and two more brought. Finally Porter was to be tried for embezzling $299.60 and $554.48. And who was to be tried for embezzling the other $3,400 that had disappeared according to Examiner Gray? Nobody.

Judge T. S. Maxey presided over the court. The defense counsel struck from the juror list three names, all Germanic, because of Editor Porter's quarrel with the German community in the days of *The Rolling Stone*. But that was not the only reason. German jurors in central Texas property cases were known in the lawyer trade as "State's jurors" who were most likely to vote to convict anyone charged with taking anything. The prosecution also struck off three potential jurors, for reasons unknown. The jury was then impaneled, and the lawyers began.[2]

District Attorney Culberson made the government's case. Attorneys Ward and James represented the defendant. The dreary recitation of the facts began. It was dreary because it could have been nothing else: the whole government case hinged on proving that money paid in at the bank by depositors had not been credited to them properly. Even before the recital could begin, the lawyers had to use up all their technical weapons. Ward and James said the indictments did not charge any offense against federal law. The judge overruled that, but he had to cite the national banking regulations to do it.

The defense attorneys then said the indictments failed to describe the bank involved so that the jurors could be sure it was the First National Bank of Austin they all knew. Judge Maxey said there was only one First National Bank of Austin.

The defense counsel said the indictment did not charge the defendant with converting the funds to his own use or of any fraudulent intent whatsoever. That was a little better, but the district attorney said the government would prove that as a part of the trial.

Ward and James then said the indictment was indefinite, uncertain, and insufficient. The judge ruled that since Will Porter was in a position of trust as teller, the indictment was sufficient.

They charged as well that the indictment did not say how the money or funds came into Porter's hands, and in what capacity he held them. The judge ruled that again, as teller, he was responsible for all the money in the bank.

The lawyers then said that the indictments did not indicate any relationship between these sums and the defendant. Again the Judge reminded them that the defendant was the teller of the bank.

Finally, the lawyers said the indictments were faulty because they did not say whether the property was money or funds. The judge said this was specious argument, property was missing, the teller was the responsible party.

So all the motions to quash the indictments were lost. Then the lawyers turned to the statute of limitations: the alleged crimes were committed in October 1894. It was now February 1898. The three years had passed. The government had offered no testimony that at any time had the defendant been a fugitive from justice.[3]

Arguments developed as to whether or not Porter had been a fugitive from justice. He was missing from Austin from early July 1896 until February 1897, that was true. Technically, his bail had been forfeit, but no move had ever actually been made to collect it. To the defense this meant the government was not concerned about Will Porter's absence. Further, he had returned voluntarily in February 1897 and was standing trial. How could he be called a fugitive?

For the purposes of this trial, said Judge Maxey, Will Porter became a fugitive when he did not appear in Austin when expected in the summer of 1897. The judge did not go into this matter further than to rule that the trial could be held.

Then Judge Maxey overruled the last two arguments of the defending counsel: that the government had confused indictments brought in by two different grand juries, and that the prosecution had not offered any proof of embezzlement of anything. The judge said the indictments had been straightened out and that the purpose of the trial was to determine if something had been embezzled as charged, and if the defendant seemed beyond a reasonable doubt to have done the embezzling.

In the testimony that followed, it appeared that a bank customer named E. L. Gwartney had come into the bank and put down $554.48 for a draft on the San Antonio National Bank. As far as Gwartney could recall he had bought the draft from Teller Porter because he usually did. Bank employees testified that Porter was *never* absent from the bank except at lunch, and Gwartney testified that he *never* went to the bank at lunch hour. Two days later the draft was presented at the San Antonio bank and paid. But at the end of the month, the San Antonio bank complained loudly that its account with the Austin National Bank showed no evidence of that payment. The Austin bank's auditor testified that until the San Antonio bank complained, there was no record of the transaction. The error had then been corrected and the San Antonio bank made happy with its money. But who was responsible? Will Porter, the bank teller.[4]

Four days after the San Antonio bank draft was drawn, a credit slip and letter were sent by Teller Porter to the First National Bank of Waco. But when the accounts came up at the end of the month, the Waco bank complained, the credit of $299.60 had not been given that bank, although they had Porter's credit slip and signed letter. Also, said the Waco bank, there was a further discrepancy of $100 in the accounts. President R. J. Brackenridge of the First National Bank of Austin wrote back to the Waco bank showing that an error had been made and that it was being corrected.

The government charged that the credit slip had been issued in Porter's handwriting. Bank witnesses so testified. They also testified that the proper procedure would have been to post the entry in the bank's books that day or the next, but that this was not done. Someone had accepted $299.60 and Will Porter had sent a credit slip to the Waco bank.

Porter's attorney tried to show that the First National Bank of Austin used such shoddy bookkeeping practices that no one could tell precisely what was happening at any given time. They also tried to show that Will Porter was highly respected in the community as a person of impeccable character. This latter move would have worked better had Will not asked all his friends to stay away from the trial as a personal favor to him. The absence of a "cheering section" did not help, particularly since the government's case rested on destroying Will Porter's character, and part of the process of destruction was implication that he had taken the money to further his failing newspaper, *The Rolling Stone,* and that part of the reason it was failing was because of the high living and roistering of the editor and his friends. Dick Hall wrote a letter to the prosecutor asking him to go easy on Will Porter, but that didn't help. The bank officials, who had earlier said they had the highest trust in Will Porter, now closed ranks and testified against him.[5]

Will Porter would have been his own best witness had he not been so set in his belief that the fates were against him. Following Athol's death he had withdrawn and indicated that he did not care whether he lived or died, went to prison or went free, and seemed determined on self-destruction.

If he knew the circumstances under which the money had been taken within one week as he said he did, then his testimony might well have changed the tide in the courtroom. His later indication was that George Brackenridge and Frank Hamilton were the culprits; that he, Will Porter, had sent the credit slip to Waco and had concealed the San Antonio transaction on his friends' promise to make restitution. He had, he said, been betrayed by one of his friends. He did not say which.[6]

But he said not a word in court.

There was no question that Will Porter was in a position of trust concerning the two sums of money. The question was whether or not he had converted the money to his own use. Suspicion derived from Will's love of the high life, and his resignation from the bank just about a month after the irregularities occurred. The allegations and implications were made by others, and oh, how easy it was. His erstwhile circulation manager compiled figures by which he "proved" that the paper had to be losing money, and came up with figures just about justifying the "embezzlements." Of course, the old employee had no way of knowing how much money Mr. Roach had sunk in, or what other earnings Will had had from his newspaper correspondence, or how big were his bar bills at the Bismarck Cafe, but in the absence of the defendant's testimony or desire to defend himself, any and all fairy stories gained credence.

On February 17, 1898, Judge Maxey instructed the jury, and defined embezzlement for them:

There must be actual and lawful possession or custody of the property of another, by virtue of some trust, duty, agency, or employment, committed to the party charged; and while so lawfully in the possession and custody of such property, the person must unlawfully and wrongfully convert the same to his own use, in order to commit the crime of embezzlement.[7]

Further, said Judge Maxey, the known character of the defendant must be examined, and where ever the testimony appeared doubtful, he should be given consideration as to his character. If there seemed to be a reasonable doubt of guilt, then the accused should be acquitted.

Had the jury been convinced of the upright character of Will Porter, then there must be a reasonable doubt as to his guilt. But he had two factors against him; he had been accused of sprinting for cover and ending up in Honduras, which he had never denied or explained. The bank certainly did not give him a good character reference, and the implication was clear that he had stolen the money to support his failing newspaper and bad habits. Then, when accused, he had fled.

Later, the *Dictionary of American Biography* put the trial within the framework of its time:

From Houston he was summoned in 1896 to Austin to stand trial for the alleged embezzlement of funds from the First National Bank in which he had been teller. Had he obeyed the summons he probably would have been acquited, for the bank had been managed very loosely and the loss of not much over a thousand dollars seems to have been due to him only in a technical sense. But instead, unnerved by the prospect, he acted like a guilty man . . .

And so with very little ado, the jury found Will Porter guilty as charged on all counts (including one count of embezzling the same money twice).

So Judge Maxey, who seemed to hold a good deal of sympathy for the accused as well as some doubts of his own, had no recourse but to sentence Porter to a prison term. He could have given him ten years, he had to give him at least five years, and he did, but he suspended the sentence temporarily, thus giving the defense attorneys every opportunity to appeal. After his conviction, O. Henry went to jail however, for that is the way the law worked in 1898. He remained in Travis County jail as the lawyers did their work.

Unfortunately the lawyers missed the one legal point that might have gotten Will off scot-free, or at least secured him a new trial. At a new trial the question of whether or not he had fled from justice would not have been brought to the attention of the jury, as it was in his trial, since the charge was included in one indictment, later dropped.[8]

The lawyers made their plea and the appellate court in New Orleans turned it down. But the judge who wrote the opinion pointed out that had the lawyers requested the trial judge to submit the question of the defendant's "flight" to the jury as a matter of substance in the case, and had Judge Maxey refused to do so, then there would have been serious question about the legality of the whole trial. Since the lawyers had not mentioned the issue, the appellate court could not rule on it, and the judges affirmed the verdict and the trial.

Will Porter was held in the Travis County jail until April 22, 1898. Mrs. Roach sent him a writing table and chairs. Friends came to call. But the prisoner aroused no more interest in Austin town than had his trial, which went virtually unnoticed in the press because it all came at the time of the outbreak of the Spanish-American War. In fact, the jury selection began on the day that someone or something blew up the battleship *Maine* in Havana Harbor, and Mr. William Randolph Hearst and Mr. Joseph Pulitzer almost double-handedly bought themselves a war in their drive to sell copies of the *New York American* and the *New York World*. With all that excitement, with Captain Lee Hall hurrying forth to organize a unit of Rough Riders, and the smell of action in the air, who was to worry about the fate of one undistinguished newspaper writer?

From his cell in the county calabozo, Will Porter wrote many letters and apparently nothing else. He wrote one letter to his mother-in-law.

> I want to state solemnly to you that in spite of the jury's verdict, I am absolutely innocent of wrongdoing, except so far as foolishly keeping a position that I could not successfully fill. Any intelligent person who heard the evidence presented knows that I should have been acquitted. After I saw the jury I had very little hopes of their understanding enough of the technical matters presented to be fair. I naturally am crushed by the result, but it is not on my own account. I care not so much for the opinion of the general public, but I would have a few of my friends still believe that there is some good in me.[9]

As to the matter of his innocence, much later his daughter, Margaret, attempted to unravel the mystery at which Will hinted here and in his conversation with Lollie Cave Wilson earlier. But she was then living in California, she was not well, and she was unable to secure the help she wanted. Consequently the matter was never probed while all the participants were alive. One final word on the subject was said by Federal Judge Duval West just before his death in 1949. Judge West had been assistant to Federal District Attorney Culberson in the handling of the Porter trial. He had been asked several times about the matter and had refused to comment but apparently it remained on his conscience, and in those last days he volunteered a statement:

"I do not believe that William Sydney Porter was dishonest. Banking laws at that time were such that any employee could "borrow" from the bank, provided that he returned it promptly. It was a common practice and I think he was just an unlucky example in order to stop this practice."[10]

So the reader must decide, and if he wants further subject for cogitation, let him read "Friends in San Rosario," which appeared in book form in the volume *Roads of Destiny,* of O. Henry's collected works. The key lies in the long-winded tale told by Major Tom Kingman of the First National Bank. There are all the clues to give the reader of America's greatest short story writer the solution to the crime.

But in the spring of 1898, there were no clues, Will Porter would not open his mouth, and the bankers of the First National Bank of Austin were still shuddering over their narrow escape. They did not shudder too long, word of the shoddy character of the bank finally led to the dwindling away of the institution. Will Porter, the victim of circumstance and misplaced friendship, could hardly have cared at all. He had left Austin that April and had become Federal Prisoner 30664 held in the state prison at Columbus, Ohio.

# 8

# Prison

After William Sydney Porter's sentence to five years imprisonment, he was immediately placed in the custody of a federal marshal. His guardian was Deputy United States Marshal Al Musgrave, whom Will had known for a long time. The federal authorities had no custodial facilities in Austin so while waiting for the train that would take the marshal and his charge to Columbus, Ohio, Musgrave took a room in a hotel and stayed there with Will Porter, rather than keep him in the Travis County jail.

The next morning Musgrave awoke to find his prisoner gone. He was just wondering what to do when Will Porter opened the door to the room and came in bearing a tray with two mint juleps on it. The prisoner looked at his warder's discomfiture:

"Uncle Al, what's the matter? You surely didn't think I would run off?"[1]

In view of the past, Deputy Marshal Musgrave might well have thought just that, but in fact Will Porter had no intention of fleeing again. Why would he? His life in Austin was over. His beloved wife was dead. His daughter was living with her maternal grandparents, and they would care for her during the next few years. His reputation was blasted. He could not return to Houston or to New Orleans, the federal authorities would be sure to search him out there. He had tasted the delights of expatriation and found them wanting. He had no future as far as he knew, and he had fallen into so deep a depression that before and during the trial he did nothing to save himself. All that mattered to Will Porter was his daughter Margaret, and at this time, even that relationship seemed to have little meaning to him. Margaret was living with the Roaches. The scandal of the trial had been kept from her. Will asked the Roaches to tell

Margaret that her father had been forced to go away for a long time on business. For the child, this word was easy to accept because he had already been gone twice for long times on business, once in Houston, after her mother had become too ill to keep house there, and then for months when he had fled rather than face the ignominy of the trial.[2]

Will Porter's depression and refusal to discuss the embezzlement case convinced some of his friends that he was, indeed, guilty. He should have been shouting his innocence and claiming he was the victim of injustices. Herman Pressler, who had gone his bond, said he had first believed Will innocent, but when he made no moves to defend himself, Pressler came to the conclusion that his friend must be guilty. That came to be the general conclusion in Austin. Only the Roaches maintained their absolute faith in his innocence and integrity.

ON APRIL 22, Deputy Marshal Musgrave and his prisoner boarded the northbound train for the Ohio penitentiary, where Will Porter would serve his sentence. The train trip took three days. Then, at Columbus the prisoner was delivered to the prison on the day that the United State declared war against Spain. At the prison the doors shut behind him, he was stopped behind the first set of bars in the "bullpen" and there he was searched and his extra clothing, including a handsome tweed suit, was taken from him. His shirt, trousers, shoes and socks, and underwear were left to him and he was told that he would have to supply his own linens.

In half an hour he was no longer William Sydney Porter, but a numbered prisoner. He was no longer Will Porter and he was not yet O. Henry.

NO. 30664 WAS thirty-five years old, five feet seven inches tall, and his chestnut-colored hair was now sprinkled with gray. He brought to prison a history of "intemperance," which was duly noted in the records. His education was better than that of most of the prisoners; he had two skills, that of newspaper writer and pharmacist. The former was not an occupation regarded as useful by the prison authorities but the latter was quite the opposite, and it determined the course of No. 30664's life in prison. He was assigned to work in the prison pharmacy.[3]

From the outset, No. 30664 proved to be a model prisoner. Why not? At that moment he thought his life was over. The shock of betrayal by his old associates at the bank had thrown him into that depression, and it remained, the deepest ever seen by Dr. John M. Thomas, chief physician of the prison.

"In my experience of handling over ten thousand prisoners in the eight years I was physician at the prison, I have never known a man who was as deeply humiliated."[4]

At first, also, No. 30664 was treated as just another one of the "fish"; his mail was strictly censored, and he found that prisoners were regarded as scarcely human. They were not allowed to discuss the prison or affairs such as appeals they might be launching. "I never imagined human life was held as cheap as it is here."[5] Penology in these days was the science of keeping prisoners penned up. Plenty of attention was given to discipline. Virtually no attention was given to "rehabilitation," which was regarded in the nineteenth century by most prison officials as coddling.

"The men are regarded as animals without soul or feeling," No. 30664 said. The work day was thirteen hours long, and any man who did not meet his quota was punished.

"If a man gets sick and can't work they take him into a cellar and turn a powerful stream of water on him from a hose that knocks the breath out of him. Then a doctor revives him and they hang him up by his hands with his feet off the floor for an hour or two. This generally makes him go to work again, and when he gives out and can't stand up they bring him on a stretcher to the hospital ward to get well or die as the case may be."[6]

At the time of this writing, No. 30664 was in despair. He had embraced the hope that his appeal on grounds of legal irregularity would free him from prison. Even that hope was scarcely enough to sustain him and he was seriously considering suicide.

"I can stand any kind of hardships or privations on the outside, but I am utterly unable to continue the life I lead here. I know all the arguments that could be advanced as to why I should endure it, but I have reached the limit of endurance. It will be better for everyone else and a thousand times better for me to end the trouble instead of dragging it out longer."[7]

Suicide. He had access to the means—the drugs of the hospital. Why then did he not kill himself?

He was indeed banking heavily on the appeal. He mentioned it four times in that single letter, and he closed the letter in a welter of emotions:

"Please let me hear from you or get Mrs. Roach to write to tell you me [sic] how you all are, and let me know about that appeal, as every day and hour is getting to be a drag and a burden worse than the one before it, and I want an end of some kind to come soon."[8]

That letter, written just three weeks after the Ohio prison doors shut behind him, indicates that even as No. 30664 let himself go in his misery, he was learning the prison ropes, and his life was already improving. He had made arrangements with a prison employee to handle his mail.

"If you write me any letter that comes through the Warden's office, *be sure not to mention in it having heard anything from me, except in the first letter I wrote you.*[9]

Here was the procedure he outlined for sending and receiving private mail:

"There is a man in here who gets letters in from a private way, and you can write that way. Follow the directions carefully. Put your letter to me in an envelope and seal it and write just my name on it. Then put that letter into another envelope and seal it and write on it—'Mr. Jess McGregor.' Then put the whole thing in another envelope and mail it to Mr. G. McGregor, Wellesville, Ohio, enclosing a little slip with it asking that the letter to Jess McGregor be delivered to him *by private means.* You needn't sign your name. This is perfectly safe, as G. McGregor is the father of Jess who is in here and is a reliable man. You can write to me in this way when you have anything to say of a private nature. Of course you can write any time through the office . . ."

THIS ORIGINAL POSTAL arrangement did not last long. Perhaps it was discovered, or perhaps Jess McGregor was released. A few weeks later No. 30664 was using a different method. Now the letters were going through Dr. E. Reinert, the night physician at the prison hospital, who seemed immediately to have recognized in this prisoner a gentle soul, completely out of place among the hard-bitten ne'er-do-wells, robbers, and killers of the prison population. Consequently the doctor offered to act as private post office.

That was the first sign of hope. It gave No. 30664 the courage to go on, awaiting the outcome of the appeal, which would be heard by the Circuit Court of Appeals in New Orleans. So he waited.[10]

From the Roaches in Austin came words of encouragement. He must remember, his mother-in-law wrote, that he had more to live for than just himself. He had a daughter to care for and educate. Furthermore, he had friends: Mr. Roach believed in him and so did she. Herman Presser and others on the outside had lent him money to go bond, and had supported him in every way. He must not forget these friends.

By the time No. 30664 received his first "outside" letter from Mrs. Roach, his spirit was already on the way to recovery. His hopes for success of the appeal were high.

They were subdued a little in July, when he learned that his appeal would not be heard until the fall term of the circuit court began in November. He had been hoping for much faster action.

"It is going to be a very weary wait until then, but I shall try to endure it until the appeal is decided."[11]

While No. 30664 waited he began to look around him. There were others of gentle nature in the Ohio state prison for crimes, and at first 30664 sought their company. One was Jimmie Consedine, who had been proprietor of the Hotel Metropole in New York before he fell afoul of the law. Consedine was a privileged character who spent most of his time practicing his personally proclaimed skill as an artist. One day he painted a picture of a cow with its tail touching the ground. No. 30664 took one look and protested. No cow he ever saw had a tail that touched the ground, said the retired cowboy. Jimmie Consedine took exception to the critic's words and a friendship was lost. As for most of the others in the prison, they were "niggers" who were relegated by this new prisoner to their own special limbo, or hard types. He got on best with the prisoners from the West, many of them old cowmen and sheep-herders turned outlaw. These were men he could understand, and he spent many hours listening to their tales. He also renewed his acquaintance with Al Jennings, the bank robber, who had come back from Honduras also and who had been captured, tried, and sent to prison. In a month, No. 30664 was beginning to take a brighter view of life. He had his "blue periods" but three months after he entered prison he had adjusted well enough to live with his situation.

"I often . . . feel as thoroughly miserable as it is possible to feel, but I consider that my future efforts belong to others and I have no right to give way to my own troubles and feelings."[12]

He had discovered, only after two months, that daughter Margaret had been sick, and that was why Mrs. Roach had not written him until June. He pleaded for regular information so that he could rest easy about her.

WHEN 30664 DID feel blue, all he had to do was consider his situation as compared to the others. Because of his experience in his uncle's drugstore he had fallen into a prison job that was responsible, and hence bearable. He perked up a bit and wrote to the Roaches to send some of his clothes, because he could wear them "inside." The clothing of the prison was plain gray "and would not appear at all remarkable on the street, so they could send almost anything from his old clothing except white shirts, which were not allowed."

"Send underclothes . . . all my old summer ones . . . and two or three pairs of socks, two or three shirts and some collars and a tie or two. I have to preserve as respectable appearance as I can in the drug store and you know I have nothing with me but one shirt. One or two men have lent me some shirts, which I am wearing now. I have no way to have them laundered at present. There are two laundries but everybody has to pay to have their work done, and I am clean broke. I am going to try to get a little newspaper work out by a private source and get a little money if I can."[13]

What he wanted money for was primarily to get his wash done and for postage stamps. All during his stay in the Ohio prison the problem of postage kept recurring.

Soon he was assigned as night druggist in the hospital.

The Ohio state prison hospital was quite modern for its day. The wards accommodated more than two hundred patients, and twice each day between two hundred and three hundred prisoners reported for "sick call." They came marching in, past a doctor, and he prescribed for them "on the fly." They took the prescriptions to the drug counter and they were filled, the line scarcely stopping. But there were really sick people in the hospital as well. The most prevalent disease was tuberculosis ("consumption here is more common than bad colds are at home").

The night druggist's closest associate was the night physician, an employee from outside the walls. The druggist's life, as he admitted, was at least 100 percent more livable than that of the other twenty-five hundred prisoners, since the hospital staff, doctors, nurses, specialists, and orderlies, whether civilian or prisoner, worked together in the hospital, which was a building separate from the cell blocks, and ate together in the hospital dining room, where the food served was like that of the hospitals outside and not like that of the prison.

Everything about the hospital was different from the rest of the prison. The big, new building was as large as the Austin city hall, surrounded by a lawn and flower beds and shaded by trees.

If one had to be in prison this was the best way.

The night druggist's job sent him to work from 5 P.M. to 5 A.M.

"The work is about the same as in any drug store, filling prescriptions [for the four prison doctors] etc. and is pretty lively up to about ten o'clock. At seven P.M. I take a medicine case and go the rounds with the night physician to see the ones in the main building who have become sick during the day."[14]

The night physician went to bed at about ten o'clock and then the druggist was on his own, prescribing for patients and going out on call. If he found someone really sick, he had them brought to the hospital and woke up the doctor. Otherwise he dosed them as his civil counterparts were doing on the outside.

HE WROTE TO the Maddoxes, the brothers who had befriended him in the early days in Austin, and asked them to do what they could to hasten his appeal. But he had no answer. Five months after entering prison, No. 30664 still had not heard the results of his appeal. It all seemed so long ago. He waited with growing pessimism and acceptance of his fate. The Ohio weather turned cold and he got the Roaches to send his overcoat. Even so he caught a cold and was ill in bed for four days.

Up and about, he returned to his routine, and waited. By mid-November his hopes for a reversal of his conviction by the U.S. Circuit Court of Appeals at New Orleans were waning. "Until I learn the facts I am hoping for a little luck in the N.O. case, but am prepared for disappointment—my usual fortune."[15]

Somehow No. 30664 got a subscription to the *New Orleans Picayune,* and read it every day. The issue of November 14 carried an account of the argument of the Porter case before the circuit court, but then there was nothing more. Letters to former friends in Austin produced no replies. He was hard put to find stamps to send letters. He needed stamps for more than letters: he was now writing sketches that he hoped to sell to the *Detroit Free Press* and the *New York World,* as he had in those days in Austin when he was awaiting trial. The reason, he told Mrs. Roach in a letter, was that he wanted to start repaying the Roaches for all their help to him and to daughter Margaret.

A month later No. 30664 was growing impatient. If the appeal failed, he proposed to launch an attempt to secure a presidential pardon. But he must first know the facts about the appeal.

The bad news about the appeal came in January. But No. 30664 did not meet it with despair. The days of despair were long behind him. Already he was working to secure that pardon. Frank Maddox was his best bet, he felt—at least Frank had answered one of his letters.[16]

No. 30664 was again hopeful.

"I am told by reliable persons that if my application is properly presented I won't have any trouble in having it granted and I want to have it done as soon as possible."

BY APRIL 1899, the prisoner had very high hopes, the result of talking to Al Jennings, the perennial optimist. He had at last heard from John Maddox as well as Frank, and both old friends had promised to do all they could to further his appeal. Since John Maddox, in particular, was a familiar figure in Washington and seemed to have considerable influence, the future looked bright. They planned to secure the aid of Texas Congressmen Bailey and Hawley to press for the pardon. They had begun circulating a petition of important Texans for the pardon. One approached was Judge Maxey, the trial judge who had sentenced Will Porter. He did not say yes. He did not say no. "Not just yet," he said. It was an odd reply, one that conjured up visions of the First National Bank crowd. For a pardon for the teller convicted of embezzlement would most certainly reflect badly on the bank.[17]

The prisoner was sagacious enough to know that the matter of the pardon depended less on the merits of his case than the political effort that could be put forth in his behalf.

The time dragged on. The prisoner waited.

THE NIGHT PHYSICIAN, Dr. Reinert, had grown so confident in his druggist assistant that he seldom responded to night calls, letting his pharmacist handle all but surgical needs. He became, in fact, a practicing physician. The druggist had his own desk and chair inside the drugstore railing, gas lights with which to work, and all sorts of reading materials: novels, four daily newspapers, and magazines. He began scribbling on bits of paper, first notes and then stories. At night, he ate at his desk, meals sent down on the dumb waiter from the kitchen at ten o'clock and at three.

Still, he was in prison, and that could not be gainsaid even though he slept on a cot in the hospital during the daylight hours and except for his official rounds, never entered the cell blocks.

"It's a melancholy place, however—misery and death and all kinds of suffering around one all the one all the time."

Men died every week.

"One of the nurses will come from a ward and say

"'Well, So and So has croaked.'

"Ten minutes later they tramp in with So and So on a stretcher and take him to the dead house. If he has no friends to claim him—which is generally the case—the next day the doctors have a dissecting bee and that ends it.

"Suicides are as common as picnics here. Every few nights the doctor and I have to strike out at a trot to see some unfortunate who has tried to get rid of his troubles. They cut their throats and hang themselves and stop up their cells and turn the gas on and try all kinds of ways. Most of them plan it well enough to succeed.

"Night before last, a professional pugilist went crazy in his cell and the doctor and I, of course, were sent for. The man was in good training and it took eight of us to tie him. Seven held him down while the doctor climbed up on top and got his hypodermic syringe into him.

"These little things are our only amusement."[18]

The irony of that last line was an indication of the druggist's spiritual recovery.

As father, he wrote frequently to Margaret, carefully maintaining the fiction that he was working in a big city drugstore. The United States continued to suffer from monetary problems, in spite of the euphoria of a successful war. The bankers began calling more loans than they liked, bankruptcies surged, the Populists and the radical Democrats and Republicans agitated for a policy of inflation; the conservatives fought it tooth and nail. Mr. Roach's business enterprises did not fail, but like many another, they suffered.

A few weeks after Prisoner No. 30664 had entered the penitentiary, fearful that the secret would out at school in Austin, Mrs. Roach took Margaret to Nashville to stay with her brother. Mr. Roach stayed on in Austin for a time, but in a few months he tired of the separation and found that his business was not really good enough to keep him in Austin. Ultimately the Roaches moved to Pittsburgh, where he assumed management of a small hotel. They had to sell their Austin property to support the enterprise in these difficult times. Still, they raised little Margaret with never a hint as to the truth of her father's absence. The fable of "business" was maintained all through his prison years and afterwards. Daughter Margaret learned of the prison experience six years after O. Henry died.[19]

PRISONER NO. 30664'S life settled down to a routine with a different kind of time than that spent outside. It was as though reality was suspended, to be remembered only by consultation of a calendar and countoff of the hundreds of days of durance ahead. He had plenty of time to read again and he did. He also stopped on his night rounds to talk to some of the prisoners and learned the stories of many of them, particularly the Western outlaws.

The scribbling continued. In the spring of 1899 a crisis approached with the pending resignation of Dr. Reinert, the night druggist's friend and protector, as well as his mail drop. The doctor was quitting the prison job to take a much better position as a police surgeon in Columbus. The problem for Will Porter was how to retain his favored position in the hospital, for he and all the others fortunate enough to work there were the envy of the prison population. Money talked in the Ohio penitentiary of the 1890s. Some well-to-do prisoners had their own "valets" who ran errands for them, cooked for them, and procured all sorts of luxuries. The prisoner said his job as pharmacist was worth at least $1,000. He knew that much had been offered for other hospital positions—and paid to the prison authorities. Fortunately his specialty was not that common, and he had the goodwill of Dr. Thomas. He also had the goodwill of Warden E. G. Coffin.

The warden, like everyone else in the prison, came to the doctors for his aches and pains. One day when he had some ailment the doctor prescribed for him, the medicine was sent over from the pharmacy, and the warden drank it down. But late that afternoon, the warden came down with violent pains; by mistake he had been given an overdose of solution of arsenic. The day drug clerk, who had made the error, was a safecracker by trade, and when he discovered the error, he did not know the antidote. The warden and the doctors around him were very worried, when someone informed the night pharmacist of the problem. He went into the pharmacy and mixed up "a little drink, just like mixing soda water."

It was rushed to the bed of the warden, who drank it down.

Presto!

"In an hour the warden was out of danger."[20]

So, Dr. Reinert left and was replaced as night physician by Dr. George W. Williard, and No. 30664 kept his job as night druggist. Dr. Williard also soon became the night druggist's confidant and letter drop, although they never became really intimate friends. The doctor's recollection was:

"He was the last man in the world you would ever pick for a crook. Toward every one he was quiet, reserved, almost taciturn. He seldom spoke unless in answer. He never told me of his hopes, his aims, his family, his crime, his views of life, his writing, in fact he spoke of little save the details of his pharmaceutical work in which he was exceptionally careful and efficient . . .

"I respected him for his strict attention to business, his blameless conduct, and his refusal to mix into the affairs of other prisoners. He seemed to like me personally because I did not ask him personal questions and because I showed that I felt as one intelligent man must feel toward another under such circumstances."

That friendship was cemented one night when a large black convict was refused a certain drug he wanted and became abusive to Dr. Williard. The guard who had brought the man in had stepped away, and the doctor was afraid that he was about to be attacked. The druggist leaped across the railing of his druggist's office, hit the man squarely on the jaw with one mighty blow, which felled him, and then jumped back across the railing as the guard came up. He did not say a word, but only smiled in answer to the doctor's thanks.

On another occasion, a valuable piece of medical equipment was stolen from the prison hospital one night. Dr. Williard was responsible for everything in the hospital during nighttime hours, and he was under suspicion of having pirated the equipment. No. 30664's ear was tuned to the prison grapevine, and when the doctor mentioned the theft to him and his dubious prospects, the night pharmacist named the thief, a minor prison official. The doctor told the warden the name of the man and the warden announced to the staff that the equipment had better be back in the hospital before the day's end. Next morning it had reappeared in its proper place.

"So," said Dr. Williard, "we grew to be friends."[21]

NO. 30664'S CIRCUMSPECTION in prison extended even to his personal habits. The reports that accompanied him from Austin put him down as a heavy drinker, but in prison he seemed to have abstained completely. As pharmacist he had the keys to cabinets where alcohol and drugs such as morphine were kept, but nothing ever turned up missing during his hours of responsibility.

At one point Chief Physician Thomas discovered that medical alcohol was disappearing from the cabinet at a far greater rate than it ought to, and he set out to discover the reason. A little discussion with the daytime workers brought suspicion on the night pharmacist, and Dr. Thomas held him over one morning for questioning.

The doctor asked how much alcohol he had been using on his nighttime rounds. The pharmacist grew very excited.

"I am not a thief," he said, "and I never stole a thing in my life. I was sent here for embezzling bank funds, not one cent of which I ever got. Some one else got it all, and I am doing time for it."

There it was again, the bitterness of the wronged. The night pharmacist kept careful records and so was able to produce proof of his usage of alcohol and in a few days Dr. Thomas found the guilty party on the day shift. But even afterward, when they met, No. 30664 would ask the doctor if he really was convinced that he was not the thief.

"You can tell when a prisoner is lying as well as you can in the case of anybody else," said Dr. Thomas. "I believed him implicitly."

That faith was returned by a confidence that the pharmacist showed in no one else at the prison. Once or twice he talked about Austin and the trial to Dr. Thomas as he never did to any other person. He told of that crossroads at Hempstead, where he had panicked and gotten on the train to New Orleans, to end up in Honduras. What a mistake it had been! Immediately even in the minds of old friends, the accusation had become conviction. After that, there was no hope, no point in trying to launch a defense against the powers arrayed against him.[22]

THE NIGHT PHARMACIST soaked up stories and atmosphere like a sponge. He spent many an hour with Jimmy Connors, the day drug clerk, a safecracker who had been sent up for blowing a post office safe. The irony was, Jimmy Connors confided, that he had not done that particular job, although he had cracked plenty of other safes. He knew who had done the job all right, but if he "squealed" on the other man, he was likely to be squealed on in turn, and sent up for other jobs he did commit. So what was the difference?

In time, the detective who had sent him up discovered the real culprit and got a confession. He did everything he could to get Jimmy Connors "sprung," even going to Washington to the Department of Justice. But in Washington the federal officials, in their wisdom, agreed with Connors. If he was in prison for a job he had not done, he still wasn't in prison for a lot of very professional jobs he had done. They decided that keeping Jimmy Connors in jail was the best way of keeping post office safes safe. And so Connors stayed in prison and finally died there a few months after No. 30664 left.[23]

By the end of his first prison year, No. 30664 had begun to write, and to send articles to newspapers and magazines.

His first story, which McClure's syndicate bought, entitled "The Miracle of Lava Canyon" (retitled "An Afternoon Miracle" in the collection *Heart of the West*), written in Austin in 1897, had appeared under the William Sydney Porter name. In prison, No. 30664 at first used various names for sketches sold to newspapers and for stories. Many tales were later told about his selection of the name O. Henry for his writing. He contributed to the mystery by telling several different tales himself at different times. But it was established in the Austin years that the name O. Henry meant something to him, and eventually he settled on it. There must have been two reasons: (1) to start a new career under a new name without the sullying stain of the "jailbird" on it; (2) to avoid any complications with authority while he was in prison, because his use of his private mail system for letters and manuscripts was definitely outside the law.

Several of his associates during the prison years recalled O. Henry's writing practices. The doctors remembered that he had written first drafts on many bits of paper of varying sizes. Dr. Thomas recalled that No. 30664 had often put stories on his desk before he went off in the mornings, so the doctor could read them and comment on them. J. B. Rumer, a night guard at the prison hospital, recalled that O. Henry wrote mostly late at night, after they had finished their midnight meal.

"He always wrote with pen and ink and would often work for two hours continuously without rising. . . . After he had written for perhaps two hours, he would rise, make a round of the hospital, and then come back to his work again. He got checks at different times and once told me that he had only two stories rejected while he was in prison."[24]

Two and a half years passed, not quickly, obviously, but not as slowly as they might have gone. He sold several stories and got the checks. He had a little money to send to Mrs. Roach and a little more to send to Margaret. He was able to send out for presents for her birthday and have them forwarded to Pittsburgh. In June 1900, his story "Georgia's Ruling" was published by *Outlook* magazine.

For this story, the author had gone back to draw from his experiences in the Texas state land office. The character of the commissioner was so closely modeled on Dick Hall that when O. Henry saw the story in print he refused to allow its publication in book form.

"Georgia's Ruling" has a life of its own as a story, and could not be improved upon by briefing it here. It was a tale out of Austin and out of O. Henry's knowledge of Texas history, shaped by one of the tragedies of his own life, a tender tale of big business and common people and a government official who rises above himself to do the greater good.

So the checks began to come, and No. 30664 began to hope that he could, indeed, make a new life for himself after prison.

In the fall of 1900 came a new opportunity. C. N. Wilcox, the prison steward, managed the affairs of the Ohio prison from an office outside the walls. His secretary, a "trusty" prisoner, was being released in October after serving his time, and the job was up for grabs. No. 30664 wanted it and went to Dr. Thomas for help.

"I have never asked a favor of you but there is one I should like to ask now. I can be private secretary to the steward outside. It depends on your recommendation."

"I called up the steward," said Dr. Thomas, "and in twenty minutes he was outside."[25]

Trusty! Outside the wall! It was not the new life, but it was a beginning good enough to raise a lonely writer's confidence.

# 9

# Outside the Wall

To achieve his new "almost freedom," Prisoner No. 30664 had drawn upon another aspect of his experience, that of bookkeeper. His job as the Ohio prison steward's secretary was primarily the keeping of the prison books. To an outsider it might seem ironic that the steward would choose a convicted embezzler to help keep the books, but such is life. One of the steward's assistants was a bank president who had been sent to durance vile for stealing a great deal of money. He was easily the most dignified and distinguished citizen of the jail, and that included officialdom.

No. 30664's lot was marvelously improved by this change. The steward's office and warehouse were located in a two-story building on the same street as the prison but quite a distance from it. He had a big desk in an office, "well-furnished," he called it, with electric lights, gas heat, and a telephone. The steward and storekeeper, both officials, left at four o'clock every afternoon, and then Trusty Porter was in charge. If someone at the prison needed supplies, Porter provided them. He also worked on the books. But he was free to come and go in Columbus, and he went walking in the streets whenever he pleased. Sometimes he went down to the river and walked along the paths. He only had to do his job and be back at work by the next morning. Best of all, of course, was that he was now outside the thirty-foot wall that reminded the inmates every day of their status.[1]

There are many tales of Trusty Porter in prison, but all of them except those told in his letters to the Roaches, come from outside sources. O. Henry never spoke of his life in prison once he got out of it. But others did, especially Al Jennings, the train robber, later turned Oklahoma lawyer, lecturer, and raconteur. Jennings made much of his own life as criminal and convict and also told so many tales about O. Henry, after the latter had achieved renown, that he finally made a book of them, called *Through the Shadows With O. Henry.* He also wrote his memoirs, *Beating Back,* in which O. Henry figures. Jennings' reliability as personal historian is questionable. His work is reminiscent of that of another Western writer, Gene Fowler, who was known to admit that many of his best tales were highly embroidered.

Judge Trueman E. O'Quinn of Austin, the most knowledgeable student of O. Henryiana in Texas, and a stickler for the verifiable fact, indicates that Jennings is not to be believed, but there is one Jennings tale about O. Henry in prison that has the ring of truth.

Train-robber Jennings was obviously a man of great personal charm. He, too, managed to get himself made a trusty,* to live in that building outside the prison yard along with Will Porter and four others: another train robber, the bank president in for embezzling, another embezzler, and a forger. The group formed the Recluse Club, said Jennings, and Trusty Porter was the president. The major purpose of the club was to produce and eat a dinner each Sunday that was as far from prison fare as they could get. This involved scrounging and purloining food from the prison and the officials' kitchen, and even buying it on the outside.[2]

Jennings described Porter as the prince of the scroungers, who "from his position and his talents could get more provisions in a day than all the rest in a week. He had made slits in the lining of his coat, and there he carried his plunder. I can see him yet, walking through the gate, looking neither to right or left, his coat bulging with a Mother Hubbard effect. As he passed the patrol guard, he would cast one quiet glance, and the guard would look in the opposite direction. Had the gate closed on him suddenly, his coat would have resembled the wreck of a grocery wagon. Once he even brought in six bottles of wine."[3]

It reads like hyperbole and probably is, for Jennings was given to that sort of statement. But what is known is that Will Porter, the man who became O. Henry, did love good food and good drink and talk, and that was the purpose of the Recluse dinners. In Jennings's account the trusties brave official wrath by artfully constructing a miniature kitchen built in a loft above the office, concealed by a false wall and fitted out with a gas stove connected to the prison gas system. But why? In a letter to Mrs. Roach Will Porter said "We have a fine cook out here and set a table as good as a hotel."

Even in the days when he had been night druggist inside the wall, No.

---

*He ended up as secretary to the warden.

30664 had the run of the hospital kitchen. He often cooked up chili con carne or a beef stew, two of his favorite dishes, for himself and the night guard and night nurse. But the dinner meetings of the Recluse Club were truly special. The trusties all wore white shirts to these banquets. The rules of the club were written up and a copy placed at each table setting. The groaning board was set with linen and silver and place cards, all drawn by Will Porter. "For the place cards of the four members who proclaimed that they were innocent— including himself, presumably—he drew a cherub or a lily."

Now, there was a gesture worthy of O. Henry.

Best of all for Trusty Porter outside the wall was "a big fine desk with worlds of stationery and everything I need." Here, given far more time than in the prison drugstore and his quarters in the ward, Will accelerated his production of tales.[4] More money began to come in.

During the prison years, the author wrote many sketches that brought in small sums from newspapers. He also wrote a number of short stories, three of which were published before he left Columbus. As noted, "Georgia's Ruling," was the first story. The second was "Whistling Dick's Christmas Stocking," a tale for which he dredged back into the brief New Orleans weeks, but brought forth a German policemen who had to be from the Austin days. Whistling Dick was a professional tramp, and there were other tramps. Did they come from his wanderings after he bolted the Houston-Austin train? Perhaps Will Porter had invaded a planter's domain, supped with his fellow hoboes (Boston Harry, Deaf Pete, Blinky, Goggles, and Indiana Tom), around an open fire, from a five-gallon kerosene tin filled with beef stew. But the story he spun, of the good-hearted hobo Whistling Dick and the manner in which he saved the planter and his family from robbery—that is strictly the art of O. Henry the storyteller. The ending, in which Whistling Dick is offered good fortune and security but opts for the open road, that, too, is the magic of the storyteller, as sheer as the stocking of the young lady whose pleasant greeting brought about the entire turn of events.

Yet another story saw publication before the author left the prison: "Money Maze," which dredged back into the brief months he spent in Honduras. The story tells much about the author's vivid imagination and ability to soak up background information: the beautiful señora, the sturdy American "businessman" Goodwin, the handsome Colonel Falcon from the capital city, who searches in behalf of President Losada for missing government funds, which Goodwin is suspected of having been the last to see. But above all, the story is captured by one character, Beelzebub Blythe, a man of a sort O. Henry had known well, and would always know well. For Beelzebub Blythe was a part of O. Henry himself, as the following dialogue shows very well. Remember, as you read, that these paragraphs were written by a drinking man who had escaped American law and hidden himself in the tangle of Latin America. He was a man who had fallen far from a genteel estate, who had tasted too often the grape, but yet a man who retained a dignity all his own:

Blythe had been rechristened Beelzebub as an acknowledgement of the greatness of his fall. Once in some distant Paradise Lost, he had foregathered with the angels of the earth. But Fate had hurled him headlong down to the tropics, where flamed in his bosom a fire that was seldom quenched. In Coralio they called him a beachcomber; but he was, in reality, a categorical idealist who strove to anamorphosize the dull verities of life by the means of brandy and rum. As Beelzebub might have held in his clutch with unwitting tenacity his harp or crown during his tremendous fall, so his namesake had clung to his gold-rimmed eyeglasses as the only souvenir of his lost estate. These he wore with impressiveness and distinction while he combed beaches and extracted toll from his friends. By some mysterious means he kept his drink-reddened face always smoothly shaven. For the rest he sponged gracefully upon whomsoever he could for enough to keep him pretty drunk, and sheltered from the rains and night dews.

"Hallo Goodwin," called the derelict airily. "I was hoping I'd strike you. I wanted to see you particularly. Suppose we go where we can talk. Of course you know there's a chap down here looking up the money old Miraflores lost?"

"Yes," said Goodwin.

"I've been talking with him. Let's go into Espada's place. I can spare you ten minutes."

They went into the pulperia and sat at a little table upon stools with rawhide tops.

"Have a drink?" said Goodwin.

"They can't bring it too quickly," said Blythe. "I've been in a drought ever since morning. Hi—muchacho! *El aguardiente por aca.*"

"Now, what do you want to see me about?" asked Goodwin when the drinks were before them.

"Confound it, old man," drawled Blythe. "Why do you spoil a golden moment like this with business? I wanted to see you—well, this has the preference." He gulped down his brandy and gazed longingly into the empty glass.

"Have another?" suggested Goodwin.

"Between gentlemen," said the fallen angel, "I don't quite like your use of that word 'another.' It isn't delicate. But the concrete idea that the word represents is not displeasing."

The glasses were refilled. Blythe sipped blissfully from his, as he began to enter the state of a true idealist.

"I must trot along in a minute or two," hinted Goodwin. "Was there anything in particular?"

Blythe did not reply at once.

"Old Losada would make it a hot country," he replied at length, "for the man who swiped the gripsack of treasury boodle, don't you think?"

"Undoubtedly he would," agreed Goodwin calmly, as he rose leisurely to his feet. "I'll be running over to the house now, old man. Mrs. Goodwin is alone. There was nothing important you had to say, was there?"

"That's all," said Blythe, "Unless you wouldn't mind sending in another drink from the bar as you go out. Old Espada has closed my account to profit and loss. And pay for the lot, will you, like a good fellow?"

"All right," said Goodwin. *"Buenas noches."*

Beelzebub Blythe lingered over his cups, polishing his eye glasses with a disreputable handkerchief.

"I thought I could do it, but I couldn't," he muttered to himself after a time. "A gentleman can't blackmail the man that he drinks with."

Three tales, one of Texas officialdom, reminiscent of the pioneer days, one about new tramps and old gentility in the deep South, and a third that dealt with the wasting of the Americano in the tropics. They were all new subjects to the eager readers of the new leisure magazines, tales to grip the imagination and transport the reader to environments far from his own, to meet new sorts of people, whose characters were suggested, no more than that, by the magic pen of the writer. Let the reader see the use of language: the high-falluting verb "anamorphosize," followed by the slangy "swiped." The reader did not have to understand the former to know where it was leading him, and the second kept the story distinctly within the realm of his American consciousness. Long had O. Henry labored over Mr. Webster's dictionary to achieve this easy flow; long, too, had he worked on his command of Spanish, just as had his ear caught the cadences of the German policeman who set Whistling Dick on his Christmas road. Atmosphere, language, superb storytelling. These were the new qualities that O. Henry brought to the American literary scene in 1900.

The magazines began to reward him with money, even though it had to reach him by circuitous routings. His stories were sent to a friend in New Orleans, who readdressed them and sent them to the magazines. The editors replied to New Orleans, and ultimately the letters reached the author by way of his private post office.[5]

There were more stories.

"A Blackjack Bargainer" is a complicated story, one of O. Henry's most complex, involving a feud of Southern families, an upstanding district attorney, and a down-at-the-heels drinking man. The young man of Texas and North Carolina looks out from every word.

"The Enchanted Kiss" begins: "But a clerk in the Cut-rate drug store was Samuel Tansey, yet his slender frame was a pad that enfolded the passion of Romeo, the gloom of Lara, the romance of D'Artagnan, and the desperate inspiration of Melnotte." The reader knows he is in O. Henry country.

"Hygeia at the Solito" is set in San Antonio, another town from Will Porter's past and the characters are cattlemen and cowboys, Mexicans, and an Irish fighter suffering from tuberculosis—all out of that past.

"Rouge et Noir" is again set in a banana republic like Honduras.

All these were written during the prison years, although not published until afterward.

IN NOVEMBER 1900, Will Porter sent $25 to John Maddox in Austin, to encourage Maddox in the effort to secure the pardon. But the old Austin friends seem now to have forgotten William Sydney Porter. Maddox did not reply and by January Will was losing confidence in him. But not in the idea of the pardon.

"I have some valuable pointers in regard to it that have been given me here, and can get some specially valuable letters from the doctors that might assist a great deal. It seems to be an undoubted fact that a pardon can be attained through political influence more quickly . . ."[6]

He had been talking to Al Jennings again. The terms of the two men were about the same. If there was ever a "jailhouse lawyer" Jennings was the man, and he had schemed and figured "angles" during all his stay in the prison. Now, facing the almost certainly negative future of the "ex-con," what roads were the two men to follow?

Jennings announced that he was going to go to Oklahoma. He had been born in the Indian Territory and they knew him there, knew all about his raucous, rip-roaring past. He was going to "grow up with the country," said Jennings, tell everyone he met exactly who and what he had been, get a pardon, continue his study of the law, and then hang out his shingle. He recommended that same approach to O. Henry. Go home to Austin and face the music.[7]

But the thought of the confrontations made Will Porter shiver. He could not. He would follow a different route; he would create a new personality to carry his future, the personality of the writer, and the man would be hidden beneath the anonymous writer with the brand-new name. And thus, finally, was developed the mechanism by which William Sydney Porter would be submerged to become the handyman for the writer. Will Porter would be the signer of contracts, the payer of school bills, the engager of hotel accommodations, the good time Charlie who loved to go out on the town with his friends, the bon vivant and heavy drinker who spent money like water and gave much of it away. O. Henry, as his editors and readers would ultimately learn, never existed. But the point was coming when neither would William Sydney Porter exist any more except as the cocoon of the writer. The change was not immediate. In the Austin days, the author's first real short story, "The Miracle at Lava Canyon," had been published under the name W. S. Porter. The stories published in prison were under the name Sydney Porter, and thus did the McClure company address him in correspondence. Preparing to leave prison, the author did not yet devote much time to what he was to do to avoid the embarrassment of confrontation with his past. In this spring of 1900 he was still more concerned with the problem of getting out of prison. He had not yet decided what to do about whatever the future might hold for him.

The weeks of spring swept on. Will Porter wrote to the Roaches: "The answer lies in Washington. . . . I hope that I can get John Maddox or someone to push things. Something ought to be accomplished by summer."[8]

But nothing happened in the summer of 1900. It was an election year, the Republican candidate, William McKinley, triumphed in the autumn election, which meant he would replace Democratic President Grover Cleveland in the White House in 1901. All the political fences had to be built up again.

THE CHANGE IN Washington was accompanied by a change in the politics of Ohio and meant a new prison administration at Columbus. Prisoner Porter was worried about his situation "outside the walls" and was careful not to send anything through his personal "pony express" lest it create problems. But by May 1901 all was well. "I am as solid as ever with the new crowd," he wrote Mrs. Roach.[9]

By that time, the concern about a pardon was overshadowed. With time off for "good behavior," Prisoner No. 30664 was eligible for release in July. On July 24, 1901, he left the Ohio state prison by the front gate, clothed in a worsted suit and carrying a small bag of belongings, the gifts of the people of the United States. He had been in prison for three years, three months, and thirty days. He had little money, but some contracts and promises from magazine editors.

Behind the walls Prisoner No. 30664 had seen a great deal of the corruption of power, the life or death control of the warders over the prisoners, the power of favors to alleviate his own condition, and the politics of prison. He had been

113

extremely fortunate to have in his background a skill the prison managers needed, and this had saved him. It had allowed him to retain the wry, ironic sense of humor that had been a mark of the young William Sydney Porter. The humor, of course, had matured, deepened, and become more ironic and less comic. From good men and bad he had learned how ordinary men went wrong, and how good men were wronged by society. He came to have a cynical disbelief in the society of movers and shakers, a contempt for money and power, and a deep compassion for the victims of society, the poor, the downtrodden, and the down-and-out.

In short, a youngish thirty-five-year-old man named William Sydney Porter went into prison in 1898, and three years later emerged a man as old as the hills, with wisdom beyond his years, his soul hardened in the most pitiless of crucibles. In went William Sydney Porter, and in the prison he quite disappeared except in name. Out came a character who will hereafter be known as O. Henry, a writer, a mysterious figure who would remain mysterious even to his closest associates, to the daughter who really never was to know him, and, ultimately, to a wife to whom he would always be a stranger, only reminiscent to her somehow of someone from the past.

# 10

# The Way Up

That summer day of 1901, when O. Henry took the train from Columbus to Pittsburgh, the Roaches and Margaret were living at the Iron Front Hotel, a run-down establishment in the heart of the red-light district of the steel city. O. Henry had no very clear view of the future. More short stories were "in the works." All had been written and sent off. Some of them had been accepted for publication, others were under editorial consideration. Hundreds more were in his head. What he needed was a place and the time to compose them. These he hoped to find in Pittsburgh.

The problem of identity still burdened him. To old friends he was still Will Porter. To some new friends he would be Sydney or Sid. To very close friends, including those from prison, he eschewed formal names, and was often called "colonel" and called them "colonel" in return. He kept up a correspondence after prison with Al Jennings, and sometimes addressed him as "colonel," sometimes as Al, sometimes as "Dear Friend," sometimes as Jennings. This had always been his way. Back in the Austin days when one of his friends had gone off to make his fortune in the West, O. Henry had written him a long, humorous letter about affairs in Austin, which he signed "William Shakespeare, Ingomar Junius Brutus Calliope, Six-Handed Euchre, Grover Cleveland Hill City Quartette Johnson."[1]

WHEN O. HENRY arrived in Pittsburgh, and after the initial exhilaration of freedom and family wore off, he settled down to work. He made an office in the family living quarters in the hotel, and there he began to write. More than a dozen stories had been written in prison, many of them for *Ainslee's*. The

115

stories were now coming out under various names: Sydney Porter, Olivier Henry, S. H. Peters, James L. Bliss, T. B. Dowd, and Howard Clark. There was more than one reason for the changing of the name: to be sure, O. Henry did not yet feel the value of a name as a writer, that was one. Another was his "jailbird" sensitivity. A third was the practice of editors, faced with two stories by the same author for an issue of a magazine, of publishing one story under the author's name and the second under a pen name.

When O. Henry reached Pittsburgh, he was still hoping to get a newspaper job and support himself thus. He soon acquired a connection with the *Pittsburgh Dispatch,* writing at "space rates," which meant so much per column inch of editorial material. Editors in those days did not inquire into the antecedents of space-rate writers, or for that matter very deeply into the histories of any of the reporters who drifted from city to city, usually leaving behind them air redolent of stale alcohol. Writing for a paper gave O. Henry an excuse to keep unconventional hours. It also soon gave him an excuse to move out of the Iron Front Hotel.[2]

He moved into a rooming house in the district known then as Pittsburgh's Little Harlem, where he shared a room and a double bed with a young man named Samuel C. Jamison. They had much in common; young Jamison was a student at the Pittsburgh College of Pharmacy, and clerk in a drugstore across the street from their rooming house. The roommates did not see a lot of each other. Jamison went to school in the daytime and worked evenings. O. Henry "worked" evenings, and usually rolled into the room at about 3 A.M. Once in a while they played poker on a weekend. Usually O. Henry ate in a saloon called Angloch's, where a sandwich, a glass of beer, and a bowl of soup cost ten cents. Mrs. Roach could wonder then, why it was that O. Henry never seemed to have any money although he was making it.[3]

One reason was certainly the clothing bill. O. Henry wore yellow kid gloves, a good suit, and spats, and he carried a cane. He was the finest-looking creature in the editorial rooms of the *Dispatch.* Obviously such sartorial splendor did not come cheap.

He told friends back in the Columbus prison that Washington beckoned him, because he had some contacts there. In fact he had been negotiating for a Washington job back in Austin in the fall of 1895 when the offer from the *Houston Post* came in. Early in September it seemed certain he would be going to Washington, and he so told Al Jennings.

A new problem had arisen. O. Henry was doing very well with the magazines. ("I have been doing quite a deal of business with the editors since I got down to work and have made more than I could at any other business.")

At this point the editors were paying him about $75 for each story, and he was producing at the rate of more than a story a week.

It was, then, apparently an idyllic life for O. Henry, reunited with his daughter and the in-laws he liked and respected, and able to make a comfortable living from his writing, was it not?

Not quite.

O. Henry had some sort of run-in with Pittsburgh, not specified, but onorous enough to persuade him to write Jennings:

> I want to say that Pittsburg is the "low-downedest" hole on the surface of the earth. The people here are the most ignorant, ill-bred, contemptible, boorish, drunken, dirty, mean, depraved curs that I have ever imagined could exist. Columbus people are models of chivalry compared with them. I shall linger here no longer than necessary.[4]

How much of this feeling, if any, was prompted by O. Henry's discomfort in the presence of daughter Margaret and his in-laws was never said. But it was obvious from the first that O. Henry was not comfortable in Pittsburgh, nor was he then or ever to be very close to Margaret. Despite his undeniable amiability, he had always been something of a "loner" and the prison years had enhanced that characteristic. He felt an enormous responsibility to Margaret and to the Roaches but it was primarily a financial responsibility, and this could not be managed at all at the moment. Later, when he achieved his hoped-for success, it could be managed from anywhere. So Washington called, and O. Henry was about to answer.

In the interim, he had dozens of ideas to pursue, including one for an article that he and Al Jennings would create. It was a study of "the art and humor of holding up a man" by an expert who had done so. He wrote Jennings, who was still in prison, and they collaborated on the piece. It did not work out quite as anticipated, but ultimately became "Holding Up a Train," published with a prefatory note by O. Henry:

> The man who told me these things was for several years an outlaw in the Southwest and a follower of the pursuit he so frankly describes. His description of the modus operandi should prove interesting, his counsel of value to the potential passenger in some future "hold-up," while his estimate of the pleasures of train robbing will hardly influence any one to adopt it as a profession. I give the story almost exactly in his own words.[5]

117

Then in his own words, with a little rearranging and literary cleanup by O. Henry, Al Jennings (never named) told the tale of the holdup of the Santa Fe flyer at a water tank at the end of a bridge in Oklahoma.

Not then, but much later they sold that tale to *McClure's Magazine.* Most of O. Henry's effort that summer and fall of 1901 was devoted to the short story. Four short stories were published that year. In May, before O. Henry had left prison, *Ainslee's Magazine* published "Money Maze," which was signed O. Henry, and in December they published "Rouge et Noir," which was signed Olivier Henry.

The reason for the change was a questionnaire.

"Money Maze" had been set in O. Henry's mythical Central American Republic of Anchuria. It had reached the editors of *Ainslee's* via O. Henry's underground post office from prison, from Columbus to New Orleans to New York. The editors' acceptance and further correspondence had gone the same way. When they accepted "Rouge et Noir" they also asked O. Henry for some information about himself, including his first name. It was not fashionable to use just an initial. Richard Harding Davis didn't, did he? That comparison seemed apt because Davis was then all the rage for his stories about Latin America, a field in which he had virtual monopoly until O. Henry came along. Triple-barreled names were all the rage.

The author replied from Pittsburgh that his name was Olivier Henry.[6]

The publishers received the letter, and then tried to find Olivier Henry. They failed. He was not listed in the Pittsburgh city directory. They wrote again to the address he had given. This time they suggested an idea to him: why did he not write a story with a real setting in Panama? They also sent a questionnaire. Olivier Henry seemed to be an assumed name. Who was he, really?

Further, said the editors, if the author would fill out this questionnaire they proposed to get some publicity for him in one of the literary magazines. Would he please send his real name, certain facts about himself, and a recent photograph?

That letter aroused a number of emotions in O. Henry. First was fright that the unhappy secret of his past be revealed. Second was anger—all his life he would be furious when someone offered him either an idea or a plot for a story. For some reason that he could not explain this seemed demeaning. Not that he did not "steal" plots all the time. Many of his stories are rewrites and recastings of classic situations. But that was his business as a writer, and no editor or anyone else had any right to interfere. So his reply to *Ainslee's* was a combination of humor and irritation.

O. Henry replied:

Gents:

Your extremely unsolicited but nevertheless dastardly favor of even date herewith has been received and contents fumigated.

The damnable savoir faire with which you insinuate that you do not know my real name leads me to believe that it is assumed. As to what I believe to have been assumed is purely a matter for the grammarians and plain clothes men to solve.

Your request that I send you a story about the Isthmus of Panama, followed by a lot of personal questions for civil service examination forces me to the conclusion that Mark Hanna is now editor. Before going any further I would like to propound one interrogatory.

In case I should be able to write a story about Panama, thus gaining sufficient funds to pay my next week's board, would I be justified in referring to the proposed isthmus improvements as my alimentary canal?

I will endeavor to answer your questions in order as they are given:

Q. What is your real name?

Ans. Alphonse McClure.

Q. How many children have you, if any?

Ans. Refused. Not necessary to incriminate oneself.

Q. Have you ever been married?

Ans. On occasions.

Q. Why?

Ans. God knows.

Q. Are you Bohemian by nature or merely by extraction?

Ans. By extraction. Never like to drain kegs. Prefer the bottled.

Q. Photo?

Ans. Certainly.

You say you will try to have an article about me printed in one of the literary magazines. Please have it stated that I am of a sedentary but slightly corpulent disposition. I compose with greater ease on unruled paper and Fridays. My morning meal consists of grape shot and potatoes a la Kimosco. My favorite authors are Carolyn and Artesian Wells. I believe the finest passage in English literature to be the expressive "noch einst." Generally feverish with thirst of mornings. Admire writings of Billy Burgundy and the prophet Jeremiah. Presbyterian. Bilious. Slightly ignorant. Favorite flower? Self-rising.

Hoping you get your story and that you are not talking through your isthmus.

I am, yours as usual,

O. Henry.

To follow? O. Henry never did the story with the isthmus setting.

In January 1902, *Ainslee's* published "The Flag Paramount," another story from O. Henry's mythical Latin American Republic of Anchuria. The signature was Olivier Henry, and so it would be for some time.

That same month *The Smart Set* published another Anchuria story, "The Lotus and the Bottle." The name at *The Smart Set* was O. Henry. In February *Munsey's* published "The Duplicity of Hargraves." Again it was O. Henry. In March and April *Ainslee's* published "The Passing of Black Eagle" and "Friends in San Rosario." The latter story must have given O. Henry many wrenching moments. For "Friends in San Rosario" was the story of two bankers, and how the one, beset by the bank examiner, with a definite shortage that could cause trouble with Washington if not a run on the bank, was saved by the other banker, who broke the law quite cheerfully in pulling the wool over the eyes of the man from Washington. The story hinges on the O. Henry feeling that the artificiality of bank examination was to be (1) lamented, and (2) subverted. As a study in attitudes, it is most revealing.

By spring, *The Smart Set* had accepted "By Courier" and "Madame Bo-Peep," and *Black Cat* had taken "The Marionettes." *Everybody's* had five stories, written then or earlier, published under O. Henry and the Sydney Porter names.

Indeed, *Everybody's* was to be O. Henry's best market for 1902 with five stories: "An Afternoon Miracle," "The Struggle of the Outliers," "The Cactus," "Round the Circle," and "Hearts and Hands." The last was by far the most poignant: a handsome young man and a run-down citizen are riding the train from Denver east, when they encounter a handsome young woman the young man has known before. She sees that the young man is handcuffed to the older man, and her eyes rise in horror. But the scruffy fellow says she has it all wrong: the young man is accompanying him to Leavenworth prison. "If you'll ask him to speak a word for me when we get to the pen he'll do it and it'll make things easier for me there. He's taking me to Leavenworth prison. It's seven years for counterfeiting."

So the story goes along, and the reader is treated to an ending that could only have come from O. Henry's very soul.

To a romantic, "The Cactus" might as equally have come from the recesses of O. Henry's heart. Austin was the setting, with a wedding of the society in which O. Henry moved. The tale is one of flummery and love and the whole depends on O. Henry's intimate knowledge of place and time and language. Could the disappointed lover Trysdale be O. Henry? Perhaps, for in the Austin days he was a gay blade and wooed several girls before Athol came into his life. Is this what had finally happened between O. Henry and Lollie Cave?

It might well have been. But the poignancy of the ending might just as easily have come from O. Henry's vivid imagination, and then been linked with the background he knew so well.

O. Henry stories had now been accepted by *Everybody's, McClure's, Ainslee's, Munsey's, Youth's Companion, The Smart Set, Era, Town Topics, Black Cat,* and the *Outlook.* Now, from Pittsburgh, he began enlarging his outlets and sent stories to other magazines as well. All fall he waited for something to happen in Washington. It did not. His irons in Washington had grown stone cold. He detested Pittsburgh. But as O. Henry was the first to recognize, he had a special problem. The label of "ex-con" was not one that wore well in the American society of the early twentieth century. Rare was the employer who would take a chance on a man who had been in prison. Almost as rare was the landlord or banker who would trust a convict. Even in casual relationships, the knowledge that a man was an "ex-con" brought contempt and a desire by the average citizen to avoid the pariah. It was not too many months before O. Henry realized that he was not going to be able to get a job with a newspaper.

He decided to write a novel. It was to be fiction of a new sort, seeking "truth" through the unveiling of a human character. "I want to make it something that it won't or can't be—but as near as I can make it—the *true* record of a man's thought, his description of his mischances and adventures, his *true* opinion of life as he has seen it and his *absolutely honest* deductions, comments and views upon the different phases of life that he passes through."[7]

Gilman Hall and Richard Duffy of *Ainslee's* magazine were much taken by the O. Henry stories they read. They liked the idea of a novel and talked with G. P. Putnam's publishing house about it. Putnam's was encouraging. But O. Henry really could not come to grips with the form. He did not have the sort of view of humanity that gave rise to a long story. His outlook was quite special: he regarded life as a series of pastiches, one scene following another, all self-contained. An O. Henry story was like a novel in its two to four thousand words, with beginning, middle, and end. But the end referred back to the beginning, and snapped it around with a completely unexpected conclusion.

This was not novel technique.

FOR VARIOUS REASONS, in the early months of 1902 O. Henry decided he must go to New York to make his way. In the anonymity of the great city he would be able to avoid the stigma of his past.

O. Henry suggested to Gilman Hall that he might come to New York. Hall was enthusiastic and hinted that *Ainslee's* would make the writer's decision worthwhile.[8]

Then came the rub. How would O. Henry finance the move to New York?

P. G. Roach could not help him more. The sleazy hotel was not prospering. He was seriously considering moving back to Austin now that O. Henry was out of jail and could be expected to take care of Margaret. In Austin Roach had been a figure of importance, a member of the Board of Trade and pillar of the Presbyterian church. In Pittsburgh he was manager of a seedy hotel. No, O. Henry could not look to that source for more assistance, and he so said in a letter to Frank Maddox in Austin, to whom he now turned.

The problem, said O. Henry, was that "I have been so completely absorbed in my work on it (the novel) I have not done any short story work for some months. Consequently funds are scarce. I want to make that novel count the best I can. . . . I would have had the means had I kept up my short story writing but I am anxious to get along with the novel which promises so much in the way of reputation and emolument that I have found myself without the means to make the move I want to."[9]

The net was that O. Henry wanted to borrow $75 from Frank Maddox. He enclosed several letters from magazines, including one from *McClure's* accepting one of his stories and promising payment of $75 within six weeks, and an acceptance of the story "The Renaissance at Charleroi" from *Era,* which was a new market for him. It was also something new in atmosphere, a tale from New Orleans.

The letter, like so much of O. Henry's contact with the outside world, was not quite honest and aboveboard. It was part fairy story. As he said himself, "all of us have to be prevaricators, hypocrites, and liars every day of our lives; otherwise the social structure would fall in pieces. . . . We must act in one another's presence just as we must wear clothes."

To strengthen his case with Frank Maddox, O. Henry indulged in a bit of hyperbole: "It is absolutely necessary that I get where I can have the advantage of books of reference and the advice of others of the craft, and the letter from Mr. Hall will corroborate my statement."

But the fact was that in the Carnegie Institute at least, O. Henry had plenty of reference books in Pittsburgh, and that when Messrs. Hall and Duffy suggested that O. Henry "come to New York" they did not mean that he should come there to live. The fact was also that O. Henry had planned from the prison days to submerge the "ex-con" in New York, and before he left Columbus had told Al Jennings that he would see him there. So, O. Henry was joining other writers: "Rousseau & Zola and George Moore and various memoirs that were supposed to be window panes in their respective breasts; but mostly, all of them were either liars, actors, or posers."

He was posing for Frank Maddox. But just a little bit. Anyone could feel the ring of truth in his argument that "this work of mine in New York means a new life and a resurrection of my old ambitions to me. I feel that I can do work that will be a success, and now is my opportunity. My unfortunate condition prevents me from taking advantage of it as another might, but I can crush down the past and make something of myself if I can seize the chance."

Another part of the truth, however, was that the real reason O. Henry was "broke" was those nightly forays into the darker corners of Pittsburgh, corner bars and the tough saloons down by the railroad tracks and the red-light district. This way, he said, he learned to know a city. He must have had some rousing adventures, for one night Mrs. Roach found him roaming in the street and expressed alarm for his safety. Pittsburgh, she said, was no place to roam in at night.

"I can handle it," he said. "You don't know how genteel some thieves are."

Another part of the truth was that O. Henry was then and always had been a "toff," a lover of stylish clothing and the high life as well as the low.

He also owed a great deal of money to the Roaches. (P. G. Roach estimated that he advanced or spent for O. Henry and Margaret $10,000 between 1887 and 1901.)[10] There was pressure on O. Henry now not only to support himself and Margaret, but to begin to repay the debt, and those costs were undoubtedly taking a share of his income from writing.

In fact, the "work" he was doing on the "the novel" was largely cerebral; he was turning out short stories and selling them regularly. But payment was often delayed, and in March 1902, when O. Henry wrote to Frank Maddox, he was in a hurry. He had been in Pittsburgh for seven months. The newness of his relationship with Margaret had worn off, and the problem now was to get her into boarding school, another big expense. Also, it is not hard to see that in addition to the people who had caused O. Henry to dislike Pittsburgh, he was beginning to feel stifled by the Roaches.

The letter to Frank Maddox produced nothing but a stony silence. After a month O. Henry wrote him again, a stilted letter, asking for the return of the specimen "publishers' letters" he had sent along to buttress his case for the loan.

O. Henry then wrote the editors of *Ainslee's* and told them he was eager to come to New York but had no money for the trip. Hall advanced him $100. Weeks went by but no O. Henry appeared in New York. Then came a message, virtually the same as the earlier one: vicissitudes had attacked O. Henry (read saloon fever) and his hardships had been beyond belief. He could come to New York immediately but he did not have the funds. A half dozen of the author's short stories had now appeared in the magazine, and all of them had been hits with the reading public. So Mr. Hall consulted Mr. Duffy and they agreed to advance O. Henry another $100 for the trip. This time he vowed to make it.[11]

One spring day O. Henry got on the train to New York. There was no looking back.

# 11

# Joining the Four Million

One fine spring afternoon in New York, one of those days when the sun reflecting off the buildings hides the dirt that covers the brick and stone and concrete beneath, when the girls on the street seem to smile invitingly, when the cops twirl their sticks expansively, and when even the bank branch managers look up and out the window to suddenly discover that there is a tree growing across the street and real people on the sidewalks—on one of those halcyon days, O. Henry appeared in New York.

Actually, he had come in the night before, gotten off the Pennsylvania Railroad train in New Jersey, taken the ferry across to Manhattan, and put up at a frowsy hotel near the ferry station. Then he spent the morning looking around the town. He had indicated that he would call on the two editors in the afternoon, and they had come back from an early lunch, but no O. Henry arrived. The hours wore on until it was nearly time for the editors to take their daily stroll uptown to Madison Square, where they then parted and went their ways to meet again next day at Duane and William streets. They wondered if the writer would show up. He had already disappointed them for several weeks after their first infusion of money. Was this going to be a repeat performance?[1]

The Messrs. Hall and Duffy had their necks out a mile for this man. Mr. Smith, the chief executive of Street and Smith, owners of *Ainslee's,* was not a man with eleemosynary inclinations, and they had dipped into his pocket for $200. As they had assured him, they had great hopes for this new writer, who had produced for them several more than acceptable short stories about the southwest and about Central America. Duffy later recalled that they had looked upon O. Henry as the most exciting writer who had come their way in a long time, accepting seven of the first eight stories he sent them.

Now, late on the afternoon of this remarkable, gorgeous spring day, a short, neatly dressed man in a well-fitting gray suit appeared at the offices of *Ainslee's Magazine.* He was wearing gloves and carrying a cane, and he gave his card to the man at the outer gate. He was obviously an out-of-towner for no New Yorker would be caught wearing so flamboyant a four-in-hand cravat. The necktie also marked him as of the lower middle class, certainly not the upper. All this was immediately apparent to the moody office boy, who could tell a New Yorker from a Jerseyite at forty paces.

The stranger gave the office boy his card. That is, he gave the office boy the engraved calling card, manufactured in Pittsburgh, of William Sydney Porter. The office boy looked unimpressed as he took the card, an engraved card that once again had the feel of the stranger, as opposed to the Manhattanite about it. The name meant nothing to the office boy, a jaded figure, long used to the names of Jack London, Booth Tarkington, Bret Harte, and that great master of the alias, Samuel Langhorne Clemens. Wearily, the boy delivered the bit of pasteboard to his employers. *William Sydney Porter.* For a moment, Messrs. Hall and Duffy drew a blank, then the light dawned. The name was indeed meaningful to the editors of *Ainslee's*: it meant that their long-lost author, the man in whom they had placed enough trust to advance the payment allocated for at least four ordinary short stories, had arrived.

HE DID NOT look much like an author, the two editors thought, mirroring the office boy's impressions. Not only was he dressed as described, but he also carried in with him a black derby hat, a headpiece much favored in London's City district by bankers, but in New York by prizefight managers when worn square on the head, and by gents from the Bowery when tipped back over one ear.

After the amenities, the editors took their new author on a walk from Duane Street to Madison Square, pointing out the sights. They showed him Morgan Robertson, a very famous writer of the day, who was passing by at Sixth Avenue and Twenty-third Street. Many an eye was turned on Mr. Robertson that fine spring afternoon, for in top hat and frock coat he made a princely figure. There, said the rig, was a real New Yorker. The editors silently urged their new acquaintance to look. But O. Henry was shy of meeting strangers, and instead of taking the hint and inquiring about Mr. Robertson, and perhaps showing a desire to make his acquaintance, which the editors were hoping to honor, O. Henry looked upward at the elevated railway and watched a snorting steam engine go by, hauling its smoky cars.

"Why," asked O. Henry, "aren't people scared to ride up so high?"[2]

Mr. Hall and Mr. Duffy were real New Yorkers—that is, they had lived in the city for at least a year—and, as such, nothing that happened in the city seemed unusual to them. They looked at O. Henry suspiciously. Was this Pittsburgher trying to pull their collective leg? But O. Henry gazed back with his most liquid and engaging shy smile, the one that made this chubby thirty-nine-year-old man look like a cherub, and they decided no, he could not so dissimulate. He must really be afraid of it. They were quite wrong about the dissimulation but quite right about O. Henry and the elevated. All his life O. Henry detested the elevated railway, sometimes he castigated it in his stories, and to get around town he took the slower streetcar or the subway.

As the editors escorted O. Henry uptown, they plied him with suggestions about this hotel and that, this restaurant as opposed to its fellow across the avenue, this shop over that one. He said very little and smiled a lot, a very shy man, they decided. But later they confided in one another that it was not precisely shyness that they meant, but a sort of deliberate summing up of what they said, what they pointed at, and what they ignored.

That day Mr. Hall and Mr. Duffy gave O. Henry all the advice they could spare about changing his abode from the hotel down by the ferry station, and at Madison Square they parted company with him. Next day, into the offices at Duane and William streets strode O. Henry, bouncing every step of the way as he did when he was pleased, to doff his hat and tender the youth at the railing another calling card. He had changed his necktie to one of slightly more somber hue. When the editors again deigned to receive him he announced that he had found a home, in Madame Marty's French *table d'hôte* hotel on Twenty-fourth Street between Broadway and Sixth Avenue. He also brought them a story, one he had knocked out that very morning (although he did not tell them so much: one of O. Henry's major efforts during his writing career was to conceal the ease and speed with which he composed his stories, on that soundest of literary principles, that genius receives plenty of lip service; if the editors think the prose is written easily, they will denigrate, if they believe it has been composed in the blood of the author, they will appreciate it more).[3]

The editors of *Ainslee's* were very pleased. They promised to give the story their promptest attention. At O.Henry's request they advanced more money, and with many protestations of mutual respect, editors and author parted company once again. In the days that followed, O. Henry produced several other stories for *Ainslee's,* plus a few sketches and some light verse, and bought some more stiff-collared shirts and some more neckties.

As quickly as the magazine could accommodate this material, the editors put it in. In the May 1903 issue appeared three contributions from O. Henry, one signed by the author, and two under pseudonyms. One of the pseudonyms was Sydney Porter.[4]

One of the pseudonymous stories Editor Duffy called "an unusually clever short story." This was "While the Auto Waits," a tragic tale of failed romance, in which the two romantics destroy the future with little white lies that play out their fantasies. It marked a new high point in O. Henry's writing; before, his tales had come out of his experience in the Southwest, in Central America, and from what he learned in prison. Now he was observing the four million people of the great metropolis, Baghdad on the Hudson he would come to call it, and in seeing the interplay of rich and poor, shopgirls and playboys, society men and seamstresses, he began to create a whole new body of literature, which he sometimes called the song of the city.

"While the Auto Waits" might have speeded O. Henry's name to fame, had that name been used on the story. But in his eagerness to sell, and in his contempt for the name Sydney Porter, O. Henry had written it under the name James L. Bliss. So when the literary editor of *The New York Times* saw the story and gave it unsolicited praise, the adulation was for a man who never existed, and never would exist even in the literary world except for this one foray. It did not help the reputation of O. Henry an iota.

The editors of *Ainslee's* were indeed gentlemen to give O. Henry an advance of $200 without requiring even "first refusal of all his works," which was a common practice in the industry. They did him much better: they supplied his financial needs for a number of weeks, while he got started, again without any attempt at corraling him into exclusivity. So the new arrival from the West was free to pursue his literary career as he wished. They accepted virtually everything he offered them. Only three stories were rejected: one about a gentleman named Mike O' Bader, which gave the editors a sense of *déjà vu* as a variation on the tale of the Wandering Jew; one rococo story set in New Orleans, written in a manner that reminded the editors simultaneously of a Thomas De Quincy, Edgar Allan Poe, and Lafcadio Hearn, and overwhelmed them with the quite un-O. Henryish triumph of background over plot; and a story about a man left over from Louisiana's prewar days of princely pleasures, living a life "remote, unfriended, and alone" in a crumbling mansion, a story so negative that it gave the editors an unpleasant feeling.[5]

O. Henry took the latter tale to Major Orlando J. Smith, president of the Associated Press, who was just preparing to launch *Brandur's* magazine in September. O. Henry had seen the announcement that Major Smith would pay five cents a word for any story he believed to be good enough to publish.[6]

The major bought the story. He also bought "Cupid à La Carte," a tale of the roaring West. Smith also announced that he was interested in "exclusivity." He wanted everything that O. Henry could write, and he promised to buy all, paying more than any other editor. But O. Henry was too canny to throw all his eggs into one basket. He told the major he would supply him with all the stories he wanted, but he declined to become a "property" of *Brandur's* magazine. So he left Major Smith with a mutual agreement to provide a story a week for *Brandur's*. "Cupid à La Carte" was published in the first issue of the magazine, in September 1902. Unfortunately the magazine did not make it, and there were no more checks. O. Henry might not have thought of himself as much of a bookkeeper, but he certainly had a fine sense of survival. By the end of 1902 his literary efforts had spread over eleven magazines and ten of them were still alive.[7]

*Everybody's* had bought some of O. Henry's work during the prison days, and so the author went to call on Editor John O'Hara Cosgrave, who awed him promptly by taking him to dine at the Players Club in Gramercy Park—"the swellest club in the city," O. Henry called it. They drank in the handsome bar, all dark wood and black leather, and then ascended to the glittering dining room, where each evening assembled representatives of the Great White Way. "It was Edwin Booth's old club and is like a palace inside," said the country boy from North Carolina, Texas, the prison at Columbus, Ohio, and Pittsburgh, Pennsylvania.

Major Smith was not giving up on his attempt to monopolize O. Henry. The major invited the author to join one or two of his clubs. O. Henry declined. He did not tell the major why, but he wrote P. G. Roach the real reason: "I shall not be too prominent socially; I intend to keep quiet and give no one a chance to make any trouble."[8]

Half a dozen calls on half a dozen magazines produced the sort of welcome every writer envies:

"I have the entree at several of the prominent offices, going in unannounced when I please, while everybody else waits outside."

It was a bit boastful of him to say so to Mr. and Mrs. Roach in a letter, but completely pardonable in a man who has suffered so many vicissitudes in recent years that when he made an overture he half expected a kick.

All the negative past seemed now to be behind him.

Still pursuing, Major Smith insisted that O. Henry visit his country house up the Hudson at Dobbs Ferry. O. Henry went, but he was not converted. How wise O. Henry was not to become totally involved with Major Smith; the gentleman never did prosper in the magazine business.

O. Henry shunned the usual sort of social contact, and even when he accepted invitations he was on his guard. To make small talk, the editors would ask him about his background. Immediately, the antennae came up, the patient stiffened, and passed off the difficult moment as swiftly as he could. One day at lunch Richard Duffy asked him such a question, and O. Henry diverted him by relating the plot of the story he was just then working on. The little that Duffy ever learned about O. Henry's past came out in swatches, in discussions relating to what was happening in his life at the moment.

"Always he lived emphatically in the present, not looking back to yesterday, not very far ahead toward tomorrow."[9]

Duffy got a glimpse of O. Henry's father when he asked the author one day about the story he was supposed to be delivering to *Ainslee's.*

Ah, yes, said O. Henry, that reminded him of the good doctor. When anyone would ask the doctor how a patient was getting along, the doctor would look at him omnisciently and reply: "Oh, Mrs. So and So is progressing."

He never explained which way the patient was progressing, whether toward better or worse.[10]

Yes, he added, the doctor was a real character, and he told a little about the doctor's inventions. But so vague was O. Henry, even in the telling of such tales, that Duffy seemed to remember that the doctor in question was an uncle of O. Henry's. And, how was the story coming along? In the anecdote, the purpose of the question somehow got lost, and the editor went away unenlightened. So it was, when the editors of *Ainslee's* lunched with their will-o'-the-wisp writer.

Gilman Hall, the more romantic of the two editors of *Ainslee's,* was certain that O. Henry was a man with a past he wanted to hide. O. Henry never said a word that would give him that impression.

"I used to notice, however, that whenever we entered a restaurant or other public place together, he would glance quickly around him, as if expecting an attack. I thought that he had perhaps killed some one in a ranch fight, for he told me that he had lived on a ranch in Texas. This inference was strengthened by finding that he was a crack shot with a pistol."[11]

The editors were only doing their editorial duty in taking O. Henry to lunch, but in fact they enjoyed these meetings immensely, for as Gilman Hall said, the author "was a man with whom you could sit for a long time and feel no necessity for talking, though a passerby would often evoke from him a remark that later reappeared as the basis of a story."[12]

Rather than anything to do with the past or even with business, he was much more likely, said Editor Duffy, to speak about the last restaurant he had dined in, or the house where he was living.

The Hotel Marty was a very quiet place, called a hotel, but not really one in the sense that O. Henry had known before. All the guests were men, and all of them save himself were men of business, who went to offices or shops every day, leaving the hotel "as quiet as a church," much to O. Henry's satisfaction. How he could write there!

Madame Marty, the proprietress, was a kindly old lady in black. O. Henry's room was on the third floor, back, with an alcove fitted with plumbing. Although Broadway was only half a block away and Sixth Avenue lay on the other side, the street was "as quiet as a country town," said O. Henry. The dining room was large and the fare excellent, and the hotel boasted a summer garden in the back where on clement evenings the gentlemen ate alfresco.[13]

O. Henry had settled in so intensely that except for lunches with editors, sometimes he went for as long as three days without speaking to a soul except at meal time in the dining room or in a little French restaurant he had discovered on Twenty-sixth Street.

But if he did want to see someone, he was located in the middle of the literary world of New York. The offices of *The Great Round World* magazine were on Twenty-second Street. A few weeks after O. Henry came to town *Ainslee's* moved up to Fifth Avenue, three blocks away. *Everybody's* was just six blocks away. The locale, the ambience, all seemed idyllic.

The Hotel Marty had only one negative. Her name was Lena. She was the chambermaid, an human bundle of efficiency, bursting with ambition, just a few months removed from Ellis Island, the gateway to America for European immigrants.

O. Henry was following his old ways, up most of the night, writing or carousing, and abed half the day. He was the despair of Lena, who liked to get her work on the rooms done in the mornings. By nine thirty or ten she had made up all the other rooms in the house, and it was simply a question of rousting out O. Henry before her day's work was done. Every day, half in belligerence, half in despair, Lena launched her assault on O. Henry.

She would pad up the third floor hall to this holdout castle and knock on the door with her passkey. Of course, O. Henry was dead to the world inside and there would be no answer. She would knock again, and then, anticipating anything, she would quietly open the door with the passkey. Then she would rush in like the wind, past the bed in which lay the writer, past the chair on which the writer sat when composing, past the steamer trunk that was his desk, and hurl herself to the farthest corner of the room, back by the single window that looked onto the airshaft, to begin her tidying up. When she had finished with the corner she would charge on to assault the bedroom, calling out as she came:

"May I come in, Mister?"

O. Henry, lifting his head from under the pillow, would mumble and try to pull himself together. Ultimately he would stagger out of bed and out toward the bathroom, while Lena triumphantly "made up" the room. This same scene was played day after day, until at the offices of *Ainslee's* the story had been told so many times that whenever anyone on the staff wanted to do something without asking polite permission, he said "May I come in, Mister?"

The battle continued even after O. Henry's improved financial conditions allowed him to take a better room, one overlooking Twenty-fourth Street, furnished in faded elegance, with a sort of alcove that contained the necessary plumbing.[14]

By mid-July O. Henry was completely established in New York. He had written enough stories to pay off his debt to *Ainslee's*. He had several other markets and was producing at the phenomenal rate of a story a day. The stories were coming along beautifully, long stories, short stories, and multi-part stories. *Ainslee's* wanted a novelette. Doubleday, Page, and Co., the book publishers, had asked him to do a novel, and he had agreed. "I have about settled on a subject and am going to work on it at once," wrote O. Henry hopefully. It was a hope to be reiterated time and again in the years to come. He had not yet reached the point of confidence where he felt able to turn down any reasonable offer that came his way.

ON JULY 19 O. Henry wrote the Roaches that he had all he could possibly do, and that he felt he was finally on the right track. He promised that he would begin sending money to them the next month to begin the repayment of the debt he carried very heavily. The proof of his activity was there: in earlier times all O. Henry's writings had been penned with great care, in fine Spencerian hand, by a fine-point pen in black ink on white paper. But now he began writing in pencil on unlined yellow pads, and from this point on his handwriting began to deteriorate, not through any physical failures, but because of the volume of verbiage that flowed from those unceasing fingers.[15]

One editor after another discovered O. Henry and began to court him. The secretary of the Periodical Publishers' Association invited him on a sailing outing, a trip up the Hudson. He was too shy to reject the invitation. So he got aboard the big sailboat the revelers had chartered, and submitted to the endless questioning that his reticence seemed to arouse in editors. Finally, at Poughkeepsie, the sailboat put in and tied up at the pier, and O. Henry jumped ship to catch the next train back to the town he also sometimes called Gotham.[16] He hated crowds just as much as he loved the convivial table with a handful of friends around swapping lies and telling stories.[17]

McClure's newspaper syndicate, which had published the first O. Henry story back in the Austin years, had forgotten about this Texas author. But McClure's also published a magazine that had become very prominent, particularly for its exposés (muckraking) and fiction. One of McClure's first readers was a junior editor named Witter Bynner, who had just graduated from Harvard College and in the manner that was to become immemorial was out to establish himself in the literary world. One Olivier Henry had submitted a story called "Tobin's Palm," which dealt with the vicissitudes of a pair of Irish immigrant sweethearts who had lost touch with one another in the vast "melting caldron" of America. It was one of O. Henry's earliest New York tales.

Reader Bynner was taken by the tale, but the head reader did not like it, and sent it back. Bynner discovered this and took the matter to the editor in chief, S. S. McClure. The editor ought to take a look himself, he said. Editor McClure was willing and told Bynner to have the author resubmit the story. But Bynner said the story was so great that he was afraid it would be snapped up by another magazine. The only way to stop that, he said, was to go to the author (who had given his address) and retrieve the script.

McClure was so impressed by the exuberance of his young reader that he told him to go and get the manuscript, that McClure's would buy it.

Bynner hurried over to O. Henry's address, and found the author in a room equipped with a bed, chair, and a steamer trunk that he was using as a writing desk. There on the top of the trunk, he recognized the McClure's envelope and knew what was inside. He did not stop for civility:

"'Tobin's Palm'?" he asked.

"Yes."

"It's sold."

"Good. I'm flat broke," said the author.

Whereupon they began talking and soon became good friends.[18]

WHY O. HENRY should be "dead broke" seemed mysterious to some editors. After a meal or two with the author they had part of the story at least. He did himself well at the bar, quaffing several drinks before a meal, and often drinking wine or beer with it. Then, he was as likely to give the waiter a tip that matched the size of the check. And on the street he never passed a beggar without giving him a handout. One time he came upon one of those sorry figures who would later be known as Bowery bums. O. Henry dug into his pocket and found a coin, which he handed the man.

"Here's a dollar. I hope it helps."

The man went off but before O. Henry and his companion had gone far they heard a shout, and the down-and-outer came running up, holding the coin.

"Here, mister. You gave me a twenty-dollar gold piece."

O. Henry spurned the coin, and turned and walked on, giving an embarrassed look at his companion.

"Nonsense," he said over his shoulder. "Don't you think I know a dollar when I see one?"[19]

So those who came to know O. Henry began to realize that he was a compulsive giver just as he was a compulsive drinker. One of his friends noted (after O. Henry's death) that he drank two bottles of whiskey a day. He did not get drunk as far as any of his editors knew. He drank steadily, and far into the night, as he pursued his quarry: the people, just then the four million people of New York.

# 12

# O. Henry's People

Virtually every editor who worked in New York between 1901 and 1910 seemed to have an O. Henry tale, a good indication of the author's celebrity in a literary community noted for its forgetfulness and the evanescence of its heroes.

There are probably more stories connected with the emergence of the name O. Henry than any other about this man. Some say the author began using that nom de plume as a child. Some say that the author used O. Henry as an expletive so often that someone suggested he also use it as a pen name. Harry Peyton Steger of McClure's and later of Doubleday, said it came from New Orleans days, when the author, preparing to send out "some stories" picked the name out of the social pages of a New Orleans newspaper. That is how he got the Henry. The O. was half contributed by a friend, who said he needed a front name, too. O. Henry then said a plain initial would be best and the easiest of all to write was O. The only problem with Steger's tale is that O. Henry did not send out any stories while he was in New Orleans.[1]

Some say the O. Henry cognomen came from a story. Some give the tale, as noted, of the name coming from a romantic interlude with Lollie Cave in Austin. The Lollie Cave story is obviously true, the evidence exists, but whether or not that youthful gesture caused O. Henry to use the name is not certain; he was always a quixotic character and it amused him to tell tall tales to people who asked low questions. Other sources might have been quoted but, in fact, no one but O. Henry ever knew and he never told. Probably it was not very important to him in the beginning; he did use the William Sydney Porter name in its variations, but after the prison period he did not seem comfortable with the old name and used it less and less, preferring the anonymity of many pen names. And, as also noted, the editors helped by supplying him with some when two or more of his contributions were to be used in a single issue of a magazine. Thus in 1902 the author was appearing in many publications in many guises; the pattern would not be set until his success became overwhelming, and that was not yet. The man was a writer, he wrote for money, and until the value of the name became apparent he did not care what "monicker" his work wore. Get the money, that was the name of the game. He was one of the original "money writers" without any claims (at the time) to literary importance.

"Writing is my business," he once said, "it is my way of getting money to pay room rent, to buy food and clothes and Pilsener. I write for no other reason or purpose."

He was not, in other words, a social reformer. That year Ida Tarbell was doing the work for her great social exposé, *The History of the Standard Oil Company,* which would run in *McClure's* in 1903. That magazine and *Collier's, Cosmopolitan, Everybody's,* and *The American,* would open their pages to the new group of infuriated writers whom Teddy Roosevelt would characterize as "the muckrakers," after the character in *Pilgrim's Progress* who raked muck forever and could see nothing in his world but muck.

O. Henry, nightly traversing the New York Tenderloin, which ran from Fourteenth to Forty-second Street on the near west side, saw all the horrors that man could imagine: rapes, beatings, murders, and the lesser spectacles of extortion, slow starvation, prostitution (the do-gooders estimated 25,000 prostitutes roamed the streets of New York at the turn of the century), and plain misery of plain people. But unlike a Lincoln Steffens or an Upton Sinclair he did not try to change these aspects of life by screeching with a shrill pen. He felt himself always too near those at the bottom—a wage slave paid by himself for his own herculean efforts—to react thus. His reaction to poverty was to give the poor one a handout. When questioned once about where he had been the previous evening, O. Henry replied:

"I spent the evening alleviating the condition of a shopgirl, insofar as a planked steak dinner would do."

Sometimes, O. Henry wandered farther afield. One autumn day Richard Duffy of *Ainslee's* persuaded him that it would do him good to go for a walk in the country, and took him out of the city to the hills of Westchester County. They walked about a mile on a zigzag path through the woods.

"I showed him plains below us and hills stretching away so far and blue they look like the illimitable sea from the deck of an ocean liner," said Duffy.

"But it was not until we approached the station from which we were to take the train back to New York that he showed the least sign of animation.

"What's the matter, Bill?" I asked. "I thought you'd like to see some real country."

"Cunn'l, how kin you expeck me to appreciate the glories of nature when you walk me over a mountain like that an' I got new shoes on?"

He stood on one foot and then the other, nursing his feet.[2]

That exaggerated language above, described by Editor Duffy, was no exaggeration.

It was, said Duffy, one of O. Henry's affectations to speak a sort of Southern back-country style English, although as anyone who read any of his stories could see easily, it was equally a part of the man to use pinpoint precision in his selection of adjectives, many from the inner recesses of Mr. Webster's lexicon. From this came a tale O. Henry told Duffy:

A woman who had read some of his stories wrote him and asked if she and her lady friend might meet him because they admired his work so much. O. Henry was not above appreciation of flattery, particularly from ladies, so he agreed to the meeting. Later, the lady said, "You mortified me nearly to death, you talked so ungrammatical!"[3]

As noted, from the beginning of O. Henry's New York career Gilman Hall and Richard Duffy of *Ainslee's* had befriended him, and the two editors continued to do so. During the remainder of 1902 *Ainslee's* continued to be O. Henry's major market, although they did not immediately publish all the stories they bought from him that year. The "discovery" by *McClure's* meant a lot to the author, because it raised his rate for a short story from the $75 paid by *Ainslee's* to $100, paid by *McClure's*. Friendly as O. Henry was with Gilman Hall and Witter Bynner of *McClure's,* he never stopped looking for new markets. The biggest and most important magazine in America was the *Saturday Evening Post,* published in Philadelphia, and he assaulted that market as he did all the others, frequently and with finished manuscripts. They came back to him, one after another, and so high and so mighty was the *Saturday Evening Post,* and so busy were its editors, that O. Henry was not deemed worthy even of a letter, but was sent printed rejection slips with his stories.

O. HENRY ACHIEVED a degree of notoriety by the fall of 1902, said Gilman Hall, although virtually no one but a few editors knew who the writer was or where he lived.

One measure was collegiate: when the O. Henry stories began to catch on with magazine readers, and the first speculations as to the true identity of the writer trickled in, one brash college youth astounded his contemporaries by claiming that he, the undergraduate, was really the great author. This intelligence was imparted one day to Gilman Hall by a competing editor, who had just sent an invitation to "the real O. Henry," to cease his studies for a day or two and write a short story for his magazine. Editor Hall laughed and said the real O. Henry had left his office just a few minutes before the other editor called, and that the real O. Henry could be found in his room on Twenty-fourth Street. The other did not believe—until his request to the undergraduate "O. Henry" failed to produce anything at all.[4]

There was flattery in a sort of imitation. When Gilman Hall told the tale to the real man, O. Henry laughed. Very funny, said he. Just let Editor Hall make sure the checks were still sent to Twenty-fourth Street.[5]

The checks were always on his mind. They could not come fast enough for him, he seemed always to be short of cash, as just before Christmas 1902, when he wrote Witter Bynner at *McClure's.*

"P.S. By no means as a precedent, but under existing 'special circumstances' and in consideration of the horror and havoc of the approaching Christmas season, would you care to get a check put through today for that little story? It would be much appreciated, as I am quite a sufferer at the hands of some of the 'payment on publication' publications. Hope you won't think the request out of order."[6]

That was the first such request of Witter Bynner. It was far from the last. During the next four years nearly every acceptance of a manuscript of O. Henry's would be followed by a plea for immediate payment of the cash, and many times the requests came for an advance against a new—and often unnamed—story, as this one:

"I could use $100 awful nicely just now. Want to ship some dough West. Could you do that and put $25 on account.* A good 5,000 word story will come up to you extremely shortly to knock the balance off the books."[7]

The stories that were selling to the magazines were mostly those about the mythical Republic of Anchuria, and its port city of Coralio. Some of the characters repeated in new stories. The effect was to give a reader of O. Henry tales a sort of kaleidoscopic vision of the life of expatriates in Central America. The time was ripe for it. Richard Harding Davis was making capital of the same general scene in story and play. Indeed, as O. Henry gained ground in

---

*McClure's* owed O. Henry $75 for a short story at that moment. The reference to shipping "dough West" referred to sending money to the Roaches to provide for Margaret and retire some of O. Henry's debt.

New York he was often compared to Richard Harding Davis, but the only real similarities were that they were both writers and were at the time writing about Latin America. Richard Harding Davis was ever the demon journalist, and as O. Henry once told the editors of the *Sunday World,* he was not a journalist primarily but a story writer.

Still, one reason the Anchuria stories caught the eye of magazine editors was the subject matter, so new to Americans. Theodore Roosevelt was making political capital of the region and preparing to launch the Panama Canal project. O. Henry was in the right place at the right time with subject matter that appealed. His abilities were certainly appreciated all the more for this.

It was not long before book publishers began talking to him seriously. Most serious was Witter Bynner, who decided he wanted to make a book out of the Anchuria stories. The trouble was that with only four Anchuria stories published in 1902, and another four scheduled for 1903, there were not enough to make a book. O. Henry would oblige by including nine more tales never published in magazines. To a book publisher the idea was enthralling; here he had a popular author's work, given enough advance promotion by O. Henry's growing popularity in America, *and* an element of exclusivity with half the book consisting of new material.

So the work of adjusting and adding began, but it did not take nearly all of O. Henry's time or effort.

No matter what O. Henry was currently writing, in 1902 and thereafter, the city became O. Henry's world.

"When I first came to New York," he said much later, "I spent a great deal of time knocking around the streets. I used to walk at all hours of the day and night along the river fronts, through Hell's Kitchen, down the Bowery, dropping into all manner of places and talking with anyone who would hold converse with me. I have never met a man but what I could learn something from him. He's had some experiences that I have not had, he sees the world from his own viewpoint. If you got at it the right way, you can extract something of value from him."[8]


BUT, AS O. HENRY sensed, the ambience had to be exactly right. One evening, strolling through Madison Square with a friend, O. Henry came upon a young girl who was crying. The men stopped and O. Henry asked her what was wrong.

Between sobs the girl told them that she had come to New York from New Jersey, and she had run out of money and she had no friends and no place to sleep. O. Henry gave her some money and they found a policeman and put her in his charge, to be sure she got on the ferry and a train to home.

As the friends continued to walk through the square, O. Henry's companion spoke.

"Why didn't you talk to her? I'll bet there was a story in that girl."

"Old man,"* said O. Henry, "there never is a story where there seems to be one." His specialty was finding the material for stories, and he looked everywhere for it but not in the obvious places. The obvious place to find a shopgirl was in a shop, was it not? said his friend.

"Indeed not," said O. Henry. "It is not the salesgirl *in* the department store who is worth studying; it is the salesgirl *out of* it."[9]

In the beginning, he found much of his material in the public squares, the incident with the little girl from New Jersey to the contrary notwithstanding.

"By Courier," the poignant tale of a young man who is about to throw his life away because the girl he loves has rejected him, is played out in one of O. Henry's parks. He has observed his people and his scene, and the story indicates it.

O. Henry was fearless in his assault on New York, which in the early years of the century was no safer than in the later, although the population was much tougher and resilient then. One night he was walking through Hell's Kitchen, and he stopped to talk to a policeman. As they were passing the time of night, two shots suddenly rang out.

"Someone's been killed!" cried O. Henry.

"No. Don't worry," said the policeman. "Only hurt. It takes at least three bullets to kill anyone in this part of town."[10]

O. Henry told these tales to his friends, at lunch (which he had to learn to appreciate, since the long, liquid lunches of the publishing trade played hob with his working habits), and, more happily, at long liquid dinners and evenings, which he dearly loved.

One night O. Henry and two friends were walking down Broadway. Near Herald Square they were approached by a well-dressed young man who told them a "hard luck" story. One of the men was much impressed and gave the young man some money to tide him over. Like a buck frightened on the road, the young man disappeared around the corner into Thirty-sixth Street.

---

*O. Henry almost never called anyone by his proper name. In the years that he knew Witter Bynner he addressed him as Bill, Honored Sir, Colonel, Doubleyou B, B-r, Pal, Mr. Man, Brother, My Dear Person, Willie, Witt, B. Binny, and many another sobriquet. And he signed himself by all sorts of names, Panhandle Pete, Hiram Q. Smith, but most often simply S. P., the true initials of the last two-thirds of the old family name he kept for use in American social intercourse. Obviously, he was bemused by names.

"He seemed like an honest, worthy chap," said the charitable one.

"Yes," said O. Henry. "He seemed like an honest, worthy chap to me, too, last night."[11]

He would go anywhere that seemed to suggest a story. One evening he found one right at home. He had, as was so usual with him, spent all the money advanced for his most recent literary effort and was "dead broke." He worked all afternoon and into the evening, unable to afford to go out to dinner. Until the story was finished, and delivered, he could not expect any more money.

The evening wore on. Hunger stilled his pen. He got up and went out into the corridor and walked up and down. He passed a doorway from which emanated the marvelous odor of someone's cooking. He went down the hall, came back and passed the door again. This time, the door opened and a young woman came into the doorway.

"Have you had your supper?" she asked. "I've made a Hazlett stew and it's too much for me. It won't keep, so come and help me eat it."

So O. Henry gratefully went into the girl's room and ate the stew. They talked about feather curling. That was her profession in the big city, curling feathers with a dull blade for the hats of wealthy women.

They talked about life in the city. O. Henry asked what was in the stew and the girl told him, all she had been able to afford: liver, kidney, and heart of calf.

No matter, it had saved O. Henry that night. He went back to his room and finished his tale. A few days later, rich in pocket, he rapped on the girl's door, intending to reciprocate, no, not reciprocate, but reward her a dozen times by buying her the finest dinner in New York. But the girl was gone. Gone where? No one knew. The city had claimed another victim. That experience coupled with his own imagination, provided O. Henry with the idea for one of his tales of the young woman in the heartless city: "The Furnished Room."[12]

Aiming at so many markets, O. Henry had to work very hard. Many of the magazines, as he noted, paid only on publication. In 1902 O. Henry published seventeen stories in the major magazines, which brought him in about $1,200. In terms of his life style that was a fair amount of money; he could buy a four-course meal at his favorite French restaurant for thirty-five cents. Ten dollars would buy a suit of clothes. A room cost a dollar a day. But O. Henry was almost always broke. Later critics and biographers blamed his situation largely on high living. He continued to order Sazerac cocktails before a meal and was known to consume a number of them. He also liked French table wines, and one bartender said he always knew when O. Henry was going back to his digs for a long session of writing, because the writer asked that a bottle of Scotch whisky be sent to the room.

Certainly his habits ate up money, but it was his unflagging personal charity that ate up as much. A hallmark of his life was that he could never resist the unfortunate.

In this initial period, learning the ways of the city, O. Henry made many acquaintances. One was Anne Partlan, daughter of a labor leader, reformer, and advocate of women's rights, and one of the early muckrakers, whose articles about the plight of women in the cities had attracted attention.

"One evening," said Miss Partlan, "a group of department store employees were having dinner with me. Among them were sales girls, an associate buyer and one of the sales force. I asked O. Henry to join us so that he might catch the spirit of their daily life. He leavened their shop talk with genial simple expressions of mirth as they told their tales of petty intrigue and strife for place amid the antagonism and pressure which pervades the atmosphere of every big organization."[13]

And he also listened.

Out of such encounters came stories like "An Unfinished Story."

"I had a dream," wrote O. Henry. It was a dream about heaven and the "bar-of-judgment" theory.

The story was about a working girl and a man the girls called Piggy.

"Piggy needs but a word," said O. Henry. "When the girls named him, an undeserving stigma was cast upon the whole family of swine. The words-of-three-letters lesson in the old blue spelling book begins with Piggy's biography. He was fat, he had the soul of a rat, the habits of a bat and the magnanimity of a cat. . . . He wore expensive clothes; and was a connoisseur in starvation. He could look at a shopgirl and tell you to an hour how long it had been since she had eaten anything more nourishing than marshmallows and tea. He hung about the shopping districts and prowled around the department stores with his invitations to dinner. Men who escort dogs upon the street at the end of a string look down upon him . . ."

The reader now knows what Piggy wants from the shopgirl Dulcie. This time, hungry, with only a box of crackers and a pot of strawberry jam in her room, Dulcie the shopgirl resists Piggy. Although in a moment of weakness she has accepted an invitation to dinner; when he arrives, she refuses to go downstairs. And she goes to bed hungry. But, says O. Henry, there will be a next time, when Dulcie is feeling hungrier and lonelier than usual . . .

The author summed up:

"I dreamed that I was standing near a crowd of prosperous-looking angels, and a policeman took me by the wing and asked if I belonged with them.

"'Who are they?' I asked.

"'Why,' said he, 'they are the men who hired working-girls, and paid 'em five or six dollars a week to live on. Are you one of the bunch?'

"'Not on your immorality,' said I. 'I'm only a fellow that set fire to an orphan asylum, and murdered a blind man for his pennies.'"[14]

That was as about as near social commentary as O. Henry ever got.

THERE WAS, HOWEVER, more to O. Henry's nightly forays in the streets of New York than search for story material. Perhaps the real reason his tales of Manhattan ring so true is that he had a real feeling for the common men and women, and particularly those caught in the urban machinery. He would change twenty dollars into quarters at a restaurant, and after dinner would go up through one of his favorite parks, often Madison Square, handing out quarters to unfortunates he found sitting or sleeping on the benches. He might roam the streets until the twenty dollars was gone.

AS 1903 BEGAN, O. Henry was doing ever better. He added *Cosmopolitan* and *Harper's* to his string of markets. *Ainslee's* that year ran twelve of his stories. In March, they published "The Shamrock and the Palm," under the name Olivier Henry. They also published that month "Sound and Fury," under the name S. H. Peters, and "Cherchez la Femme," under James L. Bliss. By this time, O. Henry's relations with the editors were so close that they came around to his way, and began using the name he preferred: O. Henry.

Sydney Porter appeared that year, 1903, in *Munsey's* April issue, with "One Dollar's Worth," and again in the July issue with "Jimmy Hayes and Muriel." But mostly it was O. Henry, with occasional changes to accommodate the editors when necessary.

The stories were a mixture now: the subjects were Texas days and Central America, New Orleans and New York, and the postwar South. O. Henry never had any use for the "professional Confederates" who lived on in a dream world where resentment seemed to be their principal stock in trade. His stories slashed them to ribbons. His heroes might be outside the law, and often were, but they were energetic men looking to a positive future. Sometimes his stories of the shopgirls were tear-jerking, but always his vision of New York was of the great city where every emotion reigned at some point or other, where anything could happen and usually did.

One story that appeared in the spring of 1903 in *Cosmopolitan* created a lot of attention favorable to O. Henry. It was "A Retrieved Reformation," based on the story of Jimmy Connors, the safecracker he had known in prison, who had been "sent up" for a crime he did not commit. Not only did this tale make his reputation with *Cosmopolitan* (it was his first story for them) but the word about this remarkable tale spread wider. It was not really a New York story, but it was embraced by New York.

HE COULD ENJOY himself at a shooting gallery with his friend Seth Moyle, the New York literary agent, or in a long evening with Anne Partlan's father, an evening which included attendance at a labor convention.

"Where do you keep shop?" asked the wife of a Missouri mechanic.

Ann Partlan said he was an author.

"Well, I can do other things," said O. Henry. "I can rope cows and I tried sheep raising once."[15]

The stories still reflected those experiences from the West and from Central American climes. Plenty of people had written about New York; what had brought O. Henry to the attention of the editors was as much his scenery, unfamiliar to the cynical magazine editors, as his mastery of his craft. From 1900 to 1902, of twenty-two stories four were about Central America, nine were about Texas, four were set in "the south," one definitely in New Orleans, four in indefinite settings, and only one definitely in New York City. In 1903, four of O. Henry's thirty-five published tales were set in Central America, fourteen in the Southwest, four in the South, four in indefinite surroundings, one in France, one in Switzerland, one in New Orleans, and six in New York. As noted, the book that was in the works, almost novelistic in its progression of tales and repetition of characters and settings, was about the mythical Republic of Anchuria in Central America. In later years, New York reviewers would suggest that O. Henry's reputation was made in the revelation of the New York City of his time. His book publisher, Doubleday, would add to the image when a complete edition of his works was brought forth in 1927 by putting the volume *The Four Million* (about New York) ahead of all the rest. This idea was embraced by the New York literary community, which seldom ventured west of the Hudson River, and it was suggested that with only his New York stories as a guide, without any statistics or other means, a historian could recreate the city of the early part of the 1900s. Perhaps. The same could also be said of Anchuria and Texas. The fact was that O. Henry gained his fame as a writer about the exotic, and only when he was established did he write about New York. By that time he could have cast his stories in Antarctica and a happy public would read them.

(left) William Sydney Porter (then Sidney) at the age of two, in Greensboro. What can you say about a baby? Perhaps that here shows a certain melancholy that Porter carried all his life. *(O. Henry Memorial Museum, Austin)*

(below) O. Henry's parents. The good doctor seemed to be sober when this picture was taken. That was not always the case, but drunk or sober, Doc Porter was a beloved citizen of Greensboro. Mary Virginia Swain Porter was descended from important colonial families, but she married beneath her. She died young, and Porter was brought up by his aunt and grandmother. *(Doubleday & Co.)*

(above) Edgeworth Female Seminary, Greensboro. O. Henry's mother and his aunt were products of this early female educational institution. During the Civil War, his father sawed off legs there when it was made into a Confederate army hospital. O. Henry was present the night it burned down. *(Doubleday & Co.)*

(right) Where O. Henry learned the Three Rs. The little school in Greensboro, North Carolina, where the young Will Porter was taught by his aunt, Lina Porter. The drawing is by Isabella Swaim, a classmate of Porter's.

Porter, give me a little piece of ice. I'll pay you for it.
Clark, ain't you got no cigars here.

(above) This drawing of the interior of Clark Porter's drugstore was made by O. Henry in his youth. The gent crossing in front of the counter with the jug is on his way to the back room where a card game ran most of the time. Contents of jug: ice. Purpose: mix with bourbon whiskey. (Doubleday & Co.)

(right) In O. Henry's youth in Greensboro, the South was run by carpetbaggers from the North and scalawags from the South. Judge Tourgee was a well-meaning northerner who came to the South to try to help the "Reconstruction" process. But because he was a carpetbagger, everyone hated and distrusted him. Here is O. Henry's cartoon of the judge fleeing Greensboro with nothing but his carpetbag. (Doubleday & Co.)

(bottom facing page) A bunch of the boys in front of the Porter drugstore in Greensboro. Will Porter would have inherited this store from his uncle if he had not gotten sick (incipient tuberculosis) and also tired of the dullness of a small Southern town. (O. Henry Memorial Museum, Austin)

(above) The Hill City Quartette. These four young men took their singing very seriously. Night after night they appeared beneath the windows of their lady loves, with a portable organ or a guitar, which Will Porter played, and serenaded the girls until the neighbors complained. They also were available for parties and light opera. (*O. Henry Memorial Museum, Austin*)

(right) Will Porter at seventeen in Texas. This photo must have been taken at a San Antonio photographer's salon, for nobody in the raw ranch country of the Nueces River would have had a Japanese parasol for a prop, and San Antone was the nearest big city. (*O. Henry Memorial Museum, Austin*)

(above left) This picture of O. Henry at about twenty years old was taken in Texas. *(Greensboro Historical Museum)*

(above right) Athol Estes Porter, Will Porter's first wife and the mother of his only child. The marriage was relatively successful, although Athol took exception to Will's drinking and late hours in the Austin days. Like O. Henry's mother, Athol died young and of the same disease, tuberculosis. *(O. Henry Memorial Museum, Austin)*

(below) The land office in Austin. It still stands, as gray and forbidding as it was in O. Henry's day. This is where he worked as a draftsman for the Texas state government. *(Doubleday & Co.)*

(above left) Athol, daughter Margaret, and Will Porter, 1895, in Austin. When this photograph was taken, Athol knew she was dying of tuberculosis. *(O. Henry Memorial Museum, Austin)*

(above right) This is the bed that Porter and Athol slept in in their little cottage in Austin. Much of the furniture has been recaptured and the cottage has been made into a museum where visitors can see much Porter memorabil.ia. *(George Ancona, O. Henry Memorial Museum, Austin)*

(below) When he lived in Austin, Will Porter came to this barbershop every morning for his shave and a bit of conversation with some of the other young blades of the city. *(O. Henry Memorial Museum, Austin)*

THERE WAS AN OLD FELLOW FROM AUSTIN
STOPPED OVER A DAY IN BOSTON
AND HE SAIS: "THIS HERE TOWN
COVERS MOST TOO MUCH GROUND
It's JUST THE RIGHT SIZE TO GET LOST IN.

(above) Will Porter (alias O. Henry) in his cash cage. As teller of the First National Bank of Austin, Porter was the only bonded official, and that is what got him into trouble when the crooked dealings of his superiors were discovered by the Federal bank examiners. Porter sported a handlebar mustache until he went to prison, but when he got out never adopted the fashion again. (*O. Henry Memorial Museum, Austin*)

(left) An O. Henry limerick and sketch. (*University of Virginia Library*)

*[handwritten letter]*

Greensboro N.C.
May 26th 1884

To All Whom it May Concern,
I J.N. Wilson Clerk of the Superior Court
do hereby Certify that I have known intimately
acquainted with W.S. Porter for more than
ten years when I first became acquainted
with him he was Working for his uncle W.C.
Porter who kept a Drug Store and remained
with him up to the time he left for the
State of Texas and he is undoubtedly a young
man of good moral character and reputed
to be a No one druggist and a very
popular young man among his many friends

J.N. Wilson Clk

I fully endorse the above
Wm. H. Steiner
Register of Deeds

J.S. White Clk
Greensboro N.C.

## O. HENRY'S CHARACTER"

(above) Many of Will Porter's friends gave character references at his embezzlement trial.

(right) The Caledonia Hotel did not have a very imposing front, but this seven-story building was O. Henry's favorite home in New York. It was also his club. Others belonged to the Players, the Harvard Club, etcetera, but this entire hotel was O. Henry's club. He had the run of the kitchen, the services of all the waiters, and was protected loyally by the staff from curiosity seekers. *(Doubleday & Co.)*

(left) 55 Irving Place was one of O. Henry's "digs." All he needed was a bed, a table and chair, a place for the trunk in which he kept rejected manuscripts, and running water to mix with whiskey. *(Doubleday & Co.)*

(below) This is O. Henryland, which centered around Madison Square. O. Henry walked the streets at night, sitting in the parks, buying drinks and meals for the bums, and chasing shopgirls. That's how he got his New York stories. *(Doubleday & Co.)*

(above) Margaret Worth Porter, O. Henry's daughter, at about twenty years old. *(O. Henry Memorial Museum, Austin)*

(right) O. Henry on vacation in western North Carolina. *(Austin-Travis County Collection, Austin Public Library)*

(left) This portrait of O. Henry was taken by J. Carl Pehl. *(O. Henry Memorial Museum, Austin)*

(right) The last years. After O. Henry married Sara Coleman, his boyhood sweetheart, they went on their honeymoon to a resort hotel in western North Carolina. O. Henry was at the height of his fame. *(Greensboro Historical Museum)* (left) A bookmark ad by Doubleday including a poem on O. Henry by James Whitcomb Riley. *(University of Virginia Library)*

(right) Another Doubleday Page & Co. bookmark ad. *(University of Virginia Library)*

A sales report on O. Henry's book *The Gentle Grafter.* There was some confusion about the spelling of his first name because he changed it from Sidney to Sydney while in Texas. *(University of Virginia Library)*

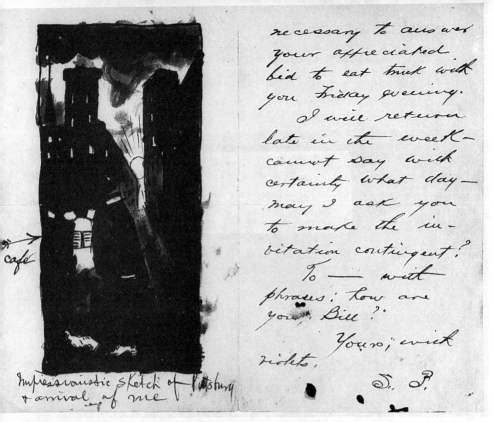

necessary to answer
your appreciated
bid to eat truck with
you Friday evening.
I will return
late in the week—
cannot say with
certainty what day—
may I ask you
to make the in-
vitation contingent?
To —— with
phrases: how are
you, Bill?
Yours, with
violets,
S. P.

café

Impressionistic sketch of Pittsburg
+ arrival of me

(above) Part of a letter to Richard Duffy of *Everyman's,* with a sketch of himself arriving in Pittsburgh. *(University of Virginia Library)*

(left) Photo of Porter in his forties. This picture was taken in New York after O. Henry had become a grand success. For years he would not allow any photos to be taken because he feared exposure as an "ex-con." Eventually he was blackmailed, finally refused to pay, and nothing happened; he then relaxed to the point of letting himself be photographed. *(Greensboro Historical Museum)*

The most celebrated photo ever taken of O. Henry, by the well-known photographer William M. Van der Weyde in the early 1900s. *(Greensboro Historical Museum)*

The Caledonia
28 4.26                    Friday

My dear Mr Davis :

Sick-abed until
yesterday since
Monday. Call
it, Monday or
Tuesday and I'll
have the story with
you, or "your money
back"
            Yours very truly
            Sydney Porter

Mr C B Davis

(left) A letter to Charles Delmont Davis, promising delivery of a manuscript. *(University of Virginia Library)*

(below) Margaret Worth Porter, O. Henry's daughter, taken at about the time of his death. She lived a sad life, always in the shadow of her famous father, and died of her mother's disease, tuberculosis. *(Greensboro Historical Museum)*

O. Henry at his writing table. He had put on fifty pounds since the prison years, mostly from drink, and was going downhill fast when this picture was taken. *(Doubleday & Co.)*

# 13

# Making It

Lo, consider the plight of the free-lance writer of 1903, dependent not only on his pen for his livelihood, but prey of the most hard-hearted of publishers, those who paid "on publication" and sometimes long after publication, for the bookkeeper was in 1903 like the computer of the 1980s, the easy excuse for a publisher to keep a tight rein on his cash. Thus *Ainslee's Magazine,* which enjoyed the immense resources of Street and Smith, the largest magazine publishing house in New York, and where the author was backed by the editors, was his salvation in 1903.

*Ainslee's* was O. Henry's principal market, publishing eleven of his stories that year. His next best market was *Everybody's* with eight stories. With thirty-five stories published that year, and the dollar worth easily twenty times in 1903 what it is worth in the 1980s, O. Henry's income had to be in excess of $3,000, or the equivalent of $60,000 in 1986.

Yet, O. Henry continued to be "broke" and constantly importuning his most friendly editors for immediate payment (usually in cash) on acceptance of a story, or an advance against stories to be written. Why?

To be sure he was beginning to pay small amounts back to his old creditors, chief among them P. G. Roach. But by Roach's accounting O. Henry owed him $10,000, and he never did pay back all of it.[1]

Daughter Margaret was also installed in a private school and he met school fees and all the usual expenses of rearing a child. But the fees at the Tennessee school, were less than $750 a year, and the other expenses were commensurate. O. Henry continued to live at the Hotel Marty, in simple surroundings. The expense, then, was in his habits. Always the fashion plate, he spent even more money on clothing. He continued to spend a great deal of money on dining and entertainment of friends, shopgirls, bums, racetrack touts, and others from whom he coaxed the material for his stories. His tips were notable and his charities to individuals were spontaneous and large.

O. Henry was constantly on the lookout for money. His favorite editors that year were Gilman Hall of *Ainslee's* and Witter Bynner of *McClure's,* because both were easy to touch for immediate payment or an advance.

> Dear Bynner:
> Can you send me $5 to chase a confounded wolf away from the portiere. This is personal, and the money will come back tomorrow. It's just a little hiatus in the mazuma, and not a case of hopeless pauperism.
> I will bring you a story tomorrow or Wednesday to fill the gap in the magazine.[2]
>
> Yours in haste,
> Sydney Porter

Although O. Henry's name was becoming very well known among New York editors, as well as the reading public, the man himself remained as elusive as a stag in autumn. For those who knew his haunts around Madison Square he was not hard to find, but he did not broadcast his whereabouts.

Thus, when F. L. H. Noble, the Sunday editor of the *New York World* wanted to find O. Henry, he could not. This was an unusual contretemps for the head of the feature sections of the most important newspaper in New York. He had seen O. Henry's work in the magazines, and it came to him that here was a man who could write introductions to articles in the feature section that would match those of William Randolph Hearst's expensive stable. That competition from the *American Weekly* had cut into the *World's* Sunday readership.

Editor Noble called in one of his minions, Robert H. Davis.

"Go out and locate this man O. Henry," he said. "He's got a breezy, snappy style. I want to get him to write introductions to Sunday stories."

Try as Davis might among the magazine crowd, all he could learn was that the writer lived over a French restaurant on West Twenty-fourth Street. He set out for that neighborhood and began to search, building by building, first the front desk, and the lobby, and where there was no front desk, then floor by floor, room by room. It took him three days. When he came to the Hotel Marty he struck pay dirt, and there found O. Henry in his little room on the third floor.

The author just then was seated by the open window, eating Bartlett pears.

"Come in and have a pear," he said with a wave, when he saw the editor. "What can I do for you?"

Editor Davis had been instructed that he was to hire O. Henry. He was to try to sign the author for $40 a week, but he was authorized to go to $60 a week if necessary. Taking a look at O. Henry, and remembering that it was Mr. Pulitzer's money, not his, Editor Davis brought out his best offer.

"The *New York World* wants you to do some work for its Sunday edition."

"How much do they want to pay for it?"

"$60 a week."

"All right, Mister. Take two pears. Take the bag. When do we begin?"

"At once."

"If that is the case we will go down stairs and have something to eat."[3]

And they did, they went down to the Hotel Marty's dining room and ate the table d'hôte dinner, at thirty-five cents, preceded by Sazeracs aplenty and accompanied by a bottle of French wine.

A few days later, O. Henry appeared in the office of the *New York World* and began his work. In a sense O. Henry had come full circle, although nobody at the *World* recognized it; how many years had passed since the youthful bank teller had written sketches that were bought on a space basis by the newspaper?

IT WAS AN easy step then, from writing prefaces to the *Sunday World's* features to contributing short stories to the *World,* and on December 6, 1903, the first one, "The Elusive Tenderloin," appeared in the paper. For the best part of the next three years, the *World* would eat up most of O. Henry's story output.

For a man who had run a newspaper himself O. Henry was very cavalier about his deadlines. Thomas Orr, an office boy at the *World* was often sent down to Twenty-fourth Street to collect O. Henry's stories. It was a task to make him flinch. One day he appeared at the Hotel Marty when O. Henry was out. He waited. The hours went by. At 6 P.M. O. Henry ambled in, and when he learned the young man's errand he was apologetic.

He promised to deliver a story that very night to the composing room, and he did.[4]

O. Henry's editor at the newspaper was William Johnston. It was Johnston's responsibility to see that the author got his prefaces and his stories finished, and on time for a weekly newspaper section. With O. Henry, as Johnston recalled, it was never easy. Deadline time came, and with it, oh too often, an excuse. Sometimes it was a visitor who had stayed too long the night before. Once he claimed that he had gotten up to finish the story and suffered "dizziness on rising" and gone back to bed. On another occasion he had gone to the doctor who said he thought he had Bright's disease.

"Good old doc says it ain't the genuine thing but it took six prescriptions and wasn't any slouch of an imitation."[5]

Often these excuses were really for a hangover O. Henry was suffering after a long night on the town. This, however, was so much an endemic ailment of newspaper offices that the reason was not given any importance at all. What was important was that he get that story in for that week's Sunday edition, and Editor Johnston was not permitted any excuses. Thus he spent many hours chasing O. Henry, or sending office boy Orr.

Johnston never forgot his favorite writer's superb circumlocutions, most of which were delivered by post or messenger:

> What you say. Let's take an evening off and strike the Cafe Francis for a slight refection. I like to be waked up suddenly by the music and look across at the red-haired woman eating smelts under an original by Glackens.
>
> Peace for Yours.

or

> I am just typewriting the closing words of the other story. I will hand it to you in the morning *en persone* between ten and eleven.[6]

William Johnston had to push and pry almost every week to get his story for the *World*. Sometimes Editor Johnston nearly lost his temper, when the story was unusually late. Once he wrote O. Henry:

> There was once a celebrated author who appeared before the judgment bar. A host of people were there saying nice things about him, when up spoke a weary editor who said:
> "He never kept a promise in his life."

When O. Henry had that letter, he sat down immediately and wrote a reply, called a messenger, and sent it back to Editor Johnston:

> Guilty, m'lud.
> And yet. . .
> Some time ago a magazine editor to whom I had promised a story at a certain minute (and strangely enough didn't get there with it) wrote to me:

"I'm coming down tomorrow to kick you thoroughly with a pair of heavy soled shoes. *I* never go back on my promises."

And I lifted up my voice and said unto him:

"It's easy to keep promises that can be pulled off with your feet."

Editor Johnston laughed, kept the letters, and they were friends again.[7]

O. Henry's contract with the *World* did not preclude him from writing for other publications. He could write for monthly magazines, and he could write books, but not for "any other weekly newspaper or newspaper-magazines."

IN 1903 McCLURE'S Editor Bynner was laboring with the book that would come out the following year. *Cabbages and Kings* was the final title. Bynner, knowing that collections of short stories did not sell as well as novels, pressed O. Henry into fabricating a loose structure for the book, making the new special stories conform to the old and giving the whole a novelistic feeling.

In the course of this work Bynner mentioned the need for a photograph for the book jacket. Did O. Henry have one?

Not only did O. Henry not have a recent photograph, but he also had an aversion (since Columbus) to having his photo taken. He stopped short, like an annoyed steer, and dug in his heels. How ridiculous it was for the editors to want a photograph of a pen name. There would be none.

The *World* stint kept O. Henry completely occupied during the last weeks of 1903. He did manage to get one story out for *Ainslee's*—"The Hypothesis of a Failure"—a tale of a lawyer and three potential clients—which fit none of the old molds of Anchuria, Texas, or New York. It was a story from anywhere in America, and an indication that O. Henry was becoming a writer of all the people.

When O. Henry presented that story to Editor Hall, as usual, he was "dead broke" in spite of now having regular and well-paid work. He wrote:

> Mon Cher Bill, can you raise the immediate goods for this, and once more rescue little Ruby from certain death?
>
> The big story will be handed in Monday for you to try on the piano.
>
> From next week I'll show you a story every week. I'm going to make some of the best special samples of 2,000 to 2,500 word stuff that's possible. That's the length that counts.
>
> I am a story ahead with the *World* now.[8]

But, as was so often to be the case, the will was good but the performance slipped somewhere along the line. When that happened, O. Henry resorted to explanations, or at least explanations of his own sort:

Dearest Bill:

Fact is—er—that—that is to say—er—er—you know—I—er—er—well, I was—er—er—I mean—the—er—er—you know.

Hoping the explanation is entirely satisfactory, I remain,

As ever thine,[9]


By 1904, propelled by the fame that accompanied his regular appearances in New York's most important newspapers, O. Henry was able to offer rejected manuscripts to magazines that were now eager to see them. One such was "The Enchanted Kiss," a very old story, with all the traces of the Texas background on it, drugstore clerk, Mexicans, and a Southwestern city. Written in 1901, it had been sitting in the bottom of O. Henry's trunk. Now, in 1904, he could dust it off and offer it to a magazine pleading for a story, and such it was with *Metropolitan Magazine,* which published the story in February.

Still the *Saturday Evening Post* rejected him and, as always, the rejections were made by some first reader who tucked a printed form in with the manuscript and sent the story back to the author.

Heartened by the success of 1903, O. Henry decided to move to larger quarters, but never completely confident of the bitch goddess Success he moved only across town to two rooms on East Twenty-fourth Street. His chosen ambience, and his most friendly bartenders, were not to be lost, nor his waiters. In one of his favorite restaurants, no matter what was on the menu, he consulted with the waiter, and was always brought something to eat that never failed to please him.

Occasionally, O. Henry could be lured out of his chosen center of Manhattan. Once a friend persuaded him to walk uptown on the west side. When they reached Seventy-second Street and Riverside Drive, O. Henry balked. "Haven't we passed Peekskill yet?" he demanded.

He had been seized by the great anonymity of New York City, where he had virtually no fear that someone from that dark past in Austin would arrive to confront him. To be lost among the four million inhabitants of America's largest city was his ideal. Now and forever his failed life in Texas and his fear of exposure as an ex-con dictated flight from the past. In New York he could keep his secret, and that, above all else in life, was what he intended to do. Thus, except for the Roaches, who had gone to Tennessee once little Margaret was off their hands, he made no attempt to keep in touch with anyone in Austin. Some of the old friends had failed him, others were now no more than distant memories. When his thoughts turned to the past, they moved to memories happier than those of Texas, to North Carolina, in those days long before the trouble began.

It was with enormous shock, then, that O. Henry responded to a call one day in January 1904, to be confronted by one of the editors of the *Critic,* a monthly literary magazine that took a great interest in writers as well as writing.

Mr. Sydney Porter? asked the editor.

Yes, said Sydney Porter.

You are O. Henry, are you not?

Yes, said O. Henry.

And then, learning that the editors proposed to write about him unveiling "the mystery of O. Henry," he made great pains to point out that there was no mystery. He was simply a person from Texas, who had come to New York, and in talking to friends had discovered that he could sell magazine editors stories based on his experiences of the past. Surely the editor could see that there was no mystery in that. Why had he begun to sign himself O. Henry? Well, that was just one of many names he had used because he was too embarrassed to put his own name on the stories. They really weren't worth it, were they?

No, it was no mystery at all, he assured the editor. He was a little shy, he did agree, and really did not want much publicity because he did not think he was or would be a real writer.

And in tones of confidentiality, he said that the really interesting thing about his writing history was that he had found "a good thing." Being naturally lazy, this had given him the chance to make money without working. Wasn't that something! As long as the string held out, it was just great, said O. Henry, playing the role of pretentious confidence man to the fullest. And then, hoping he had put out the sparks before they became a raging fire, O. Henry changed the subject and brought the meeting to a close before the editor could begin digging into his past.

HE WORRIED A good deal for the next few weeks, but there was nothing to be done but hope that the editor would be content with his little sensation, and not go any further.

Then, he picked up the February issue of the *Critic,* and saw it:

> Less than a year ago the readers of popular magazines began to be startled and delighted by certain fantastic and ingenious tales, mainly dealing with western life and bearing the strange device O. Henry as a signature. In a short time people began to talk to each other about the stories, and very soon they

began to ask who the author was. It was then that a new problem fell upon this over-puzzled age: —who is O. Henry? No one seemed to know the author's real name, and immediately vague and weird rumors began to be afloat and the nom de guerre was soon invested with as much curiousity as surrounds an author after his decease.

But, like most mysteries, when it was probed there was no mystery about it. O. Henry's real name is Mr. Sydney Porter, a gentleman from Texas, who, having seen a great deal of the world with the naked eye, happened to find himself in New York about two years ago and there discovered a market where people would buy stories of his experiences. Being of a lazy disposition he very naturally quitted active life and took to his desk. He signed the name O. Henry merely because he did not take his real self seriously as a maker of fiction. He really does shun notoriety—a most unusual characteristic among present day writers—and he disclaims any intention of having purposely created a mystery about his identity. But he is still not too old to become a professional.

There, with that last patronizing remark, the editor of the *Critic* ended his little triumph. O. Henry had guessed right and been persuasive. The real secret was still safe. The only disconcerting thing was that from someone, perhaps the person who had tipped the *Critic* to the story, the magazine had secured a photograph of William Sydney Porter taken in the Austin days. Where had they gotten it? Did the person who had it know of the trial and the conviction, and the three and a half years of Hell?

Like a man waiting for the other shoe to drop in the apartment above, O. Henry agonized for days, for weeks. But nothing—absolutely nothing— happened. The editors he knew well, who were aware of Sydney Porter, the man the checks went to, saw nothing worth talking about in this revelation. No one pursued the matter, it seemed.

Then, several months later, O. Henry had a letter from Judge Robert Hill, publisher of the *Houston Post.* He had recognized the picture in the *Critic* as that of the young William Sydney Porter who had worked as a writer for the *Post* so long ago.

The letter came to O. Henry by way of *Everybody's Magazine,* which had published his "On Behalf of the Management" in February.

Judge Hill had supplied the $200 given O. Henry by Editor Johnston of the *Post,* the money which O. Henry was supposed to use for his trial expenses, and which, instead, he took off to New Orleans when he fled. After that O. Henry had not again been in touch with the *Post* people. They were disgusted and they offered him no more help, nor did he seek any. Now, out of a blue sky, came this letter from Judge Hill. But it was a congratulatory letter, not a dun for the money. Nonetheless, O. Henry mentioned his debt, and his hope that the growing success of his writing would make it possible for him to repay all his old debts. "Yours I have not by any means forgotten, and it comes among the first."[10]

That was all. He would hear from a few people back in Texas over the next few years, but not many. And oddly enough it would be a long, long time before he really felt threatened again. The anonymity of the Great City was accomplishing just what he had hoped it would.

# 14

# Of Cabbages and Kings

When Witter Bynner of *McClure's* had digested O. Henry's tale "The Phonograph and the Graft" back in late 1902 it had started his editorial juices moving at full speed, and it was not long before he came up with an idea for the book that would be called *Cabbages and Kings.*

Like so many other book projects, this one might just as easily never have gotten off the ground. O. Henry had never written a novel and certainly was not sitting down in 1902 and 1903 for such a speculative venture. But Witter Bynner was enormously impressed with the characters O. Henry could weave on his loom. *McClure's* first story of the Republic of Anchuria, "Money Maze," introduced Colonel Emilo Falcon, the suave private secretary of President Losada of Anchuria; the American businessman Frank Goodwin, who was not above a spot of dangerous adventure; Mrs. Goodwin, nee Isabel Guilbert, once the companion of the dead Presidente Miraflores; and Beelzebub Blythe, the "categorical idealist" who was rotting away in the tropics and slowly killing himself with cadged drinks.

*Ainslee's* got the next story, "Rouge et Noir," which brought the Losada regime in Anchuria to a stunning end. This tale introduced the Vesuvius Fruit Company, several of its executives, and the concept that the placement of an export duty of so little money as one *real* on a bunch of bananas was a cause for a revolution, engineered by the fruit company. This tale introduced Dicky Malone, "a red-headed Irishman," and his beautiful wife, Pasa, who wanted to be the wife of the president of the republic. And how this came about was the tale. Frank Goodwin was there, in mention, too.

Then came "The Flag Paramount" and "The Lotus and the Bottle," the

155

former dealing with Don Sabas Placido and the ambitious Admiral Carrera, the latter with U.S. Consul Willard Geddie and his dreams. Again, *Ainslee's* had snapped these up.

But *McClure's* got "The Phonograph and the Graft," which introduced the great Keogh, confidence man extraordinary, and his sometime sidekick, Henry Horsecollar, the educated grafter, in a scheme to make a mint by selling phonographs in Latin America.

> "The Latin races," says Henry, explaining easily in the idioms he learned at college, "are peculiarly adapted to be victims of the phonograph. They have the artistic temperament. They yearn for music and color and gaiety. They give wampum to the hand-organ man and the four legged chicken in the tent when they're months behind with the grocery and the bread-fruit tree."
>
> "Then," says I [Keogh], "we'll export canned music to the Latins, but I'm mindful of Mr. Julius Caesar's account of 'em where he says *'Omnia Gallia in tres partes divisa est'*, which is the same as to say, 'We will need all of our gall in devising means to tree them parties.'"

"The Shamrock and the Palm," again in *Ainslee's,* brought back Keogh and introduced Johnny Atwood, "he who ate of the lotus, root, stem, and flower," and Clancy, a soldier of fortune, now partner with Keogh in a photography shop.

"Masters of Arts," which appeared in *Everybody's* in August 1903, returned to the adventures of Keogh and President Losada. It also included an artist named Carolus White, a scheme to mulct President Losada of $10,000, and how it failed but succeeded in the cause of virtue in taking $21,000 away from the president.

About half way along in 1903 Witter Bynner suddenly realized that O. Henry was building up these characters, and in doing so was producing a pastiche of a Central American banana republic.

"The Lotus and the Cockleburrs" appeared in *Everybody's* in October 1903. By this time Witter Bynner's ideas had become a scheme and the book, loosely novelistic in form, had taken shape. He had secured the support of his employers with the argument that not only was Richard Harding Davis mining this vein in story and play, but that the success of Owen Wister's *The Virginian* showed what could be done with such a book.

What was needed was a bit of doctoring here and there to make it all stick together. For example, the story "The Lotus and the Cockleburrs" was cut into two parts for the book. It became chapters twelve and thirteen, "Shoes," and "Ships."

In "Shoes," Johnny Atwood, U.S. consul at Coralio, stars, but Keogh, Goodwin, and Geddie reappear. They continue in "Ships," which has to do with cockleburrs creating a need for shoes in Coralia, where no need had existed before.

Author and editor working together, patched and linked and added, and O. Henry wrote nine new chapters, using these and other characters. When he was finished it was a book of chapters, not just nineteen tales strung together. Out of this fiction comes a picture that is more sympathetic to the average Latino, and more devastating to the rapacious gringo and the crooked Latino politician than a hundred times its weight in the political reportage of the period. And it is more joyous in its approach to life than anything else then being published about the area.

The McClure company was not above a little sleight of hand, in the manner of publishers perhaps since time began. The author of the new book was billed by the publisher as an expert on Latin America:

"The author, who has lived many years among the people of the South American republics, draws upon his fund of experience in this breezy story which recounts the adventures of an energetic American in the land of popular revolutions . . ."[1]

This is somewhat hyperbolic, considering the fact that O. Henry's "fund of experience" was gathered during the two or three months he spent in Honduras on the lam in 1896. He had not left Houston until July, and he was back in Austin early in February, and most of his time was spent working on newspapers in New Orleans to get the money to go to Central America.

McClure's, perhaps, did not warrant the full blame, and might not be culpable at all, for when badgered about his past, a reckless O. Henry said anything that came into his head, as long as it was not the truth. This process was never to change during his lifetime.

WHEN *CABBAGES AND Kings* appeared in the fall of 1904, it got attention, but nowhere near the attention, for example, that was given Walter Sichel's biography of Lord Beaconsfield. The latter was the lead review in *The New York Times Book Review* of December 17, 1904, while O. Henry's book was very much an also-ran, which appeared about as far back in the book section as it could go.

*The New York Times* review was favorable enough, no rave, but straight:

no faint praise, no search for anomalies, no indication by the reviewer that he would have done a better job:

> The incidents embracing as they do, a variety of subjects, hang loosely together, so loosely in fact, that at times one finds no apparent connection between them at all, and yet in the end one sees how each is intimately related to the other. . . .
>
> Written by a less able hand than O. Henry's the book might have been a sad jumble, perhaps comprehensible to none but the Walrus—but as it is, one finds a joy in its every obscurity.[2]

The reviewers were late in noticing the book, another indication of its relative unimportance on a literary scene where major attention was going to Jack London's *The Sea Wolf,* and two of Lafcadio Hearn's offerings in this year of his death: *Kwaidan,* his compilation of tales of Japanese mystery, and his celebrated *Japan: An Attempt at Interpretation.*

Stanhope Searles, who apparently did not read popular magazines, praised *Cabbages and Kings* as "a book of very unusual interest and cleverness" but passed it off as "a man's book." If one did not know it was a novel, he said, a number of the chapters "might be taken bodily from the book and held up as admirable examples of short-story telling."

That review was a very good indication of O. Henry's standing in the general literary community. He was a tyro, virtually unknown to reviewers and professors.

The reviewer for the *Critic,* however, did read popular magazines, and knew his author professionally. He did not approve of authors reworking short stories to make novels, obviously, for while he lauded O. Henry's "inimitably breezy style of story telling," he sniffed that the presentation in novel form had weakened the structure of the whole. "The characters, so delightful in the original stories, become less real, less convincing, on their new stage."

To which the reviewer of *Outlook* uttered a rhetorical "bushwah" in the tenor of the time, and said O. Henry had given the world "Pure burlesque, but lively, ingenious, and slangily humorous South American intrigue, Yankee resource, the colossal impudence of the American fakir, and the romance of unusual love complications, all worked together into a semi-connected story, parts of which have been already used as magazine tales."[3]

On balance, editor Bynner and author O. Henry had to be fairly well pleased with the results; the book was a modest success in the bookstores and that was what counted.

THE COMBINATION OF the success of *Cabbages and Kings* in the then important book pages of the newspapers and general interest magazines, and the weekly exposure of O. Henry to the growing New York literary community in the pages of the *Sunday World* raised his reputation very quickly.

O. Henry's front piece for the Sunday feature section of the newspaper had assumed a new major importance, particularly in New York, in view of the continued battle for circulation and survival between Pulitzer's *World* and William Randolph Hearst's *New York American.*

The $60 a week that Mr. Pulitzer's henchmen had invested in O. Henry was anything but charity, and they wanted, and got, their money's worth, although, as noted, sometimes they had to pry the goods out of their dilatory author. He was to produce one "piece" for each Sunday edition.[4] It need not be long. Indeed, it should be short, to capture and retain the interest of the average American newspaper reader (then estimated at an intellectual age of about twelve with an attention span of about 2,500 words. These have obviously fallen between A.D. 1904 and 33 TV).

His first story for the *World,* which appeared in the January 3, 1904, issue, was "The Transformation of Martin Burney." It was a tale of New York, and the setting was the construction site of the crosstown highway along the west bank of the Harlem River. The hero of the piece, who had the title role, was a laborer. The villain . . . or was there a villain?

At least there was a tale, one about life in the great city in the year 1904.

It was not one of O. Henry's best; it was not even one of his very good ones. But it was followed the next week by "A Little Local Color," in which a friend promised to show the author "the real New York." They began with dinner at his club in midtown. There, on the sidewalk they encountered a violent political discussion between two slangy types. Aha, said the author, taking out his notebook.

"Oh, come ahead," said Rivington, somewhat nervously. "You don't want to listen to that."

"Why man," the author whispered, "this is just what I do want to hear. These slang types are among your city's most distinguished features. Is this the Bowery variety?"

No, admitted his guide finally. Those were a university professor and a distinguished social economist.

Rivington then promised to take the author to the Bowery to get the real thing: "They talk a peculiar dialect that you won't hear anywhere else on earth."

So the investigators took a streetcar across town on the Forty-second Street line, and then south on the Third Avenue line. They got off at Houston Street.

159

"We are now on the famous Bowery," said Rivington. "the Bowery celebrated of song and story."

They passed many haberdasheries and clothing stores. The author suggested that they reminded him of such stores in Kokomo, Indiana.

"Step into one of those saloons or vaudeville shows with a large amount of money," said Rivington, "and see how quickly the Bowery will make its reputation."

"You make impossible conditions," said the author, coldly.

But they came to a cop known to Rivington, Policeman Donahue, and asked him to put them onto "one of the Bowery types—something that's got color, you know."

"Sure," said Donahue, "here comes a lad now that was born in the Bowery and knows every inch of it. If he's ever been above Bleecker Street, he's kept it to himself. Evening, Kerry," he said.

And then Policeman Donahue explained what his friends wanted.

Guide Rivington was prepared to deal with the local patois, to the admiration of the author:

"Say, cull," said Rivington, pushing back his hat. "Wot's doin? Me an my frien's taking a look down de old line—see? De copper tipped us off dat you was wise to de Bowery. Is dat right?"

"Donahue was right," said the young man. "I was brought up on the Bowery. I have been newsboy, teamster, pugilist, member of an organized gang of 'toughs,' bartender and a 'sport' in various meanings of the word. The experience certainly warrants the supposition that I have at least a passing acquaintance with a few phases of Bowery life. I will be pleased to place whatever knowledge and experience I have at the service of my friend Donahue's friends."

Rivington expressed surprise at that kind of talk coming out of the Bowery.

"I am afraid," said the Bowery boy, smiling, "that at some time you have been enticed into one of the dives of literature and had the counterfeit coin of the Bowery passed upon you. The argot to which you doubtless refer was the invention of certain of your literary 'discoverers' who invaded the unknown wilds below Third Avenue and put strange sounds into the mouths of the inhabitants."

It was true, he said, that in recent years the people of the Bowery had adopted the patois forced on them in order to deal with the tourist trade. "They supplied the demands of the market," he said.

Rivington, obviously shaken, invited the Bowery boy to have a drink with them, but Kerry said he did not drink. No, he was too busy observing life in the Bowery, and writing his second book about it. But he would be glad to show them anything, anything at all. How about starting with a trip to the East Side Kappa Delta Phi society quarters, only two blocks east?

"Awfully sorry," quavered Rivington. And the two searchers for atmosphere boarded a streetcar and went back uptown.


THIS SORT OF sketch, not quite a story, appealed enormously to New Yorkers, who liked nothing better than to spoof the do-gooders who came to town, and to turn the tables on the tourist.

But, alas, the next week's contribution, "A Newspaper Story," was much thinner, resting as it did on the great good done by a copy of a newspaper. The paper had been sold by the news vendor to his profit, bought by a young man who does not read the agony column item addressed to him, but drops the paper and his gloves, comes back and meets his estranged inamorata, and all is well. From here the paper drops and is blown onto the head of a horse, blinding him and dumping his driver in front of a brownstone mansion, from which emerges a beautiful girl to sorry over the unconscious driver and profess her love for him and her hatred of their misunderstanding. Here a cop picks up the offending paper and sticks it under the arm of a passing boy, who takes it home. His sister, pining for a real silk underskirt, takes two pieces of newspaper and attaches them under her dress, they make a satisfying swishing sound, and she goes off into the streets happy in her new opulence and one jump ahead of her jealous girl friend. The boy's father, a labor leader, gets so engrossed in the crossword puzzle that he has extracted from the paper that he misses his labor meeting, and thus a terrible strike is averted. The boy, off to school, and aware of past misdeeds, artfully arranges the newspaper in his garments, and thus the newspaper, which only in this very morning's issue has inveighed against corporal punishment, protects the lad in the end.

It was not much of a tale, but of course no writer ever got into trouble on a newspaper telling the editors what great fellows they were and what a fine institution they worked for.

On January 24, O. Henry hit a ten-strike with "A Madison Square Arabian Night," in which a rich, loving husband, who has received a photo of his absent wife and a poison-pen letter about her, invites a bum to dine. The bum turns out to be a magical character, a talented artist who has the curse of showing total truth in his portraits and has thus sunk to the level of the streets, because no one wanted the truth out.

"I painted the portrait of a very beautiful and popular society dame. When it was finished, her husband looked at it with a peculiar expression on his face, and the next week he sued for divorce."

The poor artist had tried painting only from photos, and that did not work either. The truth kept emerging. So this antithesis of Dorian Gray rode his curse to the gutter.

His host asked him to draw a picture from a photo, and the artist obliged. And that was almost the end of the story, except that the kicker brought a little gladness into the heart of every reader.

The artist took his money and went out to buy booze. The rich, loving but suspicious husband called a young artist friend who lived in the building. He showed the young artist the drawing from the photo.

"How do you find it," asked the rich man.

"As a drawing I can't praise it enough . . ."

"The face man—the subject—the original—what would you say of that?"

"The face is the face of one of God's own angels."

And thus was a marriage saved.

Texas and New York figured in the following story, a rather dull one, about a man who took the weather seriously. That was followed on February 7, 1904, by "The Adventures of Shamrock Jolnes," a spoof on the great London detective so beloved in America just then. With only a pleasant-faced man on a streetcar to work with, a mark on his face, strange scuffings on the uppers of his shoes, a sad look when he sees a woman standing on the streetcar, a boutonnier, a strange bulge in his pocket and the scent of mint in the air, Shamrock Jolnes deduces that the gent is a Virginia gentleman, just escaped from a shopping spree with his wife and three daughters, one of them a stepdaughter, and that this night he will go back to Virginia by train.

Let the reader find the magic. It was there, on the front page of the feature section of the *Sunday World*. Fifty-two times that year, 1904, editor Johnston dragged from O. Henry that weekly sketch or story, a story with a New York taste to it.

"The Sparrows in Madison Square" had both New York and newspapers in it, but not much of the magic. "Lost on Dress Parade" pursued the theme O. Henry had established in "While the Auto Waits"—the rich girl playing poor, meeting the poor man playing rich snob.

"New York by Campfire Light," which appeared in the *World* on March 6, was another of the half Texas-half New York tales, and not of the best. But it was followed on March 13 by "The Romance of a Busy Broker," which is the epitome of O. Henry's New York, a tender, laughing tale.

Thus it seemed to go, a fine story followed by one of no more than mediocre measure. On March 20 came something quite untoward: "A Matter of Mean Elevation," which had not the slightest relationship to New York, being set in Venezuela. It was out of character with all that O. Henry had before done for the *World,* and there is only one answer: that week, for some reason he had failed to produce his *Sunday World* story and the paper had been forced to content itself with something out of the O. Henry ragbag.

As if to apologize, the following week O. Henry returned to his stride with "The Brief Debut of Tildy," the story of the awakening of a hasher in Bogle's Chop House and Family Restaurant.

Oh, how O. Henry could tear the heartstrings of the reader when he tried. How he could pin down the characters of Bogle's chop house, located on "that highway of the bourgeoisie," Eighth Avenue, where Bogle, "cold, sordid, slow, smouldering," presided. And there were two waitresses, Aileen, tall, beautiful, lively, gracious, and learned in persiflage. And then there was Tildy, "dumpy, plain faced, and too anxious to please." The story, of course, is about Tildy, and New Yorkers of 1904 found it very satisfying indeed.

It was followed on April 3 by a tale of spring. Writing a weekly newspaper short story offered O. Henry a new element, timeliness, and this story about Irish men and women in New York was enough to warm the cockles of the cardinal's heart in the cathedral on Fifth Avenue.

O. Henry's milieu expanded under the aegis of the *Sunday World.* "Ulysses and the Dogman" dealt with the wretchedness of an old cowboy now entrapped by a school teacher who turned out to be a woman of New York. Wrenched from his beloved West to the city streets, living in an apartment and walking the family dog at night, a chance encounter on the street with an old comrade produces freedom for the cowboy.

On April 17 appeared a new sort of story, the tale of John Hopkins (a combination of Casper Milquetoast and Walter Mitty if there ever was one) suffering through a middle-class, middle-town, middle-apartment life, and his moment of glory.

Next came "The Caliph and the Cad," about Corny Brannigan, a truck driver from Canal Street, who discovered that he was really a gentleman in disguise.

The panoply grew, week by week, the territory spread, the characters were ever more deftly adumbrated. Whatever Bill Johnston and his assistants had to do—and it was plenty—it was worth it to his newspaper. The features section burgeoned and took on a new life that could not be matched by William Randolph Hearst's men from Mars, not even by such as Gene Fowler's foray into science with his running story of the old man who sought eternal youth by the appending of "monkey glands." There was no question about it: the O. Henry short stories brought a measure of class to the pages of the *New York World.*

# 15

# Success

The production of a short story a week for the *New York World* was curse and blessing rolled into one. It interfered with O. Henry's favorite pursuits, which were drinking and dining and observing the people of the city, especially young women, for as his favorite editors all knew, O. Henry had an active eye for young women. Editor Davis once said O. Henry was a "woman chaser."[1]

So writing cramped his style, and he wrote almost entirely under pressure for money. If he got ahead of the financial game, then he slacked off until he was again penniless and then he worked furiously to recoup.

Fortunately, O. Henry's contract with the *World* did not prevent him from selling stories to monthly magazines. His new success also enabled him to pull some tales out of the steamer trunk in his room and thus to make money from past failure. The old adage: never throw away any writing, was well known to him already. In his youth he had thrown away dozens of stories, perhaps quite properly. No one will ever know.

"The Enchanted Kiss" was one of those stories that was rejected many times. Written in 1901, it had been passed around: *Ainslee's, Harper's, Lippincott's, McClure's, Munsey's, Everybody's,* and *The Smart Set,* and had been rejected by all of them. So the author lost interest and confidence in the piece. But one day the editor of *Metropolitan Magazine* asked O. Henry for a story. He did not have one, he said. Perhaps he could find something in his files, said the editor. And so O. Henry delved into the bottom of the trunk and dusted off "The Enchanted Kiss," which was the story of a feckless youth who misses his chance at romance. It was a mark of the value of O. Henry's name in the short story field that the editors of *Metropolitan* took the story, ran it in their issue of February 1904, and were eminently satisfied. They wanted more, but O. Henry did not have more. He was as loyal as a free-lance writer could afford to be to his old editors at *Ainslee's, Everybody's* and *McClure's*. *Ainslee's* had published "The Hypothesis of Failure," a story about divorce and a lawyer, with an Austin flavor, in the January issue. *Everybody's* would have "On Behalf of the Management" for February, a funny New York tale. There just was not enough to go around, and *Metropolitan* would have to wait until the next year for another story.

This was a pleasant change of affairs for the author, being sought rather than seeking. It was represented in his climbing rate for stories, now going above the $200 mark.

"The Reformation of Calliope," sold to *Associated Sunday Magazine,* came near violation of O. Henry's contract with the *World.* It was published on February 28, 1904. It is a good story skillfully told, one of O. Henry's better Western tales, but there would be no more for this publication.

His next outside tale was for *Argosy* magazine: "Witches' Loaves," for which he delved again back into Austin days and the time when he was an architectural draftsman in the land office. Not a loving tale, this one, but a funny one, and well within the better part of the O. Henry tradition.

"The Emancipation of Billy," which *Everybody's* ran in May 1904, was not one of O. Henry's best, too long, too complicated, and not very satisfying at the end, but it was a story out of O. Henry's viscera, the tale of the long, stubborn refusal of "southern gentlemen" to accept the outcome of the Civil War. It was a subject on which O. Henry liked to discourse over a few Sazeracs, and often did.

Another of O. Henry's vagaries was a wide stretch of historical gloom. From boyhood days he had imagined various extensions of historical themes. As noted, he had written an ending to *The Mystery of Edwin Drood.* While in Texas he wrote some sketches delineating a new view of Roman history, circa the days of Julius Caesar. Now, in the spring of 1904 *Cosmopolitan* published "The Door of Unrest," based on The Wandering Jew of folklore, brought up to date and cast in a Western town. O. Henry's principal character was first known to the narrator, a small town newspaper editor, as Michob Ader, and later as Mike O'Bader, a clear tale cleverly fabricated by the master hand. This was one of the three stories that the editors of *Ainslee's* had rejected back in 1902. He could sell just about anything that had his name on it now; some wag once said that if O. Henry produced his laundry list, a magazine would take it and publish it.

"The Missing Chord" was again a Western story, out of a sheep ranch on the Nueces River, an artful mix of Texas atmosphere and human nature. It was well within the latitude of his contract, and so far he had not missed a week with the *World,* so there could be no argument when the *Century* published it.

In June, the *Critic* allowed O. Henry a chance to spoof the magazine editors of New York, who, then, as always, ran in the pack. At the time, Richard Harding Davis as depicted by Maxfield Parrish, was the beau ideal of the haute monde; his picture in white tie and tails adorned most of the magazine covers at one time or another. This was the period in which the Four Hundred of New York flourished in their mansions on Fifth Avenue, the ladies rustling in real silks, the gents exuding the odors of Havana cigars, bourbon whiskey, and Eddie Pinaud's celebrated hair elixir and the look of too much beef and baked potato. The baroche and cabriolet and matched team of mares were giving way to the electric car and the Stanley Steamer, and Mr. Olds's fiery gasoline monstrosity. O. Henry's hero, Van Sweller, is constantly trying to get free to dine at a one of the two or three most celebrated restaurants. But author O. Henry sternly holds him in check so he cannot do this. In the end, the story O. Henry has written is returned because it has no mention of any of the favorite society water holes. If he will just fix that part, said the editor in his conditional rejection letter . . .

It was a very special sketch for a very special market, but O. Henry was pleased to oblige; he always liked a chance to air his prejudices.

AS SUMMER 1904 brought the heat and humidity that made Baghdad on the Hudson miserable in those days when air conditioning meant going out into the air, O. Henry was inveigled by Editor Robert Hobart Davis of *Munsey's* into an outing.[2]

"Let's get out for a few days," said Davis. "I'll take you to a wonderful place down on Long Island, where the fishing is immense and the fish correspondingly large."

"Well," said O. Henry, "New York is a bit warm, and I'll just take you up."

So they went. The fishing tackle was produced. Collars and ties were thrown off, as well as coats. Soon they were mixing with the local citizens, almost indiscernible among them, save for the Long Islanders' ability to expectorate tobacco juice for long distances, which O. Henry admired but could not emulate.

The actual fishing, said Davis, lighting up a cigar at their digs, was about a mile away.

"We won't ride, because the exercise will do us good," he said.

Hesitantly, his guard down, O. Henry assented.

The sky was blue, with that touch of gray haze that meant a sizzling afternoon. It was already so hot, the walkers found, that at the end of three city blocks, O. Henry was drenched with perspiration. This was nothing like the heat of the Texas hills back in the ranching and prospecting days, nothing at all. The humidity was at least ninety, and most of it seemed to be running down O. Henry's backbone.

They went on, Davis a slender type, smoking his stogy, apparently unaware of the heat. O. Henry's problem was his girth, which in the past three years had expanded considerably so that he now wore a size 16½ collar. What could one expect when one's evening entertainments began with the ministrations of a succession of French and Italian chefs and sommeliers in the Madison Square area.

The author struggled on, then Davis saw him apparently staggering. But no, he had stopped and was searching his trousers pockets.

"What's wrong?" asked Davis. "What are you looking for?"

"My return ticket to New York," said O. Henry. And he found it. He then insisted on turning about and, hailing a passing wagon got a ride that took him back to their lodgings, whence he picked up his gear and began his return to the city. "There are just as good fish on the menu as there are in the sea," said he, as he headed back toward his usual haunts.

Summer and winter, O. Henry lived as much in the city streets as anywhere, and each season found it more difficult for his friends to pry him loose. With his new-found affluence he was able to move to more comfortable surroundings. He could have gone easily to Riverside Drive, the haven of the middle class, but he chose to stay in the old area. His move from Twenty-fourth Street was to 55 Irving Place, near Gramercy Park, and he stayed around there long enough that it is still known as O. Henry country. One of the neighborhood saloons he used to visit has now become a celebrated watering hole for those seeking the atmosphere of the great short story writer, particularly in summer, when the outdoor restaurant is functioning, and the breezes seem to blow away the years along with the gasoline engine fumes. The idolators are doing the same thing that O. Henry used to do when he stopped to look at the plaque announcing that Washington Irving had lived a few doors from his lodgings. He used to write about that to friends, for even at the height of his success he never considered himself a truly notable literary character. He was always approaching literary greatness, he thought, which he would achieve with novels, as soon as he could get around to it.

The old brownstone house at 55 Irving Place already had been cut up into apartments. O. Henry's was on the first floor, front, and he had a big picture window through which he could observe the passing scene. At about this time, as noted, O. Henry got to know authors' agent, Seth Moyle, who lived on Seventeenth Street near Irving Place.[3]

One requirement of friendship with O. Henry was the willingness to socialize, and drink a dram here and there. The author, when at loose ends, was not above telephoning a friend, no matter the hour. In fact, the late-hour calls were more frequent than any other. Many a time the telephone in Seth Moyle's apartment would ring, and there on the other end was his favorite short story writer.

"Is this you?"

"This is me."

"Are you there?"

"I'm here."

"I'm coming right over."

And then—within a minute—the doorbell would ring. O. Henry had not been at home, around the corner, but in the public hallway of Moyle's building, calling on the public telephone.[4]

As long as O. Henry was left alone at parties he enjoyed himself and often started telling stories. But he could not bear being bearded by someone trying to make an impression on him. It brought out the very worst.

One evening at Moyle's a young man who said he admired the author enormously learned that O. Henry had come in. There was a grand piano in Moyle's apartment and the young man had some skill as a piano player; he immediately sat down at the instrument to make his impression. He played one difficult piece, and then another, not bothering with the soft pedal. Receiving at least a little acclaim from the crowd, he forged on, his eyes seeking those of O. Henry, who, as always, when being hunted, began to look for cover.

The young man was in the middle of Franz Liszt's "Second Hungarian Rhapsody," when he looked up from an arpeggio and smiled. His hero was approaching. O. Henry came up, bent down, and tapped the pianist on the shoulder.

"I know what that is," he said.

The young piano player smiled even more broadly. He paused, then forged on, with even greater fortissimos, pianissimos, and fluttering of fingers. He had achieved his goal, he had attracted the attention of the Great One.

"Indeed I do know what it is," continued the author in the pianist's ear. "It is an awful lot of noise. Please stop and play Chopin's 'Funeral March.'"

Deflated, the pianist quit. But had he gone on to do his hero's bidding, he would have found that O. Henry really did know Chopin's "Funeral March." Back in Austin the writer had been trained in comic opera. He'd learned then classical pieces, although now he used that knowledge only as a put-down. At Seth Moyle's such a put-down was a rarity. Usually the parties at Moyle's involved theatrical or literary people, who left O. Henry pretty much alone.[5]

From there they would go out to a saloon known as Pete's or Still's, or, if the hour was respectable enough, to a famous German restaurant named Allaire's Sheffel Hall, which O. Henry memorialized in several stories, such as "The Rathskeller and the Rose."

Learning of Seth Moyle's association with O. Henry, a number of other people tried in various ways to crash through O. Henry's defenses by using Moyle. Usually the agent was successful in shucking them off, but not always.

One evening agent and author adjourned to Allaire's Sheffel Hall, anticipating a pleasant evening, organized by a successful psychiatrist who knew Moyle slightly. He had said he was having a party that included the journalist Charles Somerville; a British hero of the wars named Gilpin, who held the Victoria Cross; a pair of accommodating ladies of some reputation in the theatrical community; and a lawyer well known for his courtroom technique and his stories. It sounded like a reasonable crew, no one who might be gushing over the author, so Moyle persuaded O. Henry to attend.[6]

The evening began well enough. A few drinks were consumed, and then one of Sheffel Hall's remarkable and enormous six-course dinners was produced, to which O. Henry responded with his usual trencherman's interest.

But after the dinner the good doctor suddenly produced some books, which he put on the table, and although O. Henry could not see them very well he was accustomed to the ploy and knew that a next step would be to demand autographs, something he detested doing for people he did not know. Further, the doctor now indicated that he wanted witticisms by the author.

O. Henry seemed resigned.

"Ah," said he. "Having partaken of your food I must now pay with play."

Whereupon O. Henry dredged forth all the oldest, worst jokes he could remember.

"Why does a chicken cross the road—hurriedly?"

Before anyone could pose an answer, he obliged himself.

"To get out of the way of the automobile."

The doctor did not think that was funny, and he said so. He did not see O. Henry's wink at the assemblage.

The doctor demanded something funnier. O. Henry obliged with another old saw.

The doctor objected. He thought O. Henry was supposed to be a funny man, he complained.

"O. Henry?" asked the author. "I am afraid, Doctor, that you have made a mistake about my identity. I am not O. Henry. I am Mark Twain."

Whereupon he arose majestically and left the restaurant, followed swiftly by Seth Moyle, the British war hero, Charlie Somerville, and the lawyer, who all joined the author at Still's saloon across the way, leaving the doctor with the flowers of the evening and the bill.[7]

For the *World,* O. Henry broadened his researches into the delights and mysteries of the great city. He visited Mouquin's restaurant, one of the more expensive. Here he lingered to spy upon the very rich and write about their little adventures. He visited several of the "social clubs" on the side streets of the twenties, most notable for their Friday evening boxing matches. Here he encountered New York's Irish, the cops and hodmen, the boilermakers, and their ladies, who might be laundresses or sirens of the evening. He wrote about them all just as he wrote about the people of the theater and of Little Italy. He strayed as far as Coney Island, or anywhere that the streetcars and the subways ran. He continued to be leery of the elevated railroad, and predicted untimely ends for those who rode the flying cars by choice. Greenwich Village was in his territory, just then becoming ever more the flaming haunt of artists, but still a little town within the city.[8]

His shopgirls kept reappearing in the pages of the *World,* to amaze the readers with their street wisdom, their ignorance, and their cultural limitations. One such was Masie, one of three thousand girls in The Biggest Store, where she encountered Irving Carter, "painter, millionaire, traveller, poet, automobilist," who one day wandered into the emporium and fell for her like a ton of bricks. How Masie, who at first liked the gent, rejected him, is the subject of "A Lickpenny Lover," which ran on the cover of the *World* Sunday sections on May 29, 1904. Poor Mr. Carter—he had promised to take Masie to see foreign sights, to ride in gondolas, to see chariot races and Japanese gardens, and wonderful temples. And she had thought he proposed to take her on a honeymoon to Coney Island, and rejected him as a cheapskate.

Ah, Coney Island, the site of the action in "Tobin's Palm," repeated again and again. It was the New Coney, in July 1904, the Coney that had done in poor Irving Carter, with its Babylonian towers and Hindoo roof gardens, and the Canals of Venice, which had given little Masie the wrong impression. Gone was the Egyptian Sorceress of the Nile who told your fortune, and arrived were all the wonders of the world of fantasy, copying real ones abroad on the seven seas. O. Henry could make a story of anything, even the change, and so he did in "The Greater Coney," wherein Dennis Carnahan, a fine broth of a boy, and Norah Flynn, a fine slip of a girl, having quarreled desperately at the Dairymen and Street Sprinkler Drivers' semiannual ball, meet again by accident at Coney, dear old Coney. Yet such was O. Henry's magic with the pen that the reader is left with the distinct impression that the meeting is not by accident, but that the author shares with some great power the knowledge of the inevitability of fate.

Such a tale of the hoi polloi would be followed by a story fit for another segment of the *Sunday World*'s readership, the denizens of Fifth and Park avenues, and the corner mansions on the sidestreets in between. Or was it the other way? Was it that the stories about Masie and Mame and Norah Flynn and Dennis Carnahan were pointed at the Four Hundred, being what the Four Hundred thought the unwashed Irish would be like, and the stories of Alicia Van Der Pool, and Towers Chandler were really addressed to the Four Million, being what the unwashed thought the Four Hundred had to be like? Or were they altogether addressed to the discernment of the hardboiled eggs who had become newspaper and magazine editors, being what those romantics in unbuttoned waistcoat and untied four-in-hand believed the people of the various neighborhoods of all New York were like?

In "The Defeat of the City," O. Henry transcended even that border, taking his citified country boy, with his new Van Der Pool wife from Fifth Avenue, back to the farm, and making the girl love it all. That was the offering for the *Sunday World* of June 26, 1904. Next week, lest he had offended some of his audience, O. Henry had another offering, "The Pride of the Cities," in which he matched the home of the Great White Way with Topaz City, Nevada. It was summer, a man from each metropolis met at one of the roof gardens that made the pre-air conditioning New York summers bearable, and they began comparing the merits of their hometowns:

That great skyscraper, the Flatiron Building at Fifth Avenue and Broadway vs. ladies in short skirts climbing mountains in Topaz City.

The hotels of New York vs. sixteen stage robbers shot in 1903 in sight of downtown Topaz City.

The leisure class of New York, vs. twelve tramps in jail in Topaz City.

The Wall Street Stock Exchange vs. Red Nose Thompson's new saloon in T.C.

The great orators of New York, Chauncey DePew et al., vs. Miss Tillie Webster, who slept forty days and forty nights in T.C. without waking up.

Each to return to his marvels, the two men parted, and any who had taken umbrage at O. Henry's anti-city tale of the week before were now comforted as the rattle of an express train on the elevated drowned out the last of the Topaz City man's arguments for the capital of the hustings, way out even past the boondocks of the Hudson in New Jersey.

Union Square was one of O. Henry's newer haunts, acquired perhaps in

1904—Union Square, where off to the left of General Washington's statue resided Central Europe's contributions to the polyglot city. It was here that Katie Dempsey's mother kept a boarding house, where dwelt Katie as her mother's principal assistant, and where rented, among others, Signor Brunelli, a man who had taken to Katie con amore in his eye. Katie admitted that she liked him, but she was suspicious.

"The marnin'll coom whin he'll throt out the pictuire of his baronial halls and ax to have the week's rint hung up in the ice chist along wid all the rest of 'em."

"'Tis true," admitted Mrs. Dempsey, "that he seems to be a sort iv a Dago and too colchured in his spache for a rale gintleman. But ye may be misjudgin' him. Ye should niver suspect any wan of bein of noble descint that pays cash and pathronizes the laundry regular."

"He has the same thricks of spakin' and blarneyin' wid his hands," sighed Katy, "as the Frinch nobleman at Mrs. Toole's that ran away wid Mr. Toole's Sunday pants and left the photograph of the Bastille, his grandfather's chattaw, as security for tin weeks' rint."[9]

How Antonio (Andy to Katy) appeases the lass's every suspicion and finally makes the bid to win her hand is the tale of the *New York World* in the week of August 21, 1904; contradicting many rumors of the past, to the effect that shanty Irish and Dago might meet, but only in mortal combat. Thus did O. Henry add to the glorious theory of the melting pot that was one pride of New York.

Seldom did the master put his hand to matters even slightly political or topical; as close as anything was "The Foreign Policy of Company 99," woven for the *World* that summer. Company 99, of course, was officially NYCFD EC No 99—or New York City Fire Department Engine Company No. 99. And if anyone was under the impression that Company 99 was not an entity unto itself, why then he had not yet met John Byrnes, the hosecart driver of the company. Mr. Byrnes even had a foreign policy: Japanitis. It was, you see, the year of the Russo-Japanese War, to which elsewhere in the works of O. Henry the reader will find infrequent mention. But to Engine Company No. 99, the Russo-Japanese War had a life all its own, courtesy of Driver Byrnes. He kept a war map on a table on the second story of the engine house, stuck up with little clusters of pins that represented the troops, and he could and would discourse at any hour on the war. He was, to put it mildly, a Japanophile, forever lauding the merits of the "bow-legged bull terriers," as he called them. But then into his life came a strange non-English-speaking immigrant from God knew where on the other side of Ellis Island. This Dimitri Svangsk, all unknowing, stepped into the way of John Byrnes' hosecart when it was in motion behind its mighty steeds, causing John Byrnes to run the cart into a pillar of the elevated, to disaster; his favorite horse was killed, and John Byrnes suffered a broken shoulder.

The foreigner tried to apologize, but was kicked out of the precincts of Company No. 99, yes, really kicked, sent sprawling by the leg art of Big Mike Dowling, who left grinning. And several times the foreigner returned to apologize, and each time he was ejected with the imprint of a size 13 brogan on his backside. Then came the day when the deputy fire commissioner arrived for an inspection of Company 99, and John Byrnes' irrepressible son, who was in the firehouse that day, climbed into the deputy commissioner's auto, and mistakenly started the engine, which began racing at full speed, the car in forward gear.

The car took off down the street, and the boy was in mortal danger. Then leaping bareback upon a firehouse steed, the foreigner with the unpronounceable name flew like the wind, overhauled the auto, and rescued the lad. Thereupon Company No. 99 changed its foreign policy. For Dimitri Svangsk had then revealed that he was a cossack.

THROUGHOUT THE YEAR, week after week, O. Henry continued to probe the inner recesses of the city. He was concerned with every aspect of the Big Town, but most successfully with the problems of love in its many aspects. One such case was that of Chunk McGowan, who loved Rosy Riddle, but was unloved by Old Man Riddle. And—enter the complicating factor—Rosy was also loved secretly by Ikey Schoenstein, night clerk at the Blue Light Drug Store, between the Bowery and First Avenue. Chunk—poor, benighted, naive Chunk—comes to Ikey, his mortal enemy, unknowing, seeking a "love philtre" to strengthen Rosy's desire to elope with him. Ikey, who has professed to be Chunk's friend, tries to do him in by preparing instead a strong sleeping potion, which Rosy will take and then fold into the arms of Morpheus for twelve hours, while Chunk stands waiting beneath her window. To assure the success of the perfidious plan, Ikey then advises Old Man Riddle of the elopement plot.

There is the scene set for Chunk McGowan's tragedy.

Yet it does not happen that way, because of O. Henry's genius. What does happen is that Old Man Riddle gets the best night's rest he has had in years, Chunk McGowan gets his Rosy, and Ikey Schoenstein gets his comeuppance. Only an O. Henry, as all New York now knew, could come up with such a tale.

HOW MANY TIMES did O. Henry actually live his tales? Sometimes, certainly. One evening he spent with a young newspaperman named Lindsay Denison, touring the bars in the Madison Square area. At the end of this long saloon crawl they ended up at the door of Denison's apartment and he asked O. Henry in. His wife was entertaining two girl friends, each of whom had remarked on her admiration for O. Henry the writer. O. Henry was about to refuse, but Denison said he would introduce him as Arthur Williams of Texas, a man who knew O. Henry very well and he would keep the O. Henry secret from the girls. That way O. Henry might get a new insight into what other people thought of him. The idea appealed to O. Henry and he agreed. He came into the apartment, sat down and soon was regaling the girls with tales of O. Henry, a scoundrel who stole plots from other writers and lived by cadging money from his acquaintances and even the shopgirls he wrote about.

"And to think," said one of the girls sadly, "that a man like that could write such a beautiful thing as 'An Unfinished Story'" (the story about poor Dulcie and the wicked Piggy, the man who preyed on young girls).

"I'll tell you about that, too," said O. Henry's worst enemy, the false Mr. Williams from Texas. "O. Henry wrote that story for the sole purpose of revenging himself on a shopgirl in Wanamaker's who had turned him down."

After the girls left, O. Henry sat around with the Denisons and laughed with them over the success of his impersonation. Then, he sobered.

"In all that rigamarole," he said, "there was just one bit of truth. The real Dulcie was a shopgirl in Wanamaker's and she did turn Piggy down. And Piggy—I was Piggy."[10]

Was it true? Probably. For O. Henry was a man, and he liked women. Most of his evenings were spent at least partly in one of the cafes or what would later be called nightclubs, which provided hostesses for the entertainment of the patrons. What happened after the patrons left the premises was a matter of great delicacy, not discussed in polite places. All such establishments were a part of O. Henry's chosen beat and he extracted many a tale from the New York Tenderloin. But as to his own personal night life, he was nearly as secretive as he was about his past. By 1906 William Sydney Porter was half forgotten. He had some acquaintance with women, Anne Partlan, and others, but except with Anne Partlan there was no hint of romance, and she was too firmly committed to her causes for any permanent relationship to develop. By putting the past firmly out of his mind, the man who had been William Sydney Porter was O. Henry, a fellow without a past of any sort at all. He saw his editors and young friends marry and settle down. But in his early forties he felt he had put that sort of life behind him. O. Henry was the writer who wrote and wrote so Will Porter could eat. It was as simple as that.

# 16

# The Slide

In the autumn of 1904 O. Henry reached his stride. For the *Sunday World* that fall he surpassed himself with "The Furnished Room," perhaps the most poignant of all his stories of New York. He went on to "The Coming Out of Maggie," a celebration of the New York Irish. "The Cop and the Anthem," which appeared in the *Sunday World* on December 4, was one of his best adventures into the ironies of life. On December 11 came another of those anomalies in the *Sunday World*, "Christmas by Injunction," a story far longer than the usual 2,500 words he wrote for the newspaper, and dealing with Christmas in the West. Could it be that the liquid glories of the season had overtempted the author? It seemed so. It was followed by the enormously satisfying "The Green Door" on December 18—O. Henry was once again at his most tenderly romantic, as he was again the next Sunday, Christmas Day, with "The Badge of Policeman O'Roon." Here, in O. Henry's pages, was the sort of New York young men and women dreamed about, the magic New York where wonderful things could happen, where sadness also could come to some.

So satisfactory was O. Henry's work for the *Sunday World,* in spite of the occasional lapse, that his contract was renewed that December and his rate of pay raised to $100 per one story a week.

These were days of reform in New York, and O. Henry was taken up by the reformers as a sociological writer. Mabel Wagnalls, daughter of the dictionary emperor, was bound up in good works. She and O. Henry carried on a spirited correspondence for several months, which she later published. President

Teddy Roosevelt was an avid reader of O. Henry and later said that several of his campaigns for social reform—particularly the plight of the office girl—were sparked by his readings of O. Henry's stories of New York City.[1]

Literarily speaking, O. Henry had now "arrived" in New York. Gelett Burgess invited him to a party, but as was so usual with O. Henry, he did not go. His excuse, made in his typical fashion on the eve of the affair, when he contemplated with horror the exposure to all those strangers, was that an old lady friend from Texas was coming in unexpectedly. Perhaps. But had she not existed, probably O. Henry would have invented her. The real reason was shyness, which he revealed in a postscript to Burgess:

"I ain't any good at tea parties anyhow. I'd have been a drag on the festivities. Get a young man with the 'temperament.'"[2]

Part of the reason for the shyness was his nature. Even as a child:

"I took life mighty seriously and sentimentally—that's why I always went about looking like a monkey with the toothache."[3] But at least an equal part, which he never admitted to anyone, was his fear of being unmasked as an "ex-con." The whole period from 1898 to 1902 was expunged from his official recollection, sometimes it was elided into the ranch years, sometimes he indicated a long residence in Latin America. Usually he simply avoided all discussions of the period before his arrival in New York City.

In 1904 Robert H. Davis moved from the Pulitzer empire to the Frank A. Munsey Company on lower Fifth Avenue. He asked O. Henry about some more stories for *Munsey's* magazine. He also asked O. Henry to lunch, and they did go to lunch once or twice that fall but nothing came of their meetings. In fact, O. Henry had grown to detest the publisher's lunch, for to him it meant having several drinks, and that in turn meant no work would be accomplished in the afternoon.

"D—— the lunch," he wrote Davis one day, "noon grub puts me on the blink. Don't you ever wander in the mead after sundown? Dodge the curfew some evening, and I will prove my devotion."[4]

They did meet from time to time, but it was the spring of 1905 before anything came of their meetings.

Davis wanted stories. The author was only too glad to oblige. It was a question of getting a subject, and the *World's* demands really ate up all his New York ideas. The two of them finally came upon an acceptable idea for a story for Davis's magazine. The title was "Hostages to Momus." It referred to the Greek God of Ridicule, who, for his censures of the other gods, was banished from heaven. For this tale O. Henry delved back into the prison days in Columbus and some of the stories told him by his crook friends of their misadventures in crime. This tale was of a kidnaping in Georgia, carried out by two desperate men, who "snatched" the president of the Sunrise and Edenville Tap Railroad. Having treated the old gent royally (they spent $250 on "the most efficient and gratifying lines of grub that money could buy" in Atlanta), they called upon his friends and associates on the railroad for ransom. The president enjoyed the food and the attention, finally his assistants sold all available railroad bonds to raise the ransom, and therein lay the kicker to a typical O. Henry tale.

When the deal was made, and O. Henry described the story he would tell, he walked away with $50 of *Munsey's* money. A little later he secured another advance against the script. But he did not deliver. Editor Davis kept after him, but apparently to no avail until on April 10 he wrote:

> My Dear Bill:
> If the sun sets on Monday without—well you know the rest!
>
> As ever
> R.H.D.

When O. Henry had that letter, for some reason he was annoyed. Perhaps it was because the messenger had awakened him early in the morning after a late night. So he answered, not quite in his usual genial way:

> Dear Personal Bill:
> She will set without . . . come on with the rest.
>
> The same
> S.P.

"The rest" had to refer to the rest of the advance, of course. Here apparently a difficulty arose, for the money and story were delayed. Finally goodwill was restored, and the tale was published by *Munsey's* in the July 1905 issue. It was, however, many weeks before O. Henry and Editor Davis got together again on a story.[5]


ANYONE WHO WAS in trouble could come to O. Henry, and if he had any money he would share it in a way that would make the acquaintance feel that maybe he was doing O. Henry a favor. Here is a letter from the summer of 1905 to his young friend Witter Bynner, an underpaid editor at *McClure's.*

Dear Bill:
　This loan is conditional.
　These is the conditions:
　Some time when you are sufficiently lousy with money you repay it.
　In the meantime, both of us forget it.
　When you return it, you go away, kick yourself, and exclaim: "Well, what a sucker I was to do that!"
　And I exclaim: "Well, I never expected to see that again!"

Yours toujours,
Panhandle Pete.[6]

THE *WORLD* STINT had tired out O. Henry by the summer of 1905 and he was looking for change.

Whatever was bothering O. Henry that summer—and it seems likely that he was having internal difficulties caused by alcohol, he felt that he had to get away from the city for a time.

But "getting away from the city" was relative. He took an apartment uptown, way up in Harlem (when that area was still a white residential community), and it seemed a million miles from his usual haunts. Perhaps it was to seek new atmosphere for his stories, he did not say why. From there, he sent Witter Bynner at *McClure's* one of the spoofing letters he liked to write his friends. *McClure's,* having had some success with *Cabbages and Kings,* had now undertaken to publish a new book by O. Henry. It would be a collection of the material from the *World,* about New York, and the title would be *The Four Million.* As the months went along, O. Henry was delivering into Witter Bynner's hands portions of the manuscript. That, apparently was part of the purpose of the letter, to announce that some more copy was ready. The real purpose, however, is ascertained only in the postscript:

Home For Indigent Authors
238 West 132nd St.
New York City

Mr. Bitterwinter
C/o Mr. Sam McClure
Manhattan Island


My Dear Honored Sir:

　I have lately completed a novel whose length is under 500,000 words. Do you publish novels as short as this? The fact that this is the story of my own life, dealing principally with my first and only love, now departed this life, should make it doubly interesting to you and to the great American people. Can you assure me of enough money not only to reimpurse [sic] me but also to help found this home which is noted on the letterhead. I am now an old man, but am in a perect state of preservation, have devoted all my life to studying human nature and literature. During the reading of this soulful tale of affection you will readily see my deep-seated familiaritude [sic] with the great Masters. I have just finished reading Turgenev's "Heavenly Twins" and it is fine, don't you think?

Have you a strong and confidential Secy in who you have the greatest confidence who will call at the HOME and take confidential charge of this life's labor which I hope will not be lost. If you like this book please send me some money by same confidential Sec.

Yours respectably,<br/>Hiram Q. Smith[7]

P.S. I read with great joy your intelligible article in a recent number of the *Critic.* . . . I like your stuff and I hope you write more of it. Come up next Sunday and take dinner with me. Anyhow, whenever you are up by the Harlem River just drop in.

That last, of course, was the sort of private joke that O. Henry never could resist.

HE WAS NOT very good, however, at taking jokes on himself, or in acceptance of even legitimate criticism, and he was extremely sensitive to the latter. *McClure's* had now published "An Unfinished Story," about the shopgirl who resists—this time—the advances of one of those "men-about-town" who preyed on the poverty of young girls. A little setpiece in the story shows Heroine Dulcie's pathetic handful of possessions: "Against the wrinky mirror stood pictures of General Kitchener, William Muldoon, the Duchess of Marlborough and Benvenuto Cellini. . . ." Elsewhere in the piece, O. Henry referred to General Kitchener's powers: "General Kitchener was her only friend, he was Dulcie's ideal of a gallant knight . . ." but "she knew that General Kitchener was way over in Japan . . ."

After "An Unfinished Story" was published, *McClure's* received a letter of complaint from a reader, one W. D. Woode of Darlington, South Carolina, who pointed out acidly that General Kitchener and his British forces had never set foot in craggy Japan. It was one of those letters from readers that an editor recognized as the hallmark of the frustrated writer, who has read the work of the author sniffingly all the way, and having caught some minor error has leaped upon it to show that this author should never have been born, and if granted that privilege, should never have been allowed to set pen to paper. The implication was clear that given half a chance the complainant would have produced twice—a hundred times—as charming a tale, *and would have been completely accurate in his details at the same time.*

At *McClure's* Witter Bynner fortunately did not have to deal with this matter, since it was the magazine's policy to turn all such questions over to the author for response, and retire gallantly from the field, out of the line of fire.

O. Henry received the letter, and was, in turn, piqued by the tone.

He responded to the letter:

> Your criticism in regard to the picture was considered by both the editors and myself to be both remarkable and unique.
>
> Of course I cannot undertake to dispute or refute your strictures upon the story. Few people are gifted with the faculty of writing without making mistakes—an error in history or geography may creep into the work of any of us minor authors. . . .
>
> But do you not think, Mr. Woode, that you should have called my own attention to the mistakes instead of revealing them to the publishers who may have overlooked them in their haste? I have always admired the generosity and fairness of the Southern people. Do you think you should have "given me away" like that?[8]

And then O. Henry very deliberately did not put his address on the letter, merely the heading "New York."

O. HENRY WAS receiving much more welcome mail that summer, as his fame as story writer spread across America. It reached Greensboro, the home of his youth, and one or two old friends learned that O. Henry was really William Sydney Porter, the boy who had clerked in the Porter drugstore so long ago.

One who heard the tale was Sara Lindsay Coleman, the girl for whom he had gone walking to find magnolia blossoms in that last summer in Greensboro. Miss Coleman was still living with her mother in the parental home in Weaverville. She wrote O. Henry that summer of 1905 to find out if he was really her old suitor—if one could put a first romance so strongly—and if he remembered her.

O. Henry replied "My Dear Miss Sally,"

Indeed he did remember.

I never expected anything so nice and jolly as to hear from you. It's like finding a $5 bill in an old vest pocket. Isn't it funny that I was thinking of you a little while last week? I had a map, looking all about on it trying to decide on somewhere to go for a few weeks to get away from the hot weather.

She had told him that if he was ever around Asheville, she would be glad to see him. He said he appreciated the invitation, but he did not know when he might come. But then, toward the end of his letter, O. Henry grew more enthusiastic:

I am puzzling a good deal over your signature. It's the same old name you had when you wore your hair in a plait, and I have two very good reasons for thinking that it ought to be different. One is that somebody wrote me several years ago that you had married, and the other is that it isn't possible—it isn't POSSIBLE—that the young men of North Carolina could be so unappreciative as to have let you escape. But if you are married, please—oh, please get a divorce at once so you can be Miss Sally again.[9]

And so began a new correspondence that would be a delight to O. Henry and would reinstill in him the memories of his boyhood and North Carolina, now all coated with the unalloyed patina of pleasant reminiscence, particularly in view of the more recent past. Texas memories were not so pleasant, because the friends of his later youth had dropped away when he was convicted of his "crime"; he lost track of nearly all of them during the prison years. The Maddoxes and others had not performed well when he needed them. Now, as the rumors coursed Texas, too, that this new light of the literary world was the old Will Porter, he began to hear from Texas, but his reception was selective, and not very positive. If anything, the reentry of North Carolina and Texas into his New York life convinced him of the necessity of keeping at arms' length from most of the world, and separating the present very definitely from the past. Only in the case of "Miss Sally" was he prepared to make an exception.

O. HENRY'S HAPPY association with the *Sunday World* continued through most of 1905, until the managing editor, F. L. H. Noble, retired, and was replaced by Caleb Van Hamm, a fire-eating type of executive. When Van Hamm came into the *World* offices, one of his first acts was to go over the payroll, and when he saw enrolled there the name of a man who for $100 a week produced nothing but a single short story each Thursday, he exploded:

"Can him," said Editor Van Hamm.

And so O. Henry was canned. Of course, they could not can him until his contract ran out in December, but his stories in the *World* came to an end on November 26 with "Two Thanksgiving Gentlemen," one of his better tales, about two old men, one the giver and the other the recipient of Thanksgiving provender. At that point there was one story left over in the kitty. O. Henry was tired and O. Henry was ailing with internal miseries. What he really needed was a rest and a long absence from his favorite haunts and juices, particularly such cocktails as this, one of his favorites.[10]

Gordon Gin ½
Private Stock ½ [whiskey]
Orange Bitters, big dash
Absinthe, moderate

Mix.
And enjoy

And suffer later.[11]

This, O. Henry did far too often that season. Very little work was getting done. He was living on advances from various editors for promised stories.

THERE WAS ONE final tale in the pipeline for the *Sunday World,* the Christmas story that O. Henry had promised. And that, according to the dictates of crusty Caleb, would be the end.

O. Henry took the news calmly enough. He had already reestablished his lines with his magazine friends, with whom he had kept in touch even when he had nothing to offer them. He had made an arrangement with Editor Davis at *Munsey's* to give him first refusal on all O. Henry stories except the *Sunday World* tales. His reward was a higher rate for each story *Munsey's* bought.

That year *Munsey's* bought "Telemachus, Friend." *Everybody's* bought "A Double-Dyed Deceiver." Richard Duffy at *Ainslee's* bought "A Blind Man's Holiday," one of the longest short stories O. Henry ever wrote, set in New Orleans.

Since O. Henry was not feeling well, he went to see Dr. Wildman on Ninety-fourth Street and was given two kinds of pills and the advice to take it easy, and get out into the countryside for a rest.[12]

Freed from his obligations to the *Sunday World* and with a handful of stories in the editors' hands, in November O. Henry decided to take a little vacation. He and Richard Duffy went up to the aromatic rurality of New Paltz where O. Henry intended to relax "without being kept in a state of nightmare by the esteemed but too hebdomadal World."

He got an advance from Duffy and another from *Munsey's* Editor Davis, and the pair went off "mingling work with some fresh air and real food."[13]

Two weeks later O. Henry was back in town. It was the second week in December. The *Sunday World's* big pre-Christmas edition was planned for December 10, full of department store advertising, and tales of Christmas past in the editorial columns. For the *Sunday World*, O. Henry was to lead off with a special Christmas story.

It was not very high on his agenda, since his contract had been terminated and he had to look to the uncertainties of the month-to-month magazine world. So when the boy from the *World* came around on Thursday evening to pick up the copy, O. Henry had to tell him he had forgotten and there would be none.

"I did have a story for you but I sold it today for two hundred dollars," he explained. "I intended to write another if I could think of a subject, but I reckon they'll have to use something else . . ."

But the boy sat, staring at him, and it became evident to O. Henry that his young friend was afraid to go back to the office without a story.

"All right," he sighed. "I'll give you a Christmas story."

He went to his writing table and sat down. In his fashion, he wrote the title on one page, and handed it to the *World's* office boy.

The
Gift of the Magi

And then he began to write the story, his pencil scraping across the yellow pad he used, never stopping, never faltering. He wrote for two hours, handing the office boy each page as he finished it, not halting to correct. Finally he was finished.

"There," he said, "I reckon that will fill the space."[14]

O. Henry then went out to dinner. Next day he was dead broke again, and asking Davis for another advance for the same story on which he had collected—and not delivered—for the New Paltz trip.

"I must sell a little part of my soul to buy some bread and sharlot rust.

"Except for the Christmas story I ain't done my work for the *World* nor nobody else," he reported.

As far as the purpose was concerned, the trip had been a failure.

"I am getting some good sleep nights now, and feel like hitting out a story today. Much better. My trip never done me no good. But I will send you a story in days a very few."[15]

Editor Davis advanced another $50 as requested. He knew his man. Stall O. Henry might, but always in the end O. Henry came through with a story that was worth every penny paid.

O. HENRY'S ILLNESS persisted. It robbed him of the ability to concentrate, and the stories did not come. On February 2, 1906, he wrote Davis:

> I have sat or sot at my desk day after night, and, as Colonel J. W. [James Whitcomb] Riley says, haven't been able to think of a damned word. Perhaps you may have noticed that the columns of the World have been OHenryless. You would also discover, should you make inquiries, that no magazines, or imitations thereof have received a line of ms. from me that puts the slightest crime in our arrangement.
>
> I have explained so many times the cause of my protracted drought that it would weary you for me to repeat them.
>
> I've got a scheme in sight where by I can at least clear up all financial obligations the first of next week, anyhow, and that will help some.

The scheme seems to have involved his book publishing ventures with *McClure's*. Harry Peyton Steger, the publicity manager of *McClure's,* had high hopes for the new book which was to come out that year: *The Four Million.* This book was not a semi-novel, but a straight collection of short stories. For by 1906 O. Henry had become known among the literati as *the* leading American practitioner of the art, comparable and compared by essayists and literary reviewers to De Maupassant.

But, said Steger, how about a real novel?

O. Henry sat down and thought about that for a time, and wrote Steger in detail.

"My idea is to write the story of a man—an individual, not a type (but a man), who at the same time, I want to represent as a 'human nature type' if such a person could exist. The story will teach no lesson, inculcate no moral, advance no theory."

And so he went on, at considerable length. The result was a muddy letter, not adding up to an idea for a novel, but showing the author's struggles with the tone and theme. He had done this almost precisely the same way before; he had an idea that the sort of novel he had to write was to be "great literature" far beyond the scope or sort of writing he did for his short stories. As can be seen in *Cabbages and Kings,* he could have written charming novels by extending his characters and his plots, but he somehow conceived of the O. Henry novel as "the great American novel" and allowed himself to be trapped by that conception into immobility. He could never come up with a plot and a character; perhaps, although he denied it, his sense of the autobiographical was too great. But at that particular moment, although he might talk about novels and plays, O. Henry was really not in a position to write much at all just then, for he had a new trouble.[16]

O. HENRY LIVED in an apartment at 55 Irving Place for some time, but eventually he had to move, the sort of wrench that he truly hated. It was not just a question of money; he never wanted more than simple surroundings, a bathroom, bedroom and place to write. He did not like change, he preferred the same vista day in and out, and outside he liked to go the same way to the same bars and restaurants. But fate would have it that the landlord had other plans for No. 55 and so O. Henry had to go.

Panic set in and he expressed it to various editors. The Wandering Jew, he called himself mournfully, a new excuse for his editorial tardiness.

For a time he managed to camp at 126 Waverly Place, which was Gilman Hall's apartment, the editor being out of town for some time. There, O. Henry told Witter Bynner, he was able to stretch himself out and begin writing again after several weeks of block because of the confusions of his life. He needed money as usual. He wanted $125 in advance against his next story for *McClure's*.[17]

ALTHOUGH THE O. HENRY relationship with the *New York World* had ended, it was revived briefly in the first months of 1906. Fire-eating Editor Van Hamm was enticed by Mr. Pulitzer's deadly enemy, William Randolph Hearst, and succumbed to the lure of more money to join the Hearst organization, where he made life miserable for such as Damon Runyon and Gene Fowler. The new *Sunday World* editor, Nelson Hersh, dispatched William Walsh Williams to find O. Henry again and make a new deal. They got together and O. Henry showed no rancor. He did another ten stories for the *World* that year, but by July the relationship was ended. Times had changed. The short story was no longer so great a newspaper circulation builder for the *World.* O. Henry was back in the magazine market, and dickering with *McClure's* newspaper syndicate to take on all his old stories and put them out to the newspaper press.

# 17

# Life in the City

In 1906 when O. Henry's second book was published by McClure, Philips & Co. the book reviews indicated just how far the author had come in the four years since he assaulted New York with a steamer trunk, a sharp pencil, and an outré derby hat.

> In the four million people of New York City in their daily living and working and playing Mr. Henry has found the material for comedy and tragedy, for laughter and tears. With a few deft touches he weaves the fabric of romance in East Side tenements, Wall Street brokers' offices, or along Fifth Avenue. His sketches—they are hardly stories—are remarkable for their terseness, sympathy and humor, and for the deep insight into the inner life of the great city.

So said *Public Opinion* in its review.[1]
*The New York Times* was more restrained, less laudatory:

> The work is not even, of course, and some of it is not up to the mark—but on the whole it expresses the spirit of New York wonderfully. And it is clever and entertaining always.

The *Critic* had its encomiums: "The best thing of the kind." The *Outlook* liked the book.
All had pleasant remarks, but none of them was really good critical reviewing in the sense of examining and evaluating the author's efforts.

Perhaps all those reviewers were bemused, being city people, with the "romance of New York."

All, save *Watson's Magazine,* that is. For the *Watson's* reviewer, R. D., he signed himself (it might have been Richard Duffy of *Ainslee's Magazine*) showed that he understood as did few, just how great a contribution O. Henry was making to American letters as well as to the amusement of magazine and newspaper readers.

The reviewer lauded O. Henry for his sense of economy of words. Some critics had claimed that O. Henry's stories were too short, but *Watson's* reviewer put that plaint in perspective:

> In word limit all the stories are shorter than the average magazine story, yet it would be difficult to find as much observation and insight compacted in the short stories of any fictionist of today.

The reviewer objected to the critics who compared O. Henry to Dickens, de Maupassant, and Robert Louis Stevenson. Undoubtedly they meant well, he said, but to compare one writer to another was to demean the writer under consideration.

> Moreover, one might pick a majority of traits in the stories of O. Henry that make him quite unlike the celebrities just named.
>
> He is as much like Dickens as Broadway is like The Strand. His people are often of very humble station, and soul to soul one meets waiters of both sexes, policemen, tramps, factory workers, Bowery heroes, shop girls, messenger boys, boarding house keepers, the furnished roomers under life sentence, yaps, and a yellow dog. Not even the dog is presented in the rose-tinted vapor that most writers spray upon the Lady Romance that seems to be the genius of Manhattan island. Nor does he see them drenched in the grime that is the main denotement of the so-called realist. . . .
>
> Sometimes he seems not to be telling a story at all. The *Chorus* at his elbow always, talks uninterruptedly. One feels the case is being stated; and then comes the quirk of that last line that throws a new light on all that has gone before. With the aid of his *Chorus* he manages the paradox of telling a story without ever writing it. The quirk of the last line is factitious, but we wouldn't dispense with it, even though it does invalidate the comparison to Maupassant. He resembles all good writers in his fine instinct for the right word, whether he is writing New Yorkese or English; he is sui generis in the manifold impressions he records of the great illusion New York is—in common with other over-

advertised cities. For this reason we believe *The Four Million* to be the most interesting book of New York stories yet written.[2]

The book helped. The arrangement with *Munsey's* by which Editor Davis paid ten cents a word instead of the usual five cents a word also helped. He could quote that price quite truthfully to other editors without telling them that Davis had first refusal. O. Henry's new-found fame made it possible for him to double his rates so that for a 2,500 word story (a length he preferred) he now got $250. He told one tale of a magazine that had been paying him five cents, probably *Ainslee's* because he owed them much and was conscious of his debt. But since he was getting ten cents from all his new editors, he mentioned the new rate to them, and they agreed immediately. They had just been waiting for him to ask.

So the author's fame and prices rose, and one would believe that with some sixty stories published in 1905 he would be in clover. But that was not the fact. In 1906 O. Henry's production dropped to nineteen stories, including ten produced for the *Sunday World* in the first six months. The slowdown came for two reasons. First and by far the most important, was O. Henry's lassitude. He was a money writer, and when he did not need money he did not write. He promised and he stalled; oh, how he stalled, until the editors were ready to tear out their hair, and then he stalled some more until they were ready to tear out his hair.

There was a difference in the stories O. Henry was writing in 1906. They were somehow more introspective than in the past; they related more closely to the inner O. Henry and depended more on character for their strength than on surroundings.

The first story of the year, published by the *Sunday World* was "The Duel," in which two young men from the West, having come to New York to make their careers, come together again in a restaurant. The one, the businessman, is full of current New York gossip. He has just been introduced to John "Bet-a-million" Gates. He has heard Enrico Caruso sing and he has seen the inimitable Sarah Bernhardt, and all this in New York. You could not drag him out of it with a logging rig.

His friend argues against New York, loud and long. But then, when he goes back to his room that night and looks out over the city, he thinks again. There comes a telegram from his ladylove in the Middle West, telling him that if he will come home she will be his. "Impossible to leave here at present," he replies.

And then, soon after, came a story based on the demon rum; the process of quitting drinking.

But, it was not that O. Henry had exhausted the sights and sounds of New York, nor lost his feeling for the mysteries of the city. "The Buyer from Cactus City" is a tale of the style of the old O. Henry of 1904 and 1905: The beautiful model from the designer's shop accepts a dinner date with the buyer from Cactus City, and from the moment he picks her up she knows what he wants, or she thinks she does. But she is gloriously wrong, and it all becomes clear in the O. Henry fashion. Where this story tells so much about O. Henry is in his account of the girl's behavior. She wants a dry martini, and some wine with her dinner. Ah, where did O. Henry learn of these girlish traits?

At the Bohemia, the Berlin, and the Cairo on Twenty-ninth Street. There O. Henry would repair night after night, sometimes with a friend, and sit down at a table with several of the "hostesses." He would sit quietly, talking and drinking, and buying them their drinks of cold tea and sometimes even the sparkling grape juice from upstate that passed for "champagne," just as if he were one of the rubes. But he listened, and from his listening he earned the price of admission; the girls would forget him and when he stayed long enough the girls would begin to talk.

For a while he frequented the old Haymarket at Thirtieth Street and Sixth Avenue, where the policy was no robbing of the rubes on the premises, and if there was trouble after what ever happened late in the night, the girls had to give the money back to preserve the good name of the house.

Sometimes he went to Koster and Bial's cafe at Twenty-fourth Street and Sixth avenue, a much tougher place than the others, frequented by pimps and whores and their customers for the most part. The girls there thought he was "a nut," for he never asked for what the other men wanted: he never tried to take them out or to feel them up under the table. He paid the prices for the imitation liquor, and knew what he was doing. And when he left the cafe, any and all the girls who had been sitting at his table found that he had also left five or ten dollars for each of them.

Any and all of the night spots were grist for O. Henry's mill. He went to Tony Pastor's, which was clean as a whistle. But the tougher the joint, the better he liked it. He also went to Dewey's, where the entertainment was enough to make a Fourteenth Street whore blush. The program included a girl who swung out over the audience on a trapeze, divesting herself of her garments as she went, and climaxing the aerial striptease by tossing her garters to the men below.[3]

From at least one evening at Dewey's O. Henry got the idea for his story "The Memento," the tale of a girl who decides she is going to give up the glamor life of New York, and then . . .

So that was where O. Henry's money went, on wine, women, and song. How much of it all was for pure research, and how much for the entertainment of a lonely writer was another of the questions that O. Henry never answered, except, perhaps by innuendo, in some of the tales, and very occasionally in a report of one of his real adventures, revealed to a newspaper or magazine friend.

One evening O. Henry encountered William Wash Williams of the *World* at a cafe and asked the young newspaperman to come walking around Gramercy Park with him while he cooled off. He was furious, he told Williams, because he had just been deceived by a woman.[4]

This deceiver was one of his shopgirls, or a model from the garment district, for he often went out with both, and this was, as he said, a girl he had known for some time. Under O. Henry's usual skillful, quiet coaching, she had told him her life's story, how she came from a little town in Pennsylvania to the big city, and about her hard times. He may even have used her story to make one of his. About six weeks before his meeting with Williams, she had suddenly asked him for fifty dollars to go down to Pennsylvania to see her mother. The poor old lady was sick and not expected to live much longer. She wanted to see her daughter before she died.

O. Henry in his usual generosity had put up the money without a squeak. He had not seen the girl since, until this evening at Healy's cafe, where he was talking to another girl when she came in with another man. He had asked how long she had been back in town from Pennsylvania, and how was her mother?

His girl of the evening laughed. More, she guffawed. The other, she said, had just come back from Atlantic City where she had been on a toot. Pennsylvania? said his evening's companion, where did he get the idea she came from Pennsylvania? And if that girl ever had a mother . . .

O. Henry was stunned. He had been gulled.[5]

What infuriated O. Henry was that he had been taken, just like one of his out-of-town rubes. The money meant nothing to him. "Anybody can have my money any time; they don't have to lie to get it; just say they want it. I'm an easy mark and I know it, but that's my business." Just this once he had been gulled, and it took many hours for the bitterness to wear off.[6]

On another evening, O. Henry told a friend, he had taken one of his shopgirls to dinner at Shanley's, a very expensive fish house. As he was ordering the dinner he got the impression that the young lady was looking at someone else behind him. As the dinner continued, the impression grew that she was flirting with another man. Finally he became so annoyed that he excused himself, went to the cashier, paid his check and got his hat, and walked out.

"And that's the way to treat them, Bill," he told his friend. "No need making a fuss; just quit them cold and cut them out forever after."

The advice sounded as though it had come from long experience and stinging bitterness. Certainly there was no reason O. Henry should not have had the experience. He had no strings on him, no family to care what happened, no one who was even interested, with the possible exception of Sara Coleman, who had reentered his life so recently, and that was merely a "pen pal" relationship. He saw them all, the strumpets and the ladies and the girls in between, in his wanderings around New York at night. His behavior to women was always that of the North Carolina gentleman; his attitude toward them was something else; several of his friends had the impression that he distrusted women in general.

OCCASIONALLY, THIS LONELY man seemed ready to uncork his story. Richard Duffy felt that he had a past, through some of the casual remarks O. Henry made. Robert Davis and O. Henry got to talking one night over drinks and the subject turned to the trivial things that changed men's lives. O. Henry paused,

"Some day," he said, "I'll tell you how I fell heir to enough spare time to take up fiction seriously."

But then he realized what he was saying and stopped and stared out the window.

He said he could write his story in four lines. And later he did:

Sydney Porter
X
His Mark
O. Henry.[7]

But not having the clues, not knowing that Sydney Porter had become X and that X had become O. Henry, Davis remained mystified. Like many another he would learn the real story of O. Henry's life only after his friend was dead, although it would not be long before most editors knew one thing: that O. Henry had been in prison. That revelation was the only negative price O. Henry was going to pay for his success.

For in 1906 O. Henry was a success, but he still found it necessary to secure advances against his stories, for more than the one reason. And his demands suddenly became more strident and for greater sums than before:

To Witter Bynner at *McClure's*:

Hello Mr. Bill.

Say a fool and his money etc.

Is there anything doing for about $49.99 today for the purpose of purchasing things offered for sale in the marts? I had to send all that stuff abroad that you gave me the other day. . . . There will come to you on Monday the new story, I want it typewritten first . . .[8]

He still had not found a permanent abode, and Gilman Hall was coming back to take over his apartment at 126 Waverly Place again. That created new problems, as O. Henry wrote Robert Davis at *Munsey's*:

> I've been writing nothing for a month on account of having no abiding place in which I could work. And I've got to move from here in three or four days because Gilman Hall is coming back to town. I've got to have some money, some to send home and some for expenses. I'm not asking Munsey's for it, still less you personally, but I've got to raise $250 *today,* sure. If your magazine doesn't care to advance it I'll have to get it somewhere else, which I won't have the slightest trouble in doing.
>
> Of course I'll have to abandon the short story work to do it, but it's a case of "must." I'll have to go uptown and make an arrangement for a serial right away.*
>
> Dropping the short stories will be a big set-back for me. but I've got to have the money; and if your people object to investing it in me, I've got to get it where I can.
>
> Please give me a definite final answer at once,
>
> As ever yours,<br>Sydney Porter[9]

He meant what he said, that dropping the short story form if necessary to earn money would be a great blow to him, for he knew very well that this was peculiarly his genius. He once told a young writer seeking advice that the secret of short story writing was easy enough:

"There are two rules. The first rule is to write stories that please you. There is no second rule."[10]

But later he did invent a second rule:

"Sell the story."

It was a rule he followed always. If a story came back time and again, and some did, he kept them in his trunk, and ultimately they sold. In 1906, when he was involved with *Munsey's* on a first refusal basis, a story of his appeared

---

*Here, O. Henry's obvious threat was on offers he had constantly from various magazines to do "serial stories" that would titillate readers week after week until finished, and later be turned into cheap novels.

in *Ainslee's* and caused Editor Davis to complain that O. Henry did not seem to be living up to his agreement. O. Henry said the story was one that had been rejected so many times around New York that he had almost given up on it and was as surprised as anyone when *Ainslee's* bought it. He also sent Davis another "reject," telling him to send it back, since he was sure the editor would not like it. That was all, absolutely all, of the material he had on hand from the old days, said the writer.

The short story was his form, and he was now known as the master of it. He kept on talking about writing a novel—"the novel" he called it—but nothing came of it. Since he continued to write stories and did not go into the "serial" marketplace, it seems apparent that once more "Colonel Davis" and the others came through in a pinch.

But what was the pinch?

A few weeks later he wrote almost the same:

> In addition to the $150 I screwed out of the high browed and esteemed B. Merwin during your absence, it will make a total of $275 which will be more than covered by the moral and entertaining tale that I hereby agree to have finished and delivered to you all by 10:30 A.M. on Monday August 27 . . .
>
> Consistently,<br>Bill the Bedouin.[11]

As time went on, the stories about O. Henry's dilatory nature were multiplied. At least half a dozen men who at one time worked for the *Sunday World* wrote about dealing with O. Henry, and several of them wrote about the same thing: how "The Gift of the Magi" had been extracted.

I have accepted the tale of one of them; it is so much of a piece with all the others that one must be true, but which of the *World* newspapermen was actually involved it is impossible to say. In the 1902s it had become very popular to claim some sort of relationship with O. Henry', and that of errand boy to the great man seems to have been a favorite.

O. Henry often spoke of sending money "home." No one really knew what he meant by that. Part of home was where the Roaches were, for they still took parental responsibilities for Margaret. As noted, she went to school at the Ward-Belmont finishing school in Nashville for a time. That accounted for at least $1,000 a year of O. Henry's expenditures. He was then paying back some small amounts of the money he owed P. G. Roach and retiring a few of the other debts he had contracted in those miserable months before the trial. But as for "home" there was no home. He never set foot in Austin after 1898. Margaret was cared for, but not allowed to come close to her father. She visited him in New York only one time, and he found it difficult to pull himself away from the usual haunts, which were most unsuitable for a young lady. He finally did take her on a tour of the proper New York, and then spent days explaining to his friends that he had had to do it.

No, the pinch was not caused by Margaret's needs. They were predictable and he had been absorbing them since 1901.

There was another factor:

In 1906 O. Henry began to have symptoms that led him to believe he had some sort of kidney disease. He telephoned his doctor in the middle of one night and insisted on a house call. The doctor came, found O. Henry in a highly emotional state, and spent an hour with him to calm him down. But he found no kidney disease.

The emotional state, in 1906, might have been from something quite different.

The real O. Henry fame began to course the country in 1906, and in addition to all else it brought one new possibility to cover O. Henry's constantly growing need for cash.

Blackmail.[12]

If Judge Hill had recognized the picture of the young man from Austin as the Will Porter who had worked on the *Houston Post* in 1896, certainly others had also recognized the man. According to Al Jennings, who came to New York to visit O. Henry, the writer was being blackmailed by a woman from Austin. She was, said O. Henry, a once-respectable person, the widow of a broker, who had come on evil days. She said she had no one to turn to, so she had turned to crime, to blackmail. She had first come to see him in New York, demanding $1,000 to refrain from telling the New York press that O. Henry was really William Sydney Porter, a convicted embezzler who had served time in a federal penitentiary. O. Henry had been afraid of this development for years. He had emptied his pockets for the woman that night, he said, giving her $150 and a promise for more. She had repeated her demands for months and he had paid, time after time, until finally, he was emotionally exhausted, and said there would be no more. She could tell anyone she wanted anything she wanted. She could go to the devil but he would not pay. Perhaps realizing that she might, herself, end up in prison, the woman had then gone away and he had not been bothered again. He could not tell his editor friends the truth, of course, or he would not, hence many stories about O. Henry's wastefulness multiplied.

As noted, it was at this same time, in the summer of 1906, that O. Henry began to feel that he was ill. His physician was Dr. Collin L. Begg, who lived not far away from Irving Place, and who called to treat O. Henry from time to time. He continued to say the writer was suffering from nothing more serious than nervous exhaustion. O. Henry persisted in the belief that he had some serious disease, although many of his friends thought his real problem was too many hangovers and too much girl chasing. He continued to work, but at a greatly reduced speed. Five of his short stories in the last half of 1906 were published by *Munsey's*. *Everybody's* got two, and *McClure's* and *Ainslee's* each got only one.[13]

By the end of the year, O. Henry seems to have exhausted the patience of his favorite editors, and was admittedly deeply in debt to the magazines. His arrangement with *Munsey's* came to an end—probably because the editors did not accept his excuse that the New York story "Compliments of the Season" had not violated his agreement with them.

One of O. Henry's new problems after the literary success of *The Four Million,* was an attempt—really several attempts—to dragoon him into the literary community. He did allow himself to be persuaded to go to one or two literary dinners, but found the conversation so dull ("They talk nothing but shop.") that he carefully steered away from such gatherings thereafter. Once some newspapermen friends wanted to throw a bash for him at the Lotus Club. He refused. It was his rule, he said (if so, it was one he had just made up), never to attend a gathering with more than three other faces. Three faces he could manage and enjoy. More faces threw the whole room into a complete confusion for him.

Later, many of O. Henry's associates concluded that he led a deep, dark life, filled with sexual adventures. Perhaps he did. If so, his reticence about his private affairs covered that part of his existence, too. For the fact was that as of the end of 1906, O. Henry had been living in New York City for more than four years, and he had come to know most of the important figures in the newspaper and periodical world. But virtually no one knew anything about O. Henry except what he told them, and as in the past, it was his pleasure to tell them anything that came into his head, just as long as the real truth about the real man was kept his secret. Now, the worst part of his secret—the fact that he had spent years in prison—was becoming known. But even now he was unable to tell his whole story, which would elicit sympathy certainly to any believing listener. And so his friends and editors were subjected to the greater difficulty, forced to have trust without information. By the end of 1906, the bare facts of William Sydney Porter's career were becoming known, but O. Henry continued to hide behind his vanishing anonymity.

# 18

# Reaching Back for Happiness

The growth of O. Henry's fame was indicated by the new interest in him shown by Texas folks. In the summer of 1906 John Maddox wrote, asking him to take over a manuscript on New Mexico left to Mrs. Maddox by her father, Jonathan C. Duval. O. Henry was supposed to read it, edit it, and sell it to a publisher.

Mrs. Charles Anderson, wife of Maddox's old partner, from whom O. Henry had not heard since Austin days, wrote him when she came to New York, asking him to call. The letter had been sent to the *New York Sun*, which was then running O. Henry stories.

> Mr. Anderson and I both often speak of you and are glad your life has been so successful. I do trust this will reach you and will not be relegated to the waste basket . . .
>
> Sincerely, your friend,
> Mrs. Chas. E. Anderson[1]

Such letters might well have been relegated to the waste basket, for O. Henry might ask himself "where were all these friends when I needed them?" but he did not. He saved the letters, although usually he did not appear but sent a note (with no return address) to the correspondent, thanking him or her for the interest shown.

Requests of all sorts came in so frequently that O. Henry asked his editors not to give out his address, but it did not stop the flow; the Maddox letter had come via *Everybody's.*

With this flurry of activity from Austin, O. Henry should have known that his secret was a secret no longer and that, like his flamboyant friend Al Jennings, he had lived down his past. But as he told Jennings when the latter suggested he should have refused the lady blackmailer in the beginning, "I can't do things like that. I'm not made that way."[2]

Six years after his release from prison for the crime he did not commit, O. Henry was still tortured by that past, still living as though he had concealed his secret, although by the beginning of 1907 every editor in town knew the tale.

William Wash Williams, who had known O. Henry well during the *World* years, was approached in a saloon by another acquaintance of O. Henry's one day, after O. Henry had left the place.

"Say, Williams," said the other man. "You're keeping nice company. Do you know your pal O. Henry is an ex-convict?"

Williams said no he did not know it.

"Well," said the other, "He is. He served time in the pen at Columbus, Ohio, for embezzling the funds of a bank in Austin, Texas."[3]

So the secret was more than shopworn by the end of 1906, but never to O. Henry. He simply could not believe that if people knew that he had been a "jailbird" they would continue to speak to him. So he played his little game, pretending to be even more modest than he really was in order to prevent the prying of outsiders. But he never again was able to achieve the anonymity he sought. He had grown too famous. He was receiving letters by the score through his magazine and newspaper connections.

Some wrote asking for help, usually editorial. Some wrote asking for autographs, some for inscribed copies of one of his books (he was to supply book and inscription). Some wrote asking for photographs of the author. The former he often ignored. The latter he answered in his usual fashion, as to J. Harrigan of Boston:

> Your letter through McClure's received. Your brief submitted (in re photo) is so flattering that I almost regret being a modest man. I have had none taken for several years except one, which was secured against my wishes and printed by a magazine. I haven't one in my own possession. I don't believe in inflicting ones picture on the public unless one has done something to justify it. . . .
>
> Sorry! You'd get one if I had it.[4]

Another development was a new interest shown in adapting O. Henry's stories to the stage. A producer named Gerald Harcourt, of Los Angeles, wanted to adapt "The Caballero's Way," which appeared in *Everybody's* in the summer of 1907. But so did a well-known actor named Lorimer Johnstone. Philip Hamlin, a Denver theatrical producer, wanted O. Henry to write a twenty-minute vaudeville act for three characters.

Charles B. Dillingham, the Broadway producer, suggested that O. Henry might turn his hand to writing plays, and asked to see anything in that line that the author might put onto paper. He did have a play in mind, O. Henry said, and he met with Dillingham to discuss the matter.[5] A number of eager "playwrights" deluged him with letters, asking permission to adapt this story or that.

WHEN THE LAST *World* contract expired in 1906, O. Henry did not want to renew it. Instead, he made arrangement with McClure's to sell stories through its newspaper syndicate. The head of the syndicate was John Bradley, whom O. Henry habitually addressed as Colonel. McClure's picked up the old *World* stories and syndicated them to newspapers around the rest of the United States. The syndicate also began picking up old magazine stories and syndicating them, too. The newspapers and the magazines were avid for anything, new or old, from O. Henry's pen. He and "the colonel" negotiated a contract under which O. Henry was to have $200 a story for a series of 2,000-word pieces involving a single central character.

The outcome was successful enough that in 1907 McClure's contracted for another series of at least a dozen more short sketches. This time he was to have $300 for each.[6]

BY THE END of 1906 O. Henry was certain that he had some serious disease and nothing his various doctors said persuaded him to the contrary. His work had suffered all summer and fall as the writer found himself too often unable to concentrate long enough to turn out a story.

The O. Henry technique, as he had occasionally explained it to editor friends, consisted of getting a locale and a situation, and from that extracting a story—all this in his head before he ever sat down to put pen to paper. Once he had the story plotted out in his head, then it was only a mechanical task to transfer it to the written page, and this he did swiftly and steadily, writing hour after hour if need be until the tale was told. There was virtually no halting and no correction. The one change that came after the first few years was the typewriting of the manuscript, a matter first encouraged and later demanded by editors. O. Henry originally turned stories over to a professional typist, one of those girls who then began to creep into his stories of the great city. But in 1907 he acquired a typewriter (machine) of his own.

Still, in 1907 as in 1906, O. Henry's creativity was low. In 1906 he had been scheduled to turn out a weekly story for the *New York Sunday World* but by July had managed only ten where the year before he had done twenty-six. In the last half of April, in May, and June, he produced nothing at all. It was the same in September, except for one story ("Calloway's Code") for *Munsey's,* and in November he had been unable to write anything. Toward the end of the year he managed to pull himself together enough to do two stories, "The Seats of the Haughty," a Western tale for *Munsey's* and that Christmas tale, "Compliments of the Season," for *Ainslee's.*

He was irritable and nervous much of the time. He was also unable to settle down. He moved several times, finally to an apartment hotel called The Caledonia at 29 West 26th Street. It was the same old area, just a new address.

WITTER BYNNER OF *McClure's* was after him for some stories, and he promised willingly enough, but the turn of the year 1907 came, and the stories did not. He was heavily indebted to *McClure's,* and all they were getting from the investment just then were the compilations of the stories of the past. In 1907 there would be two such books: *Heart of the West* and *The Trimmed Lamp,* dealing with the Texas stories in the first, and the latest batch of New York tales in the second.

O. Henry was tired. Just after the beginning of 1907, when Witter Bynner asked him if he had enjoyed the holidays, the writer said he had "come through the happy season all right. I don't have those strenuous Christmases any more."

He was nearly forty-five years old, and sounding fifteen years older.

Well, he was feeling that old, too. Dr. Begg advised him that it would not hurt to cut down on his drinking, a bit of advice that was genially ignored. He wrote his editors about his adventures with pills and other nostrums. None of them seemed to do a great deal of good, however. He continued to be unable to concentrate. He had taken several trips out of New York to places in the Northeast but they did not seem to give him much inspiration or relief from his general feelings of malaise and weakness.

These persisted. His association with the *Sunday World* had ended in the summer of 1906. He produced only two magazine stories that were published in the first quarter of 1907, "Past One at Rooney's" in *Associated Sunday Magazine* in January, and "The Indian Summer of Dry Valley Johnson," in *The American Magazine* in February.

At the end of February, O. Henry decided to go down to Tennessee to visit Margaret at her school, and to try the Tennessee air for a change. He was back in New York again at the end of March.[7]

Perhaps the shortage of O. Henry stories helped the market. In any event, he wrote Witter Bynner, who had moved up to Worcester, Massachusetts, where he was employed as editor of *The Reader,* that his rate for his writing had gone up, now to fifteen cents a word. He was apologetic about it to this old friend, and said he supposed that killed the thought of writing anything for him. But he also said that he had so much work lined up that he could ill afford the time anyhow. It was not said boastingly, but simply as matter of fact.

The McClure's contract absorbed much of his energy, but many magazines were eager to offer him advance payments for stories. Too often the stories did not come. He contracted with Charles B. Davis of *Collier's* for a story in the spring of 1907 but by fall he had not delivered it, and, knowing O. Henry's reputation for procrastination, Davis asked for return of the advance. The very respectful letter was another indication of O. Henry's place in the magazine world:

> Every time I pick up a magazine and see one of your good stories, I am thoroughly envious and wish again that you had something for us. I know, however, how great are the demands on your time, and I am beginning to fear that our turn will never come.
>
> Under the circumstances . . .[8]

O. Henry's rate of production of new stories dropped sharply. He was busy revising and selecting stories for McClure's syndicate, and so as far as new work was concerned for the magazines, only eleven were published. And that year, having raised his rates so that he received at least $500 for a story, O. Henry had a new triumph. One day in the mail he received a letter from the editors of the *Saturday Evening Post* and a check for $1,000. They asked him to write anything of his choosing in exchange for the check. O. Henry picked up an envelope, addressed it to the editors of the magazine in Philadelphia, and inserted the check without comment.[9] He remembered only too well how many submissions he had made to that magazine, to receive nothing but printed rejection slips. It was a delicious moment in the life of the writer to be able to afford this little vengeance. But in fact later that year O. Henry finally did succumb to the blandishments of the most important magazine fiction market in the United States, and did write for the *Saturday Evening Post* the story "The Ransom of Red Chief," certainly one of his very funniest, one culled from the prison experience, about two "desperate men" who kidnap the son of a banker in a small town, and end up wishing they had not for reasons far from the usual. It is a tale that reads as well in the 1980s as it did in 1907.

The story came out of a little black book in which O. Henry scribbled ideas as he went along.

"Kidnapers get tough boy, and return him with a reward" was the spur for that tale for the *Saturday Evening Post*. O. Henry had long kept notes to himself. They included the names and addresses of markets: *Atlantic Monthly*, The Century Co., *Collier's Weekly, Short Story, Nickell Magazine, Criterion*, etc. etc.

Sometimes there were word lists:

> Perspicacity
> Chortle
> Cachination
> Higgledy-piggledy
> Stentorous
> Thither
> Verisimilitude
> Desideratum
> Straddle
> Stunt
> Execrably
> Tergiversation
> Amenable
> Unconscionably
> Irremediable
> Virile
> Imperturbable
> Strut
> Brainy
> Disgruntled

and

Sometimes they were random thoughts:

> Millionaire gives $10,000 on conditions that the town raises $50,000 more . . .

> Difference between personality of writer and his work

> 4th rate featherweight pugilist—can lick 9 out of 10 men—but no professionals.

> Indeed his torpid demeanor concealed nothing: it had that mysterious, almost miraculous power of producing spiking effects by means impossible of detection, which is the last word of the highest art . . .

His thoughts sometimes rambled to other fields;

> Idea for play:
> Girl or boy adopted when infant and raised in luxury, forced to go back to parents.[10]

The success of the stories, and the revelation by the *Critic* of his true identity now haunted O. Henry. Several magazines and newspapers, preparing to review his new books, asked for photographs of the author and also for biographical information. O. Henry was adamant. He told Witter Bynner that he must not honor such requests. "Nobody but a concentrated idiot would write over a pen name and then tack on a lot of d—— twaddle about himself. You will please me very much if you will refuse all information and description of that sort—*especially photos.*

He spent a good deal of time cleaning up the short stories for the books, for he had very high standards and was extremely critical of his own work. Much of what had appeared in the *World,* he chose to throw out as either time-trapped or unworthy. But the work came in starts and fits, between bouts of malaise. One day he wrote Witter Bynner thus:

Thursday

Oh,

let's

wait

till

next

week.

I

ain't

feeling

good.

**205**

Semperidem,

B
I
L
L.

The typewriter, so new to him, seemed to fascinate him, for another letter to Witter Bynner was written on thirteen folds of paper, with a word on each fold.

IN THE SPRING of 1907. O. Henry's "pen pal" relationship with Sara Lindsay Coleman progressed rapidly. She was very obviously setting her cap for him, as ladies said in those days. She admitted to thirty-six years, an admission that might be suspect by a careful student of Greensboro history. But O. Henry was so pleased to have a bit of his more respectable past reappear in his life, that he encouraged her enormously from the first, sending pictures of himself— which he never did to others. He also sent her a copy of *Cabbages and Kings*.

She wrote that she also had hopes as a writer, and she asked him to find her a literary agent. O. Henry interrupted his own routine to go out and find one for her, a female agent who sold some of her stories. He suggested that she kick over the traces of North Carolina womanhood, and come to New York to live the Bohemian life.

"There are lots of lovely women here leading beautiful and happy lives in the midst of the greatest things in this hemisphere of art and music and literature. . . . You meet the big people in every branch of art, you drink deep of the Pierian spring . . ."[11]

But Sara Lindsay Coleman was shocked. She did not wish to drink from any Pierian springs. She could find her muses right there outside Asheville. She didn't need any Greeks, or any of O. Henry's saloons either. Greenwich Village life was not for this Southern lady, and she soon made O. Henry realize it.

In the summer of 1907, when O. Henry had convinced himself (and he knew better than the doctors) that he was sick with something more than a running hangover, he began writing Sara in a different vein. He needed the love of a good woman, he said.

"I need a boss. For the last month I've been so no-account and lazy I haven't turned out a line. I've felt kind of melancholy and dreary and lonesome."[12]

This approach was precisely down Miss Coleman's alley. It appealed to the "mother" in her, and justified all the emotions she had been feeling since the moment she took pen in hand to approach the famous author. But there were the proprieties to be observed at all costs, and they were. O. Henry and Miss Coleman had been corresponding for more than a year when they finally met. She had made a trip to Boston to begin with, and just happened to stop through New York on her way home, as any lady might do.

She came at a time when O. Henry was beset. He had been making so many promises all spring and producing so little that he was in trouble with half a dozen editors. John Phillips of *The American* was complaining about an undelivered story. So was Hewitt Hanson Howland of *The Reader. Broadway Magazine* was after him. The *Pacific Monthly* wanted a Christmas story. He was way behind on his commitments to Colonel Bradley at McClure's.

One of his new collections of stories, *Heart of the West,* had appeared, and along with the usual fine reviews, lauding O. Henry's talent, had come a waspish entry from *The Nation*:

> The whole collection might be taken as an example of how conventional and tiresome the raciest slang may grow, when used in excess, as a means of enlivening flimsy and carelessly conceived commonplaces.[13]

That was not the sort of review that O. Henry was used to reading. And there was some more of it—really a sign of the New York literati's revulsion against the Western scene, an attitude that was to grow in the next few years, disappearing again in the 1920s.

THE ARRIVAL IN town of Miss Coleman gave O. Henry a chance to forget such nastiness and to escape his responsibilities. He took it. She arrived on his forty-fifth birthday, September 11, 1907, just as he was thinking of what he should say to *The American* and *Pacific Monthly*. He took her to dinner and lavished attention on her for the next few days. Before she left for Asheville, he proposed—but then before she could accept, he said there was something he had to tell her, the mystery of his life, and that he could not bring himself to speak, so she would have to read it. Miss Coleman then had to wait until she got home to Asheville and got the long letter O. Henry sent her telling in detail of his conviction and prison term for the crime he did not commit.

Miss Coleman replied that she understood all and believed that he had been wronged by society, and yes, she would be very happy to marry him.

By this time O. Henry was not quite so certain that he wanted to get married, so he wrote her again. She must reconsider, and she must be absolutely sure that his past would not affect her feelings.

But having caught her fish, Miss Coleman was not about to throw him back. Absolutely not, said Miss Coleman. When? That was the only question.

And so, after nine years O. Henry once again prepared for married life. He started looking for a New York apartment, but after checking around, decided it was not for him. It was, he said, too expensive a life. What he meant was that so long had he lived in hotels with all their services, that he was not willing to change. Gathering all the money he could squeeze out of his patient editors, he headed for North Carolina. On November 10 he wrote Colonel Bradley from the Battery Park Hotel in Asheville that he was working on stories he owed McClure's. He was invigorated by the fresh air of Asheville and said he might stay down past Thanksgiving. He had been suffering from insomnia in New York but "I'm down here in a big quiet hotel right on top of the mountains, and already feel as hearty as a syndicate and sleep as sound as justice. Finest place to work I ever saw, and the air is simply made of non-alcoholic highballs." (That latter was to assure Bradley that O. Henry was on the water wagon.)

He said nothing in that letter about his coming marriage, but the word had gotten around in New York, and Bradley mentioned it to him. A week later O. Henry admitted that it was true.

He was full of new resolutions and promises.

> I'm pretty sure to send your story next week; I've gotten it well along; and the mountain ozone is helping the work—of course, under the circumstances (as you may imagine) I do not put in exactly 24 hours every day at the desk, but the well springs of genius are booming, booming.
>
> *We* will get back to N.Y. about the middle of December; and then it's me for the work bench and no more bohemianism, procrastination or Bromo-seltzer. And there is a novel taking shape in my cerebral region. I think now is the time for a novel to follow the introductory short story volumes. More anon . . .[14]

The days of O. Henry's freedom were now numbered, but he seemed happy and determined to live a new life. Gilman Hall was to be best man, and was coming down later. O. Henry was taking this opportunity to refresh memories in Asheville, and make sure that all was well with Miss Coleman. He was prepared for domestic life, he also assured Hall, who had expressed some concern about O. Henry's wisdom in going through with this adventure, given the writer's known proclivities for the exciting life, both high and low.

"I've had all the cheap bohemia that I want," O. Henry assured him. "I can tell you, none of the 'climbers' and the cocktail crowd are going to bring their vaporings into my home. It's for the clean, merry life . . ."

And so, on November 27, 1907, Gilman Hall arrived in Asheville on the train, carrying a wedding ring, size 5⅛, which he had picked up at Tiffany's for the bridegroom; two stiff collars, size 16½; and two bouquets of flowers shipped down from MacIntosh the florist on Broadway just off Twenty-sixth Street.

He found O. Henry and they went to Miss Coleman's brother's house in Asheville for the wedding. In a few minutes it was done. Everything was changed.

# 19

# The Reformation of the Author

The future looked bright for the middle-aged honeymooners. O. Henry's income was rising all the time. In 1907 it was well over $10,000, a truly handsome sum then. He had promised to reform, to abandon his slipshod bachelor ways, and Sara was eager to reform him and make a home for him. After several weeks at a mountain hotel in Hot Springs, the happy O. Henry couple returned to New York. At first, he said, they would stay at the Chelsea Hotel on Twenty-third Street, a Victorian hostelry of wrought iron and large airy rooms. The soot and noise of Twenty-third Street were a far cry from the fresh air of Asheville, but it was all so new to the new Mrs. William Sydney Porter that she did not complain. Soon, O. Henry found that in order to work he had to get away, so he went back to his rooms at the old stand—The Caledonia Hotel, where he could come and go as he liked without inquiring glances from his better half, and where the staff had been so tipped, over-tipped, and spoiled by the author, that they would leap to do his bidding. His office, he now called it. He spent his days there from 10 A.M. to 6 P.M. with time out for refreshments, and his correspondence was directed there.

That plan sounded reasonable enough to O. Henry's friends, particularly his editors, who had some idea of his way of working. So it was settled, and he retrieved his working space, where he also had access to the ice box, the kitchen, and the vegetable room. When he was hungry and did not want to go out to a place such as Old Martin's, the Broadway restaurant frequented by luminaries like Richard Harding Davis, who kept a special table there and ate almost daily in grandeur, then O. Henry got his own lunch. It sounded very simple and homey, particularly as compared to the sort of lunching done by Davis and his friends, for no gentlemen ever completed luncheon in less than two hours at Old Martin's. First one had a sherry, or a "cocktail" if he was very modern, and then a bottle of white wine with the fish and a good red with the meat, and perhaps some champagne with dessert and fruit, and then a brandy or two, or at least a port to go with the cigar.

The fact is that the way O. Henry managed at The Caledonia quietly put the Richard Harding Davises and their showiness to shame. O. Henry had established a club so exclusive that he was the only member, with a whole hotel staff to protect him from strangers and take care of all his wishes. In the outside world only a croesus like Vanderbilt could conceive of such a way of life.

With his marriage, O. Henry opened up a little to friends who began appearing from the past. Charles Alphonso Smith was one of them, a companion from those boyhood days of playing knights in shining armor, who had grown up and become a history professor. "Phon," as he was called by friends, said he was coming to New York, to stay at the Astor Hotel. O. Henry rolled out the red carpet at The Caledonia for him, also the Chelsea. For "Phon" represented the sort of bridge that Sara needed to bring the old Will Porter and the new O. Henry together as one person.[1]

But there were not many old friends from North Carolina days coming to New York, and there were many friends and acquaintances from the bachelor days. So, with every good wish and will, the author was hard put to try to change his habits, particularly when he restored the old environment. The reform was a little slow in developing.

As usual, O. Henry managed to stay broke, in spite of the constant increase in his income. The magazines were paying more and more. His newspaper syndication meant new payment for old work, which was like clipping coupons. The *Heart of the West* had not made much money, at least for the author. His second collection of New York tales, also published in 1907, *The Trimmed Lamp,* did better financially. The critical acclaim of this collection was heartier than that of the Western stories; perhaps again this could be explained by the fact that most of the critics had never been west of the Hudson River. But it was comforting to read the *Atlantic Monthly's* comment: "The reader who skips a single story in the collection runs the risk of losing something that he would have liked quite as well as those he read if not rather better." To keep the author from getting a swelled head there was the *Literary Digest's* supercilious "For stories of their kind they are fine."

There really was no reason to fear that O. Henry's head would swell, for although he was not usually as self-depracatory as he had been just after he left prison, he had his moments of self-hatred even now. As he said one day:

"I'm a failure. I always have the feeling that I want to get back somewhere, but I just don't know where it is.

"My stories? No, they don't satisfy me. I see them in print and I wonder why people like them. I wait till they come out in book form, hoping that they may look better to me then. But they don't. It depresses me to have people point me out or introduce me as 'a celebrated author.' It seems such a big label for such picayune goods. Sometimes I feel that I'd like to get into some business . . ."[2]

But the fact was that he was doing better all the time, and in 1908 his income would hit $14,000, which was more than most company presidents earned. And how many company presidents had two New York dwellings, with hotel service; offspring in private school; and their own private club?

NOW THAT O. HENRY was married, and ostensibly settled down, P. G. Roach wrote his former son-in-law to see if he could collect some of the money owed him. In his letter he also indicated that Mrs. Roach was very upset because the first she learned of O. Henry's marriage was from others. Immediately, O. Henry sat down and wrote Mrs. Roach a long (twenty-seven-page) letter, and he explained to Mr. Roach that he had not written before because he was so sensitive about the past, and he did not know how to tell his former mother-in-law that he had married again.[3]

Roach needed money to undertake some business enterprise back in Texas. O. Henry said he had just signed a contract with McClure's to write a novel that the publisher said would earn at least $20,000, and he was to have an advance of $1,500, so he could really make some payments on the debt.

It was the O. Henry plan, urged by Sara and endorsed by all the author's friends and editors, that O. Henry would take a cottage on Long Island that summer. Gilman Hall, O. Henry's constant friend from the *Ainslee's* days, who had now become editor of *Everybody's Magazine,* had even gone out and found the cottage for them.

It seemed a sensible idea all around.

Margaret had come "home." In the fall she would attend the Dwight School for Girls at Englewood, New Jersey, under the direction of Misses Creighton and Farrar. She would spend the vacations with O. Henry and Sara.

The hope was also that the move to Long Island would force O. Henry out of his usual habitats, his park crawling, and the saloon and nightclub life he had lived for six years. All wanted him to abandon those old habits, and cut down on his drinking, for his doctors now diagnosed his various pains as diabetes and told him that liquor was poison to him, a statement about as effective as telling a fish to stop swimming.

Thus it came about that in the middle of June 1908, O. Henry and Sara and Margaret moved out eighty-two miles from New York City to Good Ground, Long Island, to a two-story twelve-room house on the water. They had a private waterfront of about a quarter of a mile; it was shady and quiet and altogether the best place in the world for a writer to get away from the hooting, snorting city. O. Henry was going to love it, right?

Wrong!

O. Henry took Sara and Margaret out to Good Ground on June 16. On June 17 he was back in New York "to finish some business," writing in the past tense as though his time on Long Island was all over: "We've got a cook and the two meals I had there were mighty good," he wrote Mrs. Roach, inviting her to come and stay with them. He was about to buy a boat and spend the summer bathing in the sea, he said. Just at the moment he was working night and day to get matters arranged, and particularly to meet the $800 payment he had agreed to make on his debt to Mr. Roach.[4]

At The Caledonia he had a complete stock of liquor into which he delved as he pleased. One day when he had some business with *Everybody's Magazine,* he invited Gilman Hall to come to lunch. Hall could not come but he sent George Barr Baker, his assignment editor. Young Baker came to The Caledonia around noon.

I arrived to find him waiting at an obscure table. The moment he saw me he indicated my chair and left for the pantry. Within two or three minutes he returned, followed by a waiter carrying a huge bowl in which, surrounded by ice, sat another bowl. In this bowl were strawberries . . . small, very red, and of a fragrance to scent the room. That is, of course, if they have come from the right gardens, and have been properly selected.

Consider, then, two quarts of these little red ones, after "Bill" had spent two hours re-selecting them, petting each one, and placing them all carefully in the bowl, layer upon layer, with barely enough fine claret to cover each new stratum as it was laid and with the least little bit of sugar between, until all were in, and sweet and moist with wine!! No ice to touch them, but ice all around. Then an hour in the refrigerator: Then placed with ceremony on a table almost bare excepting for a few leaves and pansies laid flat. Then seriously, excepting for the twinkle of those all observing eyes of the host, the production of a bottle of maraschino, from which, painstakingly, was poured teaspoonful after teaspoonful of the contents, each new lot allowed time to mix without help. Then the careful division of the fruit into two equal portions. . . .

Two hours later we left that place, filled with love of nature and all her works . . ."[5]

And probably a few Sazeracs and a couple of bottles of that fine claret O. Henry kept in stock.

AS FOR O. HENRY, where he went after lunch no one knew, but where he did not go was to Good Ground, Long Island. He was supposed to have returned to the cottage, but no. Sara was upset. O. Henry had indicated that he would be back in a day or two. Also, a local merchant called to collect a bill and she did not have the money in the house to pay it. Then she was worried, for she telephoned the Chelsea and she telephoned the Caledonia, and—no O. Henry. No one could find him. Sara tried all day and the next.

Sara telephoned Gilman Hall, asking if he had seen her husband. Hall said no, he had not, but he had a presentiment. O. Henry owed him a story, which he had promised to deliver this week and, as Hall knew, O. Henry was drawn to the hilt on his advance account at *Everybody's,* and could not expect another dime until he delivered. So, taking a page from his own experience with O. Henry, Gilman Hall sent George Barr Baker back to The Caledonia to see if the author was actually there.

"Mr. Porter?" said the desk clerk. "Why no, he is not here."

But a dollar produced a somewhat different answer and permission to go up the single flight of stairs to the front rooms of O. Henry, and the young editor hurried up. The door was ajar, and he slipped in. Inside, he found his quarry, stripped down against the summer heat to his shorts.

"On the table before him were piles of yellowish 'copy paper,' held down by weights. From the street below and the elevated railway a short distance off, came the roar of a noisy section of a noisy city. Near him on the table roared a large electric fan, blowing directly into his face. In his hand a pencil, raised as though to strike at something with the point. On his face—serenity. A few moments and he wrote a line or two, looked around, and said, 'there.'"

Barr spoke up.

"Bill, what are you doing here when your women folk took a lovely house and farm for you in the country?"

And he mentioned the fact that O. Henry's wife was frantically looking for him, and worried about money.

O. Henry addressed himself to the rural retreat;

"Noise!" O. Henry said. "Noise! There is no peace on that place, I was going mad. The barn they fixed up for me to work in is near a river that never stops running. There are birds there—irregular things. And, oh, God! why must there be cows in the world? I couldn't write or think."

In proof of what he said, he indicated the pile of manuscript.

"But here is your story. Are we square? Not that I'd ask for an advance, but women are so queer about the bills that fellows bring to the door."

Then he was off on another topic.

"Shall we eat?"

He led the young editor then to Martin's restaurant down the street, and one of those formidable luncheons. Having arranged for a new advance from *Everybody's* he was off to the country after lunch. Editor Baker returned to the office with "The Last of the Troubadors," and telephoned Sara at Good Ground. Her lost husband was on his way home and he had made arrangements about the money.

"Isn't he a dear?" said she.[6]

# 20

# How the Reformers Fared

The plan to reform the author, heartily endorsed by the "O. Henry Reformation Society," which included all his editor friends, called for the author to remain on Long Island all summer long and write his novel. He tried. But there were problems. Margaret was kicking up her heels about going back to school. She wanted to be a writer.

All right, said O. Henry. Let her finish her education in New Jersey, and go to Smith College, and, after that, become a writer or anything else she wanted to be.

But Margaret bucked like one of those Nueces River broncos out of the O. Henry past. He, O. Henry, had not even a high school education, his daughter pointed out, and look where he had gotten to.

This combination of female stubbornness and female logic was more than O. Henry could manage, and he was usually reduced to mumbling.

He called her Bill or Jim or Pete most of the time, in the same way that he invented special names for his men friends. For, as Margaret said, their relationship when she was grown was more that of friends than of father and daughter. He found it difficult to speak to her of the past, and seldom did. But she went with him on walks, and somehow they communicated without speaking; it was the same phenomenon noted by Richard Duffy of his early relations with O. Henry.[1]

The house on the Long Island shore had a piano and O. Henry would sit at it in the evenings, picking out songs of the South and singing, often in dialect. But he did this only for Margaret and Sara. He even bought a mandolin and a guitar on one of his escape trips to New York, and brought them home to the country, so the three of them could make music.

Margaret obviously had the normal child's resentment of her stepmother. She did her best to overcome it, but her success was limited. In her one published memoir of her father, Margaret did not even mention her stepmother.

The presence of the two women in the household was one distraction for the writer. The cows and birds were another of formidable proportions for the man who had chosen the asphalt jungle as his literary hunting ground. And yet another problem, forcing the muse of the novel into a corner, was the constant need for large amounts of cash. The two hotels in New York must be paid all summer, P. G. Roach's $800 put a large dent in the $1,500 advance for the novel, and so in late summer O. Henry found himself strapped. He learned of the problem early one week when he was expecting weekend visitors, and Sara said she had not enough money in the house to buy the food for the party. So O. Henry suspended operations on the novel, and wrote a quick short story, "Strictly Business," for *Hampton's Magazine,* which he then sold over the telephone, and at the same time arranged for an advance.

How O. Henry managed to spend any time at all on the novel was really a mystery, for he produced thirteen stories for magazines before autumn, including the one he owed *Collier's,* "He Also Serves." He revised twenty-four other stories for *The Voice of the City.*

Then he put together a book of the same general sort as *Cabbages and Kings.* It was the story of Jeff Peters, a confidence man, and his "unillegal graft." Mr. Peters is, by his own definition, a "reducer of surplusage," taking money from the rich, and often giving it to the poor, but keeping a bit as well. Sometimes Jeff Peters comes a cropper in the most unusual ways. The idea came from two tales O. Henry had sold to *Munsey's* in the past: "The Ethics of Pig" and "Hostages to Momus." Fourteen stories were assembled as chapters to make the book, most of them written that summer. McClure's book company brought both of these volumes out in 1908.

But the novel languished. Somehow, O. Henry just could not get going on it.

As autumn neared, Sara wanted to move out of the Chelsea Hotel and to an apartment. Editor Bradley of McClure's offered to sublet them his apartment at 88 Washington Place, and a lease was drawn. They paid $100 a month, which was a premium rent, but the whole Washington Square area was then, as now, a premium neighborhood. Margaret finally agreed that she would go back to school, to Englewood, and the marriage seemed to be working out much better. But O. Henry resumed his workdays at The Caledonia. Or, as he might have said himself, "Hell, Bill, I never left there."

And that, of course was the problem. O. Henry was simply unable to accept restraint, particularly from a woman.

"No one could manage that man," Sara said later. "He was a law unto himself, and had a deep dislike for anything that resembled nagging or fussing."[2]

This gave the lady who had married O. Henry, by his own announced wish, to reform him, a rather difficult role to play. She did her best, but the O. Henry she knew was one known perhaps only by Athol before her, a man of mercurial temper, who grew angry at nothing and seemed to pick quarrels for no good reason. One day he came home from his office at The Caledonia and saw a vase full of roses that Sara had bought at a local florist's. In the vase was one orchid. O. Henry commented on the orchid and Sara told him it had been given her as a goodwill gesture by the florist.

He grew furious and shouted that she should have had better sense than to take it.

She was upset at his violent reaction and fled into the bedroom, weeping. He came in later, to apologize, but even then his apology was conditional— "You don't know this big town as I do," he said, "I'm trying to protect you.,"[3]

O. Henry's new wife and most of O. Henry's acquaintances from the Tenderloin area did not mix at all. On one of Al Jennings's visits to New York O. Henry invited him to meet Sara. Jennings and Richard Duffy came up to the flat for an evening. Sara was most cordial to them. At midnight they got up to leave, and so did O. Henry. She objected. He stopped and the others went out, but he joined them on the sidewalk before they had gotten out of sight.

Jennings was just saying that he thought O. Henry was a fool to have gotten married again, and O. Henry overheard. She was, he told Jennings without anger, a most estimable woman, and he loved her. He recognized his own deficiencies, and that he had brought his troubles to heap on her shoulders. That was the problem of the marriage.[4]

And indeed it was, just as O. Henry had told his friend. For he was really unwilling to make the reforms he had promised in the euphoria of courtship. Indeed, to do so would have meant changing his life completely and his life was his writing. For as the principal students of O. Henry's milieu and writing have said, the characters of his Texas stories were almost all identifiable. And those who knew O. Henry's New York, have made the same claim about the New York tales.*

---

*O Henry's boyhood friend and biographer, C. Alphonso Smith, wrote at length of O. Henry's adaption of factual situations to fiction. Judge Trueman E. O'Quinn of Austin, who devoted much time to studying the Texas stories, established in virtually every one of them the real life counterparts. The relation between the stories and reality, said O'Quinn, was almost reportorial. Arthur Bartlett Maurice said that O. Henry's descriptions of streets and squares of New York was virtually photographic.

Both parties tried hard. Sara's sister-in-law from Asheville sent her six-year-old daughter, Mary Elizabeth, up to stay with their famous relatives for a visit. As O. Henry had done for daughter Margaret, he drew pictures of animals for "Lizabeth" and told her stories. All that was very well, in small doses, but in the long run, the streets of the city claimed O. Henry, and the marriage languished.[5]

Shortly after the first of the year 1909, Sara returned to North Carolina to live with her mother. It was apparently a friendly parting, a mutual agreement of failure, and not a declaration of war. O. Henry did go to Asheville from time to time. But Sara gave up trying to live with him in the city. When the seven-month lease on the Washington Place apartment ran out, O. Henry moved back to The Caledonia Hotel.

By the beginning of 1909 O. Henry's success was so great that he employed agent Seth Moyle to handle some of his literary affairs. One of Moyle's first moves was to offer future O. Henry books to a number of publishers, on a best offer basis. Thus Harper Brothers that year published the next collection of stories, *Options*. It was a collection of sixteen stories O. Henry had written in 1908 and 1909. *The Nation,* which had been unkind before, said that these were the best he had produced in the period. *The New York Times* did not agree, there were few examples of the author's best, said the *Times* reviewer. But even then the book was "full of good stories—wonderfully good stories of men and women—most of them still rather young—stories that flash upon you things which your stupidity and inattention has missed when you have looked with your own uncoached eyes upon the identical common life they are concerned to picture."[6]

This was, of course, O. Henry's genius, to be able to see, in his observation of men and women, what was really going on. Small wonder, then, that he could not give up this milieu and retire to the somnolent countryside as Sara had fondly hoped. A remarkable woman, the second Mrs. Porter, she grew to understand her husband and the impossibility of living the sort of life with him that she had expected in the beginning.

He was ailing from the first of the year. Early in January, *Ainslee's,* which had been so friendly to him, finally became upset, for he had failed for months to deliver his latest story.

But the syndication of his work continued and reached ever further. He began getting letters from all sorts of people about all sorts of things, from requests for advice about writing (by the score) to advertisements. There were many requests for autographs, and for photographs.[7]

But even at the height of his fame, O. Henry shied away from personal publicity. *Who's Who in America* asked him for a biographical sketch. He replied that there had been nothing in his life worth reporting. *Who's Who* replied (threateningly) that they would then have to rely on other sources for information about him.

"You're welcome," said O. Henry.

And here was all *Who's Who* could get:

> Henry, O. (Pen name of William Sydney Porter.) author. Born in Texas; has been cowboy, sheep herder, merchant, miner, druggist, and extensive traveler. Author: *Cabbages and Kings,* 1905, *The Four Million,* 1906; *The Trimmed Lamp,* 1907; *The Heart of the West,* 1907; Contributor to leading magazines and daily and Sunday newspapers.

*The New York Times* finally secured the only interview with O. Henry ever published, which for that reason is worth mentioning. But as a factual account of O. Henry's life and career, it is one of the great put-ons of all time, showing that even in 1909 O. Henry was still trying to conceal the truth about his life.

The *Times*'s most prominent local reporter, George MacAdam, was sent out to do the job. Armed with a letter from Doubleday, Page and Co., the reporter sought the writer. For five weeks he sought him and never found him, until finally Doubleday's Harry Steger steered the reporter to the little hotel at 28 West 26th Street, where even O. Henry's courtiers could not keep him out, armed with that letter. O. Henry was there; he had given up the apartment in Washington Square at the end of the lease, and returned to full-time bachelor living.

"Are you going to draw a pen picture of me?" asked O. Henry.

The reporter admitted that it was so.

"Then let me ask you to say that I look like a healthy butcher, just that, and no adornments."

The reporter said he had found a man he described as "healthy, short, stocky, broad shouldered, ruddy faced, clear eyed and none of his hair missing. He had none of the wan intellectuality, none of the pale aestheticisms that are conventional parts of the makeup of the literary lions that disport themselves at afternoon tea parties. One can readily see that he is the natural father of the moral reflection that life is made up of sobs, sniffles, and smiles, with sniffles predominating, which moral reflection is the thread on which most of his stories are strung."

The two pen and ink sketches of the author that an artist named Marcus drew to accompany the full-page article showed a figure who looked very much like a healthy butcher.[8]

The long interview bore no byline, as was generally the case in these days before the star system slopped over from television to make all newspaper reporters more important than their stories, but soon reporter George Mac-Adam showed how he was warming to his subject.

The reporter warned his readers that O. Henry might possibly be spoofing part of the time. All that they would be reading might not be Gospel:

"He has a way of 'smiling with both mouth and eyes when he is saying something that you are quite sure is the truth'—but of looking absolutely solemn when he was doing the reverse."

Then, the reporter began to probe, and here the interview took a distinct turn for the worse as far as Gospel was concerned.

O. Henry went to some pains to deny that he had ever been a cattle thief (true), that he had been a miner (partly false), that he had ever been a tintype artist (true), and that he had once gone into a Pittsburgh newspaper office in a ragged suit trying to sell stories and borrowed a dollar from somebody (false).

The reporter objected:

"All you've said so far about yourself has been of negative character—the things that you were not. Now won't you tell some of the things that you have been?"

"Well I was born, that is a good point to start at, in Greensboro, North Carolina [true]."

"How old?"

"Let me see, I was born in 1867 [false]. That makes me 42, almost 43 years old [false], but put it down as 42. As for my ancestors, some of them were governors of the state [true]."

"Did you go to college?"

"No [true]. That is one handicap that I went to this work of writing without. I went to Texas when I was quite a youngster [true]. Delicacy of health and not of purse was the cause of this trip [true]. I spent two and a half years on the ranch of Lee Hall the famous ranger [true]. He was a friend of my family's [false], and I was a guest at his ranch [true]. I was studying the cattle business with the idea of taking it up [false]. Then it quit raining, the pastures dried up, and I quit the cattle and sheep raising business. That's the nearest I ever came to being a cowboy or sheepherder [false]."

"Then," asked the reporter, "what did you do?"

That question evoked a long, long silence. Then O. Henry spoke:

"Why then I got a job on the Houston Post . . ." (False. And not only false, but a real red herring, now beginning the real deception.)

He skipped his entire early Austin experience and mangled his whole Texas experience glibly. He had, he said, started on the *Houston Post* at $15 a week (true) and gotten a raise in two weeks (false) and another raise two weeks later (false).

"What preparation did I have for this work? An academy education [false, it was a one-room, one-teacher schoolhouse] and books [true]. I did more reading between my thirteenth and nineteenth years than I have done in all the years since. And my taste was much better then. . . .

"As a youngster I always had an intense desire to be an artist [true]. It wasn't until I was twenty-one that I developed the idea that I'd like to write [questionable]. After about a year on the *Houston Post* I got an opportunity to exercise both these artistic yearnings. Brann had been publishing his *Iconoclast* at Houston [false, it was Austin] and failed. I bought out the whole plant, name and all for $250 and started a ten page weekly story paper. . . ."

And then he told how he had changed the name of the paper to *The Rolling Stone,* but how after two years he had given it up. Except that the place and time were mixed up, that was about as close to truth as he came in the interview.

So what did he do after *The Rolling Stone?*

"Then a friend of mine who had a little money—wonderful thing that, isn't it, suggested that I join him on a trip to Central America, whither he was going with the intention of going into the fruit business [false, false, false]. Well it takes a long time and it costs a lot of money to learn how the little banana grows. We didn't have quite enough of the latter and so never did learn the whole secret of the banana's development."

"See any revolutions?" asked the reporter.

"No, but I discovered plenty of the finest rum you ever saw [true]. Most of the time I spent in knocking around among the Consuls and the refugees [true].

"The banana plantation faded into nothing [false]. I drifted back to Texas [false]. In Austin I got a job in a drug store [false timing]. That was a rotten two weeks. They made me draw soda water and I gave it up [more or less true]."

"And, after the two weeks at the soda fountain, then what?"

This was difficult. O. Henry threatened to bog down in a morass of falsehood here, for he was dealing with that most difficult period of his life.

"Let me see: after the soda water, I think there came the high ball stage. I went to New Orleans and took up literary work in earnest. I sent stories to newspapers, weeklies, and magazines all over the country [false timing]. Rejections? Lordy, I should say I did have rejections but I never took them to heart. I just stuck new stamps on the stories and sent them out again [true]. And in their journeying to and fro, all the stories finally landed in offices where they found a welcome. I can say that I never wrote anything that, sooner or later, hasn't been accepted [true].

"As for rejections, take 'The Emancipation of Billy,' as good a story as I ever wrote. It was rejected no less than thirteen times. But like all the rest, it finally landed."

And now, O. Henry purportedly told the secret of his pen name:

"It was during these New Orleans days that I adopted my pen name of O. Henry. I said to a friend: 'I'm going to send out some stuff. I don't know if it amounts to much so I want to get a literary alias. Help me pick out a good one.' He suggested that we get a newspaper and pick a name from the first list of notables that we found in it. In the society columns we found the account of a fashionable ball. 'Here we have our notables,' said he. We looked down the list and my eye lighted on the name Henry. 'That'll do for a last name, said I. 'Now for a first name. I want something short. None of your three syllable names for me.' 'Why don't you use a plain initial letter then?' asked my friend. 'Good,' said I. 'O is about the easiest letter written, and O it is.'"

The only trouble with this explanation is that O. Henry was sending out "stuff" for a year before he hit New Orleans. And, during the six years, 1896 to 1902, he used many pen names, and his own name, without any particular regard for subject matter or assessment of quality of the sketch or story.

"A newspaper once wrote to me and asked what the O stands for. I replied 'O stands for Olivier, the French for Oliver.' And several of my stories accordingly appeared in that paper under the name Olivier Henry. [Partly true. The publication was *Ainslee's* magazine.]

"After drifting about the country, I finally came to New York about eight years ago. I have Gilman Hall, now one of the editors of *Everybody's Magazine,* to thank for this fortunate step. Mr. Hall, then the editor of *Ainslee's Magazine,* wrote me saying that if I would come to New York he would agree to take $1,200 worth of stories annually at the rate of $100 a story. This was at a time when my name had no market value [partly true].

"Yes, since I came to New York my prices have gone up. I now get $750 for a story that I would have been glad to get $75 for in my Pittsburgh days [true]."

He spoke then of his writing habits, and his manner of putting together a story, as he had in the past. But he spoke now of something new: "dry spells, sometimes I can't turn out a thing for three months. When one of these spells comes on I quit trying to work and got out and see something of life. You can't write a story that's got any life in it by sitting at a writing table and thinking. You've got to get out into the streets, into the crowds, talk with people, and feel the rush and throb of real life—that's very important for a story writer."

There was absolute truth, and the reason that O. Henry could never settle down to simple domestic life with Sara. He had to be in the streets, visiting the firehouses, talking to the cops on the beat at midnight, dancing with the bargirls in the tourist traps, and boozing with the hoi polloi in the saloons. That was his chosen life. He said otherwise:

"People say I know New York well. Just change Twenty-third Street in one of my New York stories to Main Street. Rub out the Flatiron Building, and put in the Town Hall and the story will fit just as truly in any upstate town. At least, I hope this can be said of my stories. So long as a story is true to human nature all you need do is change the local color to make it fit in any town, North, East, South, or West. If you have the right kind of an eye—the kind that can disregard high hats, cutaway coats, and trolley cars—you can see all the characters in the Arabian Nights parading up and down Broadway at midday."

And with that contradictory paragraph, ending in his admission that New York was his chosen Baghdad, the interview came to its close. He had only one more thing to say.

"I am at work on my first novel. It will be published in the Fall. In this connection you may quote me as saying that it is going to be a good one. I've always had a desire for style. In this novel I'm going to give particularly attention to style, also to character and plot. These really are the essential things in a novel. Tell the world that this novel will be worth a dollar and a half of any man's money."

With this hopeful ending, the interviewer and subject parted company. In his own way, O. Henry had triumphed: He had managed to talk for an hour about himself, without revealing virtually any personal information. The whole Austin years had been ignored, the bank experience, the prison years, even his first marriage and child had been hidden. It was a masterful performance in misleading the enemy, the whole machinery of publicity, ending on a note that had to comfort his new book publishers, Doubleday, Page and Co.

The novel had come into the hands of Doubleday, Page when they picked up all of O. Henry's books from McClure's.

That year, Seth Moyle also arranged with Doubleday to publish *Roads of Destiny,* another collection about the Texas, Louisiana, and Central America days.

But what about the celebrated novel?

O. Henry was not at all well, and in March he wrote Henry Lanier at Doubleday that "I've been ailing for a month or so—can't sleep, &c; and haven't turned out a piece of work in that time."[9]

He was apologizing for not getting any of the novel into Doubleday's hands.

THAT DISABILITY HAD also prevented him from delivering to *Everybody's* a story that was overdue, and consequently he was broke again. He asked for, and received from Lanier, $50 as an advance against the new book royalties.

In spite of all the success, now keeping up two households, one in North Carolina and one in New York, and paying school fees, O. Henry was still having money troubles, and his medical bills were rising.

At this point, even if O. Henry had wanted to go down to North Carolina, he could not. He had put himself in the hands of a new doctor, "a fine tyrant of a doctor, who makes me come and see him every other day and who has forbidden me to leave the city until he is through with me. And then only under his own auspices and direction. My doctor is a miracle worker and promises that in a few weeks he will *double* my working capacity, which sounds very good for me and for him, when the payment of his bill is considered."[10]

He managed to produce three short stories that spring, one for *Collier's* and two for *Munsey's*. Henry Lanier of Doubleday produced some more advances against book royalties, but there was a catch in that arrangement: O. Henry had to be more pliable about publicity.

For the new books and the active promotion campaign that Doubleday planned they needed a photograph of O. Henry. The matter was turned over to Harry Peyton Steger, who had now joined the Doubleday, Page firm. At first O. Henry behaved in his usual balky fashion, but Steger would not take no for an answer, and since so much publicity had already been given O. Henry, including two life drawings in *The New York Times* interview, and since the blackmailing had already come and been disposed of, there did not seem to be any abiding reason to continue to refuse.

As Richard Duffy used to say, "You could always make O. Henry do anything he wanted to do." But in this case, Harry Steger did more.[11]

He set up a photographic session with William M. Van der Weyde, a professional photographer who had all the proper credentials for New York in 1903: neat suit, white shirt, soft collar, bow tie, moustache and Van Dyke.

Van der Weyde, just then, was *the* New York photographer, a fact that meant as little to O. Henry as it did much to Harry Steger. The photographer was eager to take on O. Henry. In fact, he had been asking around the city for the ever more popular short story writer since he had discovered how elusive O. Henry was. So the appointment was set for eleven o'clock the next day.

At about nine o'clock, Steger, who also lived at the Caledonia Hotel went to O. Henry's room. He had, he announced, come to take O. Henry personally to the studio.

Here is Steger's recollection:

"He kicked like a mustang in harness in the first place."

Out of the closet came a salt-and-pepper checked suit, a white shirt with stiff, round collar, and a dark blue silk four-in-hand necktie.

"I was nearly an hour getting him dressed and out on the street, and then an hour was consumed in walking the two blocks to the studio. The last lap of the route, pulling and pushing him up the stairs, was, of course, the worst. My arms ached from it."

O. Henry began the session by announcing that this whole affair reminded him of going to the dentist (which he had just been doing).

Photographer Van der Weyde had been briefed about the manner of coming of O. Henry and what to expect. He had boned up on the author's work on the previous night and could talk knowledgeably about some of the Anchurian stories. Steger joined in, and soon they had O. Henry half forgetting where he was and why. Van der Weyde, in a superior sort of way, spoke Spanish to O. Henry and was surprised to hear it come back to him. Steger, a Texan, then dredged up a handful of "border Spanish" and made O. Henry laugh.

"He had a most delightful and contagious chuckle," said the photographer.

Still O. Henry was tense.

Perhaps, said photographer Van der Weyde to himself, he ought to amuse the author by reciting some of his experiences in trying to find him. He had spent weeks, looking in all the wrong places. But another look at that now stern face suggested this would be a disastrous ploy. Instead, he straddled a straight chair and folded his arms over the back.

"This is a 'comfy' sort of pose," he said. "Let's try it."

So O. Henry sat down in the prescribed position, and Photographer Van der Weyde busied himself under the black cloth of his big plate camera.

Van der Weyde made three or four pictures of the chair pose, and then got O. Henry to lean back in a rocking chair with a newspaper in his hands. In fact, the pose is so artificial it looks as though O. Henry is about to fall over backwards out of the chair, but it was taken, selected by Steger and became the most celebrated photograph of O. Henry ever made.

Van der Weyde took more pictures, including one double exposure that ruined a really fine portrait of the author. When it was all over, O. Henry was visibly relieved, but a few days later when he saw the proofs of the photographs he was pleased, and in his always polite, gentle fashion, wrote a note to Van der Weyde:

"Photographers are not half as bad as dentists, after all!"

THE NEW EASINESS about publicity—not so very easy, really—may have been prompted by sheer inability to cope with argument, for in that early spring of 1909 O. Henry was very sick. One day when galley proofs of the new book were due at Doubleday, he was unable to get up and to his work until 3:30 in the afternoon. But he did get them out, and sent them over by messenger that night.

The months moved along. He managed to put together about a story a month in 1909, but although he kept promising Lanier that first part of the novel, it did not come in.

Quite effectively, O. Henry concealed from Sara the true state of his health. Before she had left for the South, she recalled, he spoke a great deal of being "Oh, so tired," but she had jumped to the wrong conclusions, linking that with what she imagined to be his life outside the apartment. She was right in a sense. His lassitude was an effect of the diabetes, and the alcohol he consumed only made it much worse. But by this time there was really nothing to be done; he would not change his ways. He insisted that all he did was connected with his writing.[12]

In this spring of 1909, the O. Henry finances were becoming more tangled than ever. He was enormously in debt to *Everybody's Magazine,* for Gilman Hall went far beyond the call of editorial duty to support O. Henry in every way. In 1909, *Everybody's* got only two stories from the author, for the thousands of dollars in advances paid out.

O. Henry also got $500 from Charles Belmont Davis, editor of *Collier's,* against the first of five stories about the South promised to that magazine. The rate was to be $750 per story, but the catch was that O. Henry would have to produce them.[13]

Doubleday treated him very well, paying royalties on all his old books at a rate better than had McClure's, and keeping the books in print. Also, they gave him liberal advances. He had $1,665 advanced against the novel this spring, and another $1,250 of general advance.

He had also gotten involved in the writing of a play.

One of the stories O. Henry did for *Collier's*—"To Him Who Waits"—had caught the eye of Harry Askin, a leading play producer in Chicago. He decided it would make a fine musical comedy, and he employed a composer named A. Baldwin Sloane to write the music. He then approached Franklin Pierce Adams (FPA), who conducted the most powerful column in New York newspapers, "The Conning Tower," which ran on the front page of the *New York World.* FPA was instructed to secure the collaboration of O. Henry, and these two babes in the theatrical woods started out to write the book and the lyrics for the music of Mr. Sloane.

Each of the authors was sent an advance of $500, and they set to work, part of the time at Adams's apartment and part of the time at the Caledonia. In April, O. Henry indicated that he was feeling better—not so tired all the time.

His first contribution to the play was the title, the shortest in American theatrical history,

*Lo* from "Lo, the Poor Indian . . ." since the play as it developed turned out to be a study of an anthropological expedition that had gone to Central America to observe the Aztecs.

From there he and Adams went on to write unusual lyrics to A. Baldwin Sloane's music, as they also struggled with the story line.

With the play and with the stories for the magazines, the novel again had to be put into abeyance. The collaboration, conducted in the afternoons, involved a certain amount of liquid refreshment, and although O. Henry had been told often enough by enough people that alcohol was killing him because of his diabetes, he did not slow down his drinking. By the spring of 1909 O. Henry was as busy as his failing health would permit, and eating and drinking with the same old excess and irregularity of the past. The plan for the reformation of the author was completely off the track and he was right back where he had been when the correspondence with Sara Lindsay Coleman had begun.

# 21

# When the Train Ran
# Off the Track

O. Henry did not have a great deal of respect for the people who ran the theatrical business, and until he got involved with FPA in *Lo* he had stayed away from the producers with one or two exceptions. For friends he wrote a little skit that told all:

### Beats a Hollow Tree

All was still in the castle. The villain crept softly to the table and seized the folded paper that lay upon it.

"Ah," he muttered, "Sir Rupert's will! It must be hidden where the eye of man will never discover it!"

Hastening to his room he placed the document between the leaves of an amateur manuscript play and stealing cautiously to the post office, mailed it to a New York manager.[1]

O. Henry's first venture into the theater provided a grueling lesson for him and for collaborator FPA in the difficulties of writing and staging a musical. O. Henry had some talent as a poet, and in his earlier years had written quite a bit of verse, although not for the general market. So it was no great trick for him to think in terms of lyrics. He wrote most of the lyrics for the show, including this song, "Snap Shots":

Watch out, lovers, when you promenade;
When you kiss and coo, in the deep moon shade.

231

When you're close together in the grape vine swing,
When you are a-courting or philandering.
Mabel, Maud and Ann, Nellie, May and Fan,
Keep your eyes open for the Snap Shot Man
Snap! Shots! Hear the shutter close!
What a world of roguishness the little snapper shows!
Click! Click! Caught you unaware—
Snap Shot Man'll get you if you don't care!

The lyrics were not the worst of it by far. Three times the authors labored mightily and produced a script for the producer, and three times it was rejected. Finally, O. Henry wrote a little verse for the delectation of his partner and a few friends:

Dramatization is vexation
Revision is as bad;
This comedy perplexes me
And managers drive me mad.[2]

On the fourth try, they seemed to have it right as far as the producers were concerned, and the play went into rehearsal in Chicago. FPA took time off from his New York duties that summer to go out West and make whatever revisions were necessary. O. Henry remained in New York, working on short stories and dealing with producer George Tyler, who had been after him for several years to write a play. The play he wanted was based on the story "A Retrieved Reformation," the principal character being Jimmy Valentine. The tale itself was, in turn, based on the experience of Jimmy Connors, the safecracker from the Ohio penitentiary days.

O. Henry labored and labored over the transformation of the plot and characters from the printed page to the stage. He did not succeed. Finally, he turned the whole matter over to Tyler with an admission of failure, and Tyler bought from him the dramatic rights. Altogether, O. Henry received $750 for the effort.

In this spring and early summer of 1909, O. Henry was working to change his approach to writing. He wanted to create in the now named novel, *The Rat Trap,* the great American novel:

The "hero" of the story will be a man born and raised in a somnolent southern town. His education is about a common school one, but he learns afterward from reading and life. I'm going to try to give him a "style" in narrative and speech, the best I've got in the shop. I'm going to take him through the main phases of life—wild adventure, city, society, something of the under-world and among many characteristic planes of the phases. I want him to acquire all the sophistication that experience can give him, and always preserve his individual honest *human* view, and have him tell the *truth* about every-thing . . .[3]

He denied that it was going to be autobiographical, but everything above is precisely that. No writer ever depended more on his own life for story than O. Henry, so the novel was, when it came off, going to be very heavily drawn from his own life.

This was all set down in the long letter he wrote to Harry Peyton Steger trying to explain the inexplicable; trying to rationalize what had to be done, when as every editor whoever handled fiction knew, there was no way to do it.

A novel either has that magic element that makes it greater than the sum of its parts or it doesn't. McClure's and then Doubleday were willing to risk advance money on the hope that O. Henry could pull off the novel. O. Henry knew all that. He never finished the letter and he never sent it.

EVER MORE MAGAZINES were calling on O. Henry for contributions, and they were willing to pay his price of $750, including such publications as *The Woman,* published in St. Louis. He accepted them all, but he was unable to perform. By summer he had written only four stories, and these had been pulled out of him, piece by piece by the editors of *Collier's, Munsey's,* and *Metropolitan.* The long-suffering Gilman Hall at *Everybody's* had not had a story since "The Third Ingredient," published in the issue of December 1908.

He was stacking up advances like a woodman stacks up cordwood; the difference was that the cordwood increased in neat piles but the advances dissipated like bourbon poured from a bottle.

*Hampton's* was after him for a story. Editor William Griffiths wrote him in May about it. John S. Phillips of *The American* wrote him a half-funny-half-threatening letter ("Is it all over between us? . . . How would you like this correspondence of yours exhibited in court?") about alibis and undelivered stories against which he had paid advances.[4]

The *Saturday Evening Post* wrote, asking either for the story owed them or the return of the $500 advanced. In June *Hampton's* was again asking for a story. So was *Collier's.*

By midsummer O. Henry was so ill that he could not write at all. He decided to go to North Carolina for a change. When he reached the house in Weaverville and Sara saw him, she knew that he was very, very ill, for he had lost so much weight that his clothes hung loosely on his frame, and his gait was that of a tired old man.

He went to the doctor, a visit he described faithfully in the story "Let Me Feel Your Pulse."[5] Indeed, that story tells of the North Carolina visit that began in the summer of 1909.

He went to see Dr. William Pinckney Herbert, who took a look at him and then asked how long it had been since he had taken any alcohol into his system.

"Oh, quite a while," O. Henry lied.

The doctor then showed O. Henry the effects of alcohol on the human system by giving him a drink and then checking his blood pressure. It shot up. The doctor then pricked his finger and checked the hemoglobin. The count was all wrong. He checked O. Henry's heart. That, too, was all wrong.

Then O. Henry leveled with the doctor. He told him the sort of life he lived in New York.

"I know I smoke too much, keep late hours, and drink too much, but that's about all."

That was enough. The doctor found that he had an enlarged heart, a sick liver, and bad kidneys. What he needed was rest and a complete change of life style.

O. Henry went to a sanitarium. "Neurasthenia" was the polite word for what they said he had. "Chronic alcoholism" was a less polite word, uttered by a few.

He went from one health farm to another, and from the sea to the Blue Ridge. He learned that he had "cirrhosis of the heart, indurated arteries, neurasthenia, neuritis, and acute indigestion." He took medicines for all these ailments, and he cut out the alcohol. He went back to Weaverville and felt so much better that in the story "Let Me Feel Your Pulse" he attributed the "recovery" of his fictional patient to the ministrations of the lovely Amaryllis, who had to be Sara. They took walks in the evenings, and one evening O. Henry threw his arms around her and hugged her.

"It's just like old times, isn't it?" he said.


HE SEEMED TO grow better, as Sara told him. He was able to do a little work, not much, but a little. He opened an office in the American National Bank Building in Asheville. In the last half of the year he produced two stories for *Everybody's* and two stories for *Hampton's Magazine.*

Harry Steger wrote him asking about many bits of business between them. O. Henry replied on November 5.

Dear Colonel Steger:

I'd have answered your letter, but I've been under the weather with a slight relapse. But on the whole I'm improving vastly. I've a doctor here who says I have no physical trouble except neurasthenia (nervous debility) and that out door exercise & air will find me as good as new. As for the diagnosis of the N.Y. doctors (cirrhosis, diabetes, enlarged heart)—they are absolutely without foundation. I am twenty pounds lighter, & can climb mountains like a goat.

About the February Book *(Strictly Business)* if you will send me titles of the stories, I would like very much to select and arrange them. I will do so & return the list the next day after I receive it. There are a few of the stories of the old McClure lot that I don't think should be republished. . . .

And he closed

I think I'll be able to write a novel with each hand simultaneously in a short time.

He got on famously with Sara's relatives and their children. One day he came home from his office complaining of a splitting headache, and said he did not want any dinner. All he wanted was to be left alone. Little five-year-old Peggy Coleman, his wife's niece, followed him up to the bedroom, and when he lay down on the bed she sat in a chair, holding a newspaper upside down.

"What are you doing?" asked O. Henry.

"Don't bother me," said Peggy, aping him, "I'm busy. Can't you see I'm reading."

The exchange was magical, it cured O. Henry's headache and he picked her up and hustled downstairs calling, "What's for dinner?"[6]

That was one side, and many other stories were told by the Colemans of an affectionate friendly man who taught the children how to shoot a .22 caliber rifle, and played word games with them.[7]

But his work was the thing, and sometimes Sara annoyed him when she inquired about it or tried to keep him from overdoing. There were harsh words then, and Sara usually retired from the field of argument, crushed, knowing what was good for him but unable to manage him. No one ever could, she said, and in that many of his editors agreed. His best friends among them had for years been trying to persuade him to slow down. But all they got for their effort was a smile and a call for another drink.

In the summer and fall of 1909 O. Henry was very much in demand. Perhaps the greatest compliment of the summer was a letter from a friend at

Putnam's announcing that one Frank Sweet had stolen "The Reformation of Calliope" almost word for word and sold it to the *Black Cat* as his own, and it was published under the title "The Quicksand Terror."[8] O. Henry laughed.

The McClure syndicate wanted a new series of newspaper stories. Curtis Brown & Massie agency in London sold his stories for French translation.[9]

OFF IN NEW York, Harry Peyton Steger was busily promoting O. Henry's work. His publicity campaign averred that O. Henry was now the most popular short story writer in America, and that his work had to be compared to Balzac's *Human Comedy* as a social history of America.

Off in Illinois, FPA reported that all was as well as could be expected. *Lo* opened in Aurora, Illinois, the Hartford of the West, and the audience seemed to like it. There were the usual dull spots where the laughs were missing, and FPA did some changing of the script. The show then moved out on a fourteen-week tour. It was to end in Chicago, and then if the Chicago stand was successful, the show would come to Broadway.

It went to Waukegan, Illinois, and to Wisconsin, and then to Missouri. Unfortunately it did not arouse as much enthusiasm as it had in Aurora, and on December 5 the whole enterprise collapsed in St. Joseph, Missouri.[10]

Meanwhile, the play that O. Henry had tried to do and failed, had been turned over by George Tyler to Paul Armstrong for adaptation of the O. Henry short story. The new title of the play was *Alias Jimmy Valentine,* and it was a great success. The producer made a small fortune from it and the playwright is reported to have made $50,000. O. Henry got nothing, for he had sold the whole thing, including rights, for less than a thousand dollars.[11]

The success of *Alias Jimmy Valentine* did renew O. Henry's interest in the theater, there was no doubt about that. In 1908 he had promised George Tyler to convert another of his tales, "The World and the Door," to a play. Tyler had gone so far as to say the play was written, and had given an interview to *The New York Times* about the conversion of O. Henry to playwright. But it had never actually come about, O. Henry had never written the play. Now he decided he would do so, and began his labors while in Asheville that fall.

They were not very successful. He was too sick to do very much writing at all. The play languished. The novel was still rolling around in his head, but not on paper. He was doing so little short story work that his income vanished, and he was again begging for advances.

At the end of 1909 the advances ran out. He was so deeply in debt to his various publishers that there was no more money. His one hope, as far as he could see, was George Tyler. He proposed to Tyler that he advance $500, with the dramatic rights to all the O. Henry stories as security. O. Henry would then come up to New York, hole up, and finish the play before he did anything else.[12]

After much negotiation, Tyler finally advanced O. Henry $900 in two parts, and O. Henry left North Carolina for New York once more.

He did not return to his apartment at the Caledonia Hotel, although he kept it. He went to the Chelsea Hotel instead, apparently as he had promised Tyler; he had said he was going to hole up somewhere and no one else would know where he was.

The play was the thing. But he never wrote a line of it as far as George Tyler knew. He did not come to see Tyler or call him. Harry Steger found him one day at the Chelsea, but only because O. Henry had called on him for financial help again to stave off some immediate crisis. When Steger arrived at the hotel in the middle of the afternoon, O. Henry was in his bathrobe in a bedroom of a six-room apartment. They talked. He mumbled about his work. Then Steger left.

All sorts of propositions now came to O. Henry. A dramatic agent, Elisabeth Marbury, wrote asking to represent all his works for the theater. "I know that many of your stories are as available for dramatic use as Jimmy Valentine."

He could not respond. He had mortgaged all his rights to George Tyler for that advance against the play he could not finish.

Steger persuaded Doubleday to buy the publishing rights to *Lo* just at the time that O. Henry was desperate for money. Steger got FPA to sign a release, and sent O. Henry a check for $300. O. Henry turned around and sent the check to FPA.

"Dear Colonel:" Steger wrote O. Henry the next day when Adams reported to him. "I'm very sorry you turned that whole check over to Adams. You're inscrutable. What are you going to do for current money? It was a big thing to do, but O how silly!"

And O, how characteristic of O. Henry to give away his last dollar.

Somehow he survived, largely through the generosity of his old editors.

HE WROTE SEVERAL stories, or rather, parts of several stories. He kept in touch with Sara down in North Carolina, but he did not go home again until March. He was there for a very short time, and then he insisted on returning to New York.

In New York, he spent most of his time in the old haunts around the Madison Square area, the bars and saloons, and restaurants where the girls lined up to fleece the rubes.

He was sick almost every day. He saw a good deal of Ann Partlan at this time, enough to make some close to him believe she was his mistress. He called on her as he would have called on Sara had she been there. He began to think he was going to die, and he told Ann Partlan that he couldn't die because he had so many obligations to pay off. As to what would happen if he did die, he had been asked that question years before: what did he think about the possibility of an afterlife? He had smiled then, and recited a little poem:

> I had a little dog and his name was Rover
> And when he died, he died all over.[13]

But O. Henry recovered from this attack of illness and went back to his old ways, the bars and the whiskey.

Doubleday brought out *Strictly Business,* another collection of New York stories. The reviews were generally very respectful. Here and there came a complaint about the "strain of hurried work." But there was more talk about "his unique gift" and even the complainants spoke of the high quality of some stories, with the hope "that sometime O. Henry will have the leisure to do his best more frequently."[14]

How the author would have loved that time, that leisure, that freedom from worry about money, if he could have had it. For he knew he should be back in North Carolina, walking the trails with Sara and putting aside the pencil and the yellow foolscap, and above all, pushing away the bottle.

But that he could not do. Night after night he roused himself to roam the city as of old. He walked around Herald Square with George Jean Nathan, coeditor with H. L. Mencken of *The Smart Set.* He went up to see Richard Duffy at *Everybody's* and got another advance. Duffy came to see him several times, and little by little, pulled out of him pieces of the story—a story that he said O. Henry could have knocked off in one afternoon in the early years. Now it came to him a page or two at a time.

He had a story due to Dick Duffy and he promised faithfully (as always) to do it. But this time, he meant it.

On the first day he sent a few pages and this letter:

Dear Bill:
    This is for publication, not as good faith. The rest tomorrow if possible—anyhow, a good day's work,

Yours,

Two days later Duffy had this:

My Dear Duffy:

Here is part of the story I was reasonably sure I could have for you by 4 this afternoon. I think you know that it's better both sides not to have it spoiled by hurry. I will send in all the rest of it tomorrow afternoon, and I am sure you will like it.

Yours as ever,

Then, another day went by and this:

Mon Cher Dufe;

Here is some more of the story. I am giving all my attention to the finishing of it. I am rather sanguine of handing you all the rest of it tomorrow. All I can surely promise is that I will put all my time at it until it is completed.

No one could do less—everybody could not do more.

Am pretty sure tomorrow will wind it up. Do the best I can. It will be worth waiting a day longer for, because I think it is a good story.

Yours as ever,

And then finally, at the beginning of the following week:

My Dear Duffy:

Here's all of the story except about 200 words. It will be finished tonight. I am so sick I can't sit up. I'll go home and knock out the rest tonight if I can hold a pencil. I am hugging the radiator with an overcoat on and will be here till about six. You can call me up or come by if you want to.

Sincerely,[15]

And finally he did deliver those last two hundred words.

It was some time before Duffy saw O. Henry after that, and he asked about the author's health.

O. Henry smiled that enigmatic smile of his.

"O I am dying, Egypt, dying," he said.[16]

In the spring, he moved back to The Caledonia. The work went no more easily.

He went up to *Everybody's* several times and got more advances. John O'Hara Cosgrave, the editor, and Associate Editor Gilman Hall tried to persuade him to go into a sanitarium. They did persuade him to go see Hall's doctor, but that did not help.

He knew that he was dying, obviously. *Hampton's Magazine* had given him an advance on "The Snow Man," and the editor was quite insistent about getting all of it. O. Henry had done part, as was now his fashion. The editor sent another writer, Harrison Merton Lyons, to see him at The Caledonia. He found O. Henry sitting in a chair, gaunt and staring. "His neck stood on his collar like a stick in a pond . . ." He had the feeling that O. Henry would never finish the manuscript, and he questioned him about the way the rest of it would go in considerable detail, and he took notes.

ON THE EVENING of June 3, 1910, O. Henry was trying to work in his rooms at The Caledonia. He had been suffering for several days from great difficulty in passing water, and his kidneys had finally given up. In intense pain he called for help, and then passed out on the floor, the telephone beside him.

Dr. Charles Russell Hancock was summoned and came. He revived O. Henry and wanted to call an ambulance and did call for a room at Polyclinic Hospital on East 34th Street. O. Henry insisted that he could make it unassisted, and in spite of the pain, he and the doctor took a taxi to the hospital. He stopped in the lobby of The Caledonia to shake hands with the desk clerk.

At the hospital he insisted on registering under the assumed name Will. S. Parker. They got him into a room and into bed. An emergency operation was performed to tap his bladder and relieve the pressure. Afterward he seemed to be much improved. But the doctor found that O. Henry was suffering from advanced cirrhosis of the liver, kidney failure, diabetes, and "the most dilated heart I have ever seen."

Early on Saturday morning (June 9) Editor John O'Hara Cosgrave of *Everybody's* went to the hospital to see O. Henry. He found him lying in his little room, eyes closed. He looked up, and shook hands, feebly.[17]

"Tell Hall to telegraph at once to Mrs. Porter."

"Does he know the right address?"

"It is . . ."

Just then a nurse and an attendant rushed in, protectively.

"Has he been instructed not to talk?" Cosgrave asked.

"He must not talk to anyone."

Cosgrave turned, then turned back.

"Bill, I'll get Hall to telegraph at once and if it is going to do you any harm to talk, I'll get out."

O. Henry said nothing. Cosgrave went out of the room and down the stairs to the hospital office. There he explained just who the patient really was and that he had entered under an assumed name to avoid press publicity.

He then found Dr. Hancock, who told him that O. Henry was very ill, that he should have been in the hospital days or weeks ago, and that the prognosis was not good.

He then telephoned Gilman Hall, instructing him to telegraph Mrs. Porter. Cosgrave felt that O. Henry's thoughts were on Sara and his daughter then, and that the author did not believe he was going to die.

GILMAN HALL DID telegraph Sara Porter down in North Carolina, and she started north by train.

So, all that could be done for O. Henry had been done.

The relief of the tapping eased his pains but there was really nothing to be done about his condition. His heart had been strained too much by the events of the past few months, and the bohemian life to which he had returned. On Saturday at midnight the nurse came in and turned down the lights.

"Turn up the lights," O. Henry said, "I don't want to go home in the dark."

The nurses and doctors watched him. Dr. Hancock got a little sleep and then came back in the hours of the dawn. It was apparent that O. Henry was slipping away and he knew it. He was perfectly conscious until just two minutes before he died, shortly after 7 A.M., with the morning light streaming through his window.

By the time Sara arrived later in the day, Gilman Hall, Harry Steger, and William Griffith had made the funeral arrangements. O. Henry had once told agent Seth Moyle that he wanted the funeral at the Church of the Transfiguration on East Twenty-ninth Street—the actors and writers church known better as The Little Church Around the Corner.

The O. Henry funeral would have amused the writer immensely: The man had tried to live always in the shadows of New York. When he died, all the stops were pulled out. The pallbearers were Walter Hines Page, the publisher and later ambassador; Richard Harding Davis; John O'Hara Cosgrave; John H. Finley; Don Seitz; and Will Irwin, all notable figures in the world of letters and journalism. And—when the pallbearers began to assemble outside the church just before eleven o'clock on the day of the funeral they were overtaken by a large wedding party headed inside.

"What time is the wedding?" asked pallbearer Irwin.

"Eleven o'clock."

"But that's the time of O. Henry's funeral."

So the wedding party was delayed; they stood around outside the church, chattering in the sunshine, while inside the solemn Rev. George Clark Houghton read the Episcopal service for the dead. Then the church doors were opened and the pallbearers brought the coffin outside as the wedding people streamed in. O, what the absent short story writer could have done with that scene!

And there was one last laugh—not a laugh, really, but one of those ironic smiles with a chuckle that O. Henry used to give when he was amused by some new turn of the wheel: *Hampton's* came out with a grand flourish with "the last story" by the great short story writer—and so did three other magazines almost simultaneously.

# Notes

## 1
### The Blackest Day

1. Letter, B. F. Gray to Controller of the Currency, July 13, 1895.
2. *Ibid.*
3. Letter, R. U. Culberson to the U.S. Attorney General, July 30, 1895.
4. Letter, R. U. Culberson to the U.S. Attorney General, July 21, 1896.
5. Reports of U.S. National Bank Examiners to the Controller of the Currency, for the years 1894, 1895, 1896.
6. Letter, Herman Pressler to C. Alphonso Smith, undated, Princeton University C. A. Smith records.
7. Records of various bank examiners and comments on bank examinations of First National Bank of Austin, Texas, 1895, 1896.

## 2
### Boy, Not Poet

1. C. Alphonso Smith, *O. Henry Biography,* Chap. 1. (Hereafter Smith).
2. *Ibid.,* p. 42.
3. *Ibid.,* p. 60ff.
4. Letter, T. H. Tate to A. C. Smith, Princeton University Library.
5. A. W. Page, "O. Henry in North Carolina," *The Bookman,* July 1913.
6. Smith, p. 78.
7. Smith, p. 79.

8. Letter, J. D. Smith to A. C. Smith.
9. Smith, pp. 71–74.
10. Smith, p. 41.
11. Letter, Col. Robert Bingham to A. C. Smith.

### 3
### Ranchhand

1. Greensboro *Daily News,* Sept. 14, 1969.
2. A. W. Page, "O. Henry in North Carolina," *The Bookman,* July 1913.
3. *Ibid.*
4. Smith, pp. 96–99.
5. *Ibid.*
6. Letter, O. Henry to unknown party, Jan. 6, 1884.
7. Smith, pp. 100–105.
8. Letter, O. Henry to Mrs. Hall, Jan. 20, 1883.
9. Florence Stratton and Vincent Burke, "O. Henry's Own Short Story," *Bunker's Monthly,* July 1928.
10. *Ibid.*
11. Smith, p. 101.
12. A. W. Page, "Texan Days," *The Bookman,* July 1913.
13. *Ibid.*
14. O. Henry, "The Hiding of Black Bill."

### 4
### Oh, That Rolling Stone

1. O. Henry interview, *The New York Times,* April 9, 1909.
2. A. W. Page, "Texan Days," *The Bookman,* July 1913.
3. O. Henry story "Georgia's Ruling."
4. Trueman O'Quinn, "O. Henry in Austin," *Southwestern Historical Quarterly,* Oct. 1939.
5. *Ibid.*
6. *Ibid.*
7. Edmunds Travis, "O. Henry's Austin Years," *Bunker's Monthly,* April 1928.
8. Smith, pp. 120–21.
9. Page.
10. O'Quinn; Page.
11. Page.

12. Smith; Page; O'Quinn.
13. Page.
14. *The Rolling Stone,* various issues.

**5**

**The End of** The Rolling Stone

1. *The Rolling Stone,* various issues.
2. *The Rolling Stone,* Dec. 9, 1894.
3. Letter, O. Henry to James Crane, Dec. 20, 1894.
4. Page.
5. *Ibid.*
6. Smith, pp. 127–28.
7. Smith, p. 136.
8. Report of Federal Bank Examination of First National Bank of Austin, Texas, Feb. 23, 1895.
9. *Ibid.*
10. *Ibid.*
11. Report of Federal Bank Examination of First National Bank of Austin, Texas, July 1895.
12. Report of Federal Bank Examination of First National Bank of Austin, Texas, Dec. 1895.
13. *Ibid.*
14. Department of Justice Files, National Archives; Page.
15. *Ibid.*
16. Smith, p. 129.
17. *Houston Post* files, 1895–96; letter, O. Henry to P. G. Roach, Dec. 1895.
18. *Ibid.*
19. *Ibid.*
20. Department of Justice files, 1896, U.S. National Archives.
21. Wilson, *O. Henry's Trying Years,* p. 194.

**6**

**Honduran Interlude**

1. Letter, O. Henry to P. G. Roach, March 1896.
2. Justice Department files on O. Henry case, U.S. National Archives.
3. *Ibid.*
4. Letter, O. Henry to Herman Pressler, March 10, 1896.
5. Letter, O. Henry to Herman Pressler, April 1896.

6. Letters, O. Henry to Athol, as quoted by C. Alphonso Smith in *O. Henry, Biography,* p. 138: speaking of Honduras; "The freedom, the silence, the sense of infinite peace, that I found here, I cannot begin to put into words." Letters, Al Jennings to A. C. Smith.
7. Smith, p. 142.
8. *Ibid.*
9. Trueman O'Quinn, "O. Henry in Austin."

## 7
## Hard Times

1. Letter, S. S. McClure syndicate to O. Henry, undated, 1897.
2. Trueman O'Quinn, "O. Henry in Austin."
3. *Ibid.*
4. O'Quinn; Smith, pp. 143–45.
5. Letter, O. Henry to Herman Pressler, Jan. 1896.
6. Wilson, pp. 16–17.
7. Department of Justice Records, O. Henry case, U.S. National Archives.
8. O'Quinn. Also Howard Sartin, "Margaret and the Unknown Quantity," *Southern Humanities Review,* Winter 1976. Sartin is the stepson of Margaret Porter Sartin, and heir to O. Henry.
9. Letter, O. Henry to Mrs. Roach, undated.
10. Sartin.

## 8
## Prison

1. Travis, *Bunker's Monthly,* p. 602.
2. Smith, pp. 140–50.
3. *Ibid.*
4. Letter, Dr. John Thomas to A. C. Smith, undated.
5. Letter, O. Henry to P. G. Roach, May 18, 1898.
6. *Ibid.*
7. *Ibid.*
8. *Ibid.*
9. Letter, O. Henry to Mrs. P. G. Roach, undated.
10. Letter, O. Henry to Mrs. P. G. Roach, April 5, 1899.
11. Letter, O. Henry to Mrs. Roach, undated.
12. Letter, O. Henry to Mrs. Roach, July 8, 1898.
13. *Ibid.*

14. Letter, O. Henry to Mrs. Roach, May 18, 1898.
15. Letter, O. Henry to Mrs. Roach, Nov. 12, 1898.
16. Letters, O. Henry to Mrs. Roach, Dec. 16, 1898.
17. Letter, O. Henry to Mrs. Roach, April 1899.
18. Letter, O. Henry to Mrs. Roach, July 8, 1898.
19. Letters, O. Henry to Roaches, 1898–99; Sartin, quoting Margaret Porter in *Southern Humanities Review.*
20. Letter, Alexander Hobbs to C. A. Smith, undated.
21. Letter, Dr. Williard to A. C. Smith, undated.
22. Letter, Dr. John M. Thomas to C. A. Smith, undated.
23. Letter, Dr. Williard to C. A. Smith, undated.
24. Letter, Former guard J. B. Rumer to C. A. Smith, undated.
25. Letter, Dr. Thomas to C. A. Smith, undated.

# 9
## Outside the Wall

1. Letter, O. Henry to Mrs. Roach, Nov. 5, 1900.
2. Jennings, *Beating Back,* pp. 240–48.
3. *Ibid.*
4. Smith, pp. 162–63.
5. *Ibid.*
6. Letter, O. Henry to P. G. Roach, Jan. 1901.
7. Jennings, pp. 243–44.
8. Letter, O. Henry to Mrs. P. G. Roach, May 1901.
9. *Ibid.*

# 10
## The Way Up

1. Stenger, "Some O. Henry Letters," *Independent,* Sept. 5, 1912.
2. Margaret Porter, "My O. Henry," *The Mentor,* Feb. 1923.
3. Letter. Samuel Jamison to C. A. Smith, Smith papers.
4. Letter, O. Henry to al Jennings, quoted by Jennings in *Through the Shadows With O. Henry.*
5. *McClure's Magazine,* April 1904.
6. Letter, O. Henry to *Ainslee's,* winter 1902.
7. Letter, O. Henry to Gilman Hall, undated, Princeton.
8. Richard Duffy much later recalled that he and Hall had promised O. Henry to buy twelve stories in one year at $100 each, but that does not

square with the facts: O. Henry in 1902 was receiving $40–$75 per story. The Duffy recollection came in an article he wrote for *The Bookman* in 1913.

9. Letter, O. Henry to Frank Maddox, spring 1902.
10. Howard Sartin, "Margaret and 'the Unknown Quantity,'" *Southern Humanities Review,* winter 1976.
11. Richard Duffy recollection, *The Bookman,* Oct. 1913.

## 11
### Joining the Four Million

1. Richard Duffy recollection of O. Henry, *The Bookman,* Oct. 1913.
2. *Ibid.*
3. *Ibid.*
4. *Ibid.*
5. *Ibid.* I tracked down the stories from Duffy's minute description of them. All were later sold to other publications.
6. Letters, O. Henry with Orlando Smith, O. Henry collection.
7. *Ibid.*
8. O. Henry to P. G. Roach, July 1902.
9. Duffy recollections.
10. *Ibid.*
11. A. W. Page, "Little Pictures of O. Henry," *The Bookman,* various issues.
12. *Ibid.*
13. Duffy recollections.
14. *Ibid.*
15. Letter, O. Henry to P. G. Roach, July 19, 1902.
16. *Ibid.*
17. *Ibid.*
18. Richard O'Connor, *O. Henry, the Legendary Life of William S. Porter,* p. 103.
19. Robert H. Davis, pp. 200–210.

## 12
### O. Henry's People

1. In April 1909, Reporter George MacAdam of *The New York Times* tracked down O. Henry with the connivance of Harry Steger of Double-day, and persuaded O. Henry to submit to an interview—the only one he ever granted. The result, as noted (Chapter 19), was a compendium of

truth, outright falsehood, and a great number of red herrings, dropped by silence and innuendo. This story of how O. Henry got his name originated here.

2. Duffy reminiscences, *The Bookman,* October 1913.
3. *Ibid.*
4. A. W. Page, "Little Pictures of O. Henry."
5. *Ibid.*
6. Letter, O. Henry to Witter Bynner, undated, Dec. 1902, Harvard collection.
7. Letter, O. Henry to Witter Bynner, undated, Harvard collection.
8. MacAdam interview.
9. Page, "Little Pictures of O. Henry."
10. Travis, "O. Henry in New York."
11. Page, "Little Pictures of O. Henry."
12. Seth Moyle, "My Friend O. Henry."
13. *Ibid.*
14. O. Henry, "An Unfinished Story."
15. Moyle.

## 13
### Making It

1. Sartin.
2. Letter, O. Henry to Witter Bynner, undated, Harvard collection.
3. Davis, *The Caliph of Baghdad.*
4. Thomas Orr, "Office Boy and Caliph," *Liberty,* June 13, 1931.
5. Letter, O. Henry to Witter Bynner, undated.
6. Davis, p. 270ff.
7. Davis, pp. 258–60.
8. Letter, O. Henry to Gilman Hall, Dec. 1903.
9. Letter, O. Henry to Gilman Hall, undated.
10. Letter, O. Henry to Judge Hill, undated.

## 14
### Of *Cabbages and Kings*

1. McClure book company's promotion release for *Cabbages and Kings.*
2. *The New York Times Book Review,* Dec. 17, 1904.
3. *Outlook,* May 16, 1904.
4. Contract between O. Henry and the World Publishing Co., Dec. 1904.

## 15
### Success

1. Davis, p. 275. In the O. Henry papers are several letters that indicate that O. Henry made use of the "agony columns" of the newspapers, answering advertisements from lonely women, and inserting some of his own. In two cases these led to prolonged correspondence, but whether O. Henry was using these for story material or for his personal reasons is really not known. Several times in letters and conversation, O. Henry did indicate a lively interest in young women, in those days before he married for the second time.
2. Davis.
3. Moyle.
4. *Ibid.*
5. *Ibid.*
6. *Ibid.*
7. *Ibid.*
8. Travis.
9. This sort of dialogue drove some members of the literary community almost to distraction. Complaint about this and slang were the two most important negative factors in reviewers' judgments about O. Henry's work.
10. Davis, p. 207.

## 16
### The Slide

1. Letter, Theodore Roosevelt to C. Alphonso Smith, undated.
2. Letter, O. Henry to Gelett Burgess, undated.
3. Letter, O. Henry to Sara Coleman, 1906.
4. Letter, O. Henry to Robert Davis, undated. O. Henry had a habit of dating his letters "Tuesday" or "Saturday" and no more. Often the dates can be estimated by context, and sometimes there are envelopes with postmarks.
5. O. Henry interchange with Editor Davis, in O. Henry papers.
6. Letter, O. Henry to Witter Bynner.
7. Letter, O. Henry to Witter Bynner, Harvard collection. Note lack of date, typical of O. Henry.
8. Letter, O. Henry to W. D. Woode, undated, 1905.
9. Letter, O. Henry to Sara Coleman, summer 1905.

10. Davis, p. 201ff.
11. That O. Henry cocktail recipe was found in his papers.
12. Letter, O. Henry to Witter Bynner, undated.
13. Letter, O. Henry to Gilman Hall, undated.
14. Thomas Orr, *Liberty,* June 13, 1931. This tale of the delivery of "The Gift of the Magi" is told by several people who were associated with the *New York World* at the period, each claiming to be the person involved. Possibly none of them were, but the story persists. Also, it is known from Richard Duffy and Gilman Hall that O. Henry could sit down and write out a story in a couple of hours, and Duffy himself once waited for one in O. Henry's room. So it is probable that there is a modicum of truth in the claim, but the person probably never will be known.
15. Letter, O. Henry to Robert Davis, undated. The hand stamp on the letter, placed there by the accounting department of the *World,* shows that the advance was paid.
16. This letter to Steger was undated and was never mailed. O. Henry did make mention in his correspondence to various editors of "The Novel," but it was always just in passing, and no outline or any "treatment" exists. Probably there never was one. O. Henry's method of composing a short story was to write it out in his head and then transfer it to paper. That would have been much more difficult with a novel, and perhaps that is why he never really got started. He had begun talking about it even before he arrived in New York.
17. From O. Henry's correspondence of the period discussed it is apparent that he found not having a place to call his own extremely distressing and that it affected his work. He mentioned this to several editors as his current excuse for not delivering stories promised to them.

## 17
### Life in the City

1. *Public Opinion,* Oct. 1906.
2. *Watson's Magazine,* Sept. 1906.
3. Travis.
4. William Wash Williams, *The Quiet Lodger of Irving Place,* p. 25ff.
5. *Ibid.*
6. *Ibid.*
7. Davis, p. 362.
8. Letter, O. Henry to Witter Bynner, undated.
9. Letter, O. Henry to Robert Davis, undated.

10. MacAdam interview.
11. Letter, O. Henry to Robert Davis, Aug. 1906.
12. This material about blackmail comes from several sources. O. Henry's friendly editors were constantly amazed at his capacity for spending money. The thought of blackmail had occurred to several of them, particularly Richard Duffy, who sensed very early that O. Henry had a past he wanted to conceal, and by 1906 the secret was really out, following the publication by the *Critic* of O. Henry's picture and the reverberations from Texas. Jennings mentions his conversations with O. Henry on the subject in *Through the Shadows With O. Henry.*
13. Williams, p. 211.

## 18
### Reaching Back for Happiness

1. Letter, Mrs. Charles Anderson to O. Henry, Sept. 1907.
2. Jennings, *Through the Shadows With O. Henry,* p. 314.
3. Williams, p. 206ff.
4. Letter, O. Henry to J. Harrigan, undated.
5. Letter, C. B. Dillingham to O. Henry, Oct. 27, 1906.
6. The negotiations between McClure's and O. Henry are detailed in a series of letters from various McClure's executives to O. Henry in 1906 and 1907.
7. Letters, O. Henry to Witter Bynner, Feb. 1907.
8. Letters, C. B. Davis to O. Henry, April, May 1907.
9. As with many a tale about O. Henry, several different sources claimed to have seen this performance with their own eyes. It may have been apocryphal, but one fact is known: O. Henry sold only one short story to the *Saturday Evening Post* during his entire career, and that long after he had become famous. In his little black book of jottings, the *Saturday Evening Post* appears occasionally as a market to which this manuscript or that was sent, but the only sale was "The Ransom of Red Chief" in 1907.
10. The little black book apparently covered several years of jottings.
11. Letter, O. Henry to Sara Coleman, undated, summer 1907.
12. Letter, O. Henry to Sara Coleman, undated, summer 1907.
13. *The Nation,* Oct. 20, 1907.
14. Letters, O. Henry to William Bradley, Nov. 1907.

**19**

**The Reformation of the Author**

1. Letter, O. Henry to C. Alphonso Smith, undated, 1908.
2. MacAdam interview.
3. Letter, O. Henry to P. G. Roach, undated.
4. Letter, O. Henry to Mrs. Roach, undated.
5. Letter, George Barr Baker to Mrs. W. P. Fuller, Jr., April 5, 1927.
6. *Ibid.*

**20**

**How the Reformers Fared**

1. Margaret Porter, "My O. Henry," *The Bookman,* Oct. 1914.
2. Letter, Sara Coleman to John O'Hara Cosgrave, 1910.
3. Sara Coleman Porter, "The Gift," *Delineator,* May 1912.
4. Jennings, *Through the Shadows With O. Henry,* p. 309.
5. Greensboro *Daily News,* Sept. 14, 1969. In a full-page article about O. Henry and North Carolina, the newspaper reviews O. Henry's life there and quotes various relatives of Sara Coleman who knew O. Henry.
6. Letters, O. Henry to various publishers about publishing projects, especially to Doubleday's Henry Lanier.
7. University of Virginia O. Henry collection.
8. MacAdam interview.
9. Letter, O. Henry to Henry Lanier, undated.
10. *Ibid.*
11. William Van der Weyde, "Photographing O. Henry," *The Bookman,* Oct. 1914.
12. Letter, Sara Coleman Porter to John O'Hara Cosgrave, July 1910.
13. Letter of contract between *Collier's* and O. Henry, 1909.

**21**

**When the Train Ran Off the Track**

1. This little tale was found in O. Henry's papers after his death.
2. Alexander Woollcott, "O. Henry, Playwright," *The Bookman,* Oct. 1922.
3. This again is from the long letter written to Harry Peyton Steger,

explaining what O. Henry intended to do with his novel. But he was so inchoate on the subject that he never sent the letter.

4. These letters, dunning O. Henry for the work he had never produced were saved by the author and appeared in his papers after his death. The implication is very clear: he intended to produce the stories he owed these magazines, and was prevented from doing so only by his long illness, and then death.

5. "Let Me Feel Your Pulse" is hardly a story, more a report of O. Henry's encounters with various agencies of healing in New York and North Carolina. As much as anything he ever wrote it is autobiographical.

6. Greensboro *Daily News,* Sept. 14, 1969.

7. *Ibid.*

8. O. Henry received several letters about the "theft" of that story that appeared in the *Black Cat.* He saved them all, but made no overt effort to do anything about the matter.

9. S. S. McClure himself was the originator of the correspondence over the new O. Henry series for the newspapers syndicate. Curtis Brown was then a London agency, they sold the French translation rights for the ridiculously small sum of one pound, which O. Henry then asked them to donate to their favorite charity.

10. Franklin Pierce Adams sent several reports to O. Henry about the progress of *Lo.*

11. In several letters, George Tyler discusses this play and other plays he hopes O. Henry will do for him.

12. Alexander Woollcott, "O Henry, Playwright," *The Golden Book Magazine,* May 1934.

13. Margaret Porter, O. Henry's daughter, included this little couplet in her reminiscence of her father, which ran in *The Bookman* in 1914.

14. *The New York Times Book Review,* Nov. 17, 1909.

15. Arthur W. Page, "Little Pictures of O. Henry."

16. *Ibid.*

17. Letter, John O'Hara Cosgrave to Sara Coleman Porter, June 12, 1910.

18. *The New York Times,* June 11, 1910.

# Bibliography and Acknowledgments

I am indebted to many people for invaluable assistance in the preparation of this biography of O. Henry. They include archivists, librarians, and the heir to the O. Henry literary legacy, Mr. Howard Sartin, the stepson of Margaret Porter Sartin, O. Henry's only child.

Others, more or less in order of contact, are: Martha George, curator, O. Henry Museum, Austin, Texas; Linda Zezulka and staff of the Austin History Center, Austin Public Library; manuscripts librarians, Randolph-Macon Women's College, Lynchburg, Va.; Richard Shrader, University of North Carolina Library; manuscripts librarians, University of Southern California at Los Angeles; Mills College; The Henry E. Huntington Library, Stanford University; University of California at Berkeley; Beinecke Library, Yale University; Knox College Archives, Galesburg, Indiana; Sarah Taylor, the Lilly Library, Indiana University, Bloomington, Ind.; Giuseppe Bisaccia, Boston Public Library; Minnesota Historical Society; L. Szladits, Berg Collection, the New York Public Library; The Wagnalls Memorial, Lithopolis, Ohio; Dawes Library, Marietta College, Marietta, Ohio; manuscript librarians, Haverford College, Haverford, Penna.; manuscripts librarian, St. John's Seminary, Camarillo, Calif.; Greensboro Public Library; Bill Moore, Greensboro Historical Museum; Duke University Library; Carol Elizabeth Lee, Texas and Local History, Houston Public Library; North Carolina State Division of Archives and History, Raleigh, N.C.; Jean F. Preston, curator, manuscripts, Princeton University Library; James E. Lewis, Houghton Library, Harvard University; Gregory Johnson, University of Virginia

255

Library; and especially Olga G. Hoyt who typed all the letters to all these research organizations and managed the whole correspondence.

The Witter Bynner collection at Harvard University Library contains a good deal of correspondence between Bynner and O. Henry, most of it in the days when Bynner was an editor with *McClure's Magazine* and the same firm's book company.

The University of Virginia Library has a large collection of O Henryana, including many of his drawings, and much written in his own hand. His "little black book," actually several little notebooks of ideas and thoughts and markets is there, and I drew on it for a number of matters.

The Princeton collection of O. Henry material is very large, including items as disparate as bills for Margaret's schooling and manuscripts, and much correspondence. The C. Alphonso Smith papers are here too, and these trace the composition of Smith's "authorized" biography.

Duke University has a number of bits of O. Henry memorabilia, including an entire file on Archibald Henderson's efforts to create an O. Henry memorial in North Carolina.

The Huntington Library in California holds a number of O. Henry materials including some interesting correspondence relative to O. Henry's Honduran period. Frank Vance, Jr., Public Affairs Specialist of the Comptroller of the Currency, Administrator of National Bank was most helpful in providing documents relating to the bank examinations at the First National Bank of Austin, Texas in 1895 and 1896.

## Published Materials

Clarkson, Paul S. *A Bibliography of William Sydney Porter (O. Henry).* Caldwell, Idaho: Caxton Printers, 1938.

Current-Garcia, Eugene. *O. Henry.* New York: Twayne Publishers, 1965.

Davis, Robert H., and Arthur B. Maurice. *The Caliph of Baghdad.* New York: D. Appleton and Co., 1931.

*Dictionary of American Biography.* New York: Charles Scribner and Sons, 1909.

Henderson, Archibald. *O. Henry, A Memorial Essay,* Raleigh, N.C.: Duke University, 1914.

Henry, O. *The Complete Works.* New York: Doubleday and Co., 1928.

Jennings, Al. *Beating Back.* New York: A. L. Butt Co., 1920.

———. *Through the Shadows with O. Henry.* New York: A. L. Butt Co., 1921.

Kramer, Dale. *The Heart of O. Henry.* New York: Rinehart and Co., 1954.

Langford, Gerald. *Alias O. Henry.* New York: The Macmillan Co., 1957.

Long, E. Hudson. *O. Henry The Man and His Work.* Philadelphia: University of Pennsylvania Press, 1949.

Moyle, Seth. *My Friend O. Henry.* New York: H. K. Fly Co., 1914.

O'Connor, Richard. *O. Henry, The Legendary Life of William S. Porter.* Garden City, New York: Doubleday & Co., 1970.

Pike, Cathleen. *O. Henry in North Carolina.* Chapel Hill, N.C.: University of North Carolina Library, 1957.

Smith, C. Alphonso. *O. Henry, Biography.* New York: Doubleday, Page and Co., 1916.

Steck-Vaughn Co., eds. *O. Henry, American Regionalist.* Austin: Steck-Vaughn Co., 1969.

Williams, William Wash. *The Quiet Lodger of Irving Place.* New York: E. P. Dutton and Co., 1936.

Wilson, Lollie Cave. *O. Henry's Trying Years.* Los Angeles: Wetzel Pub. Co., 1935.

## Magazine Articles

Davis, Robert H. "I Go In Search of O. Henry." *The Golden Book Magazine,* April 1930.

Henderson, Archibald. "O. Henry After a Decade." *Southern Review,* May 1920.

Hall, Gilman, *The Bookman,* October 1913.

Irwin, Will. "O. Henry, Man and Writer," *Cosmopolitan,* September 1910.

Johnston, William. "Disciplining O. Henry." *The Bookman,* February 1921.

Maurice, Arthur Bartlett. "About New York With O. Henry." *The Bookman,* September 1913.

*Mentor, The.* Special O. Henry Number. February 1923.
      This includes an article, "The Discoverers of O. Henry"; William Van der Weyde's, "Photographing O. Henry"; Margaret Porter's "My O. Henry.

Nathan, George Jean. "O. Henry in His Own Baghdad." *The Bookman,* July 1910.

O'Quinn, Trueman. "O. Henry in Austin." *Southwestern Historical Quarterly,* October 1939.

Orr, Thomas. "Office Boy and Caliph." *Liberty,* June 13, 1931.

Page, Arthur W. "Little Pictures of O. Henry." (four articles) *The Bookman.* June, July, August 1913.

Richardson, Caroline Francis. "O. Henry and New Orleans." *The Bookman,* May 1914.

Sartin, Howard. "Margaret and 'The Unknown Quantity.'" *Southern Humanities Review,* Winter 1976.

Seibel, George. "O. Henry and the Silver Dollar." *The Bookman,* August 1931.

Steger, Harry Peyton. "On O. Henry's Trail." *Cosmopolitan,* October 1912.

––––––. "Some O. Henry Letters and the Plunkville Patriot." *Independent,* September 5, 1912.

Stratton, Florence, and Vincent Burke. "O. Henry's Own Short Story." *Bunker's Monthly,* July 1928.

Travis, Edmunds. "The Triumph of O. Henry." *Bunker's Monthly,* June 1927.

––––––. "O. Henry's Austin Years." *Bunker's Monthly,* April 1928.

––––––. "O. Henry Enters the Shadows." *Bunker's Monthly,* May 1927.

Woollcott, Alexander. "O. Henry, Playwright." *Golden Book,* May 1934.

## Newspapers

Greensboro *Daily News,* 1969.

*Houston Chronicle,* March 26, 1961.

*Houston Post,* 1895–96.

*The New York Times,* Interview with O. Henry by George MacAdam, April 9, 1909.

*The Rolling Stone,* Austin, Texas, 1894–95.

## Unpublished Manuscripts

Gano, John T. *Sidney Porter—O. Henry,* In Princeton University Library.

Robinson, Celia Myrover. *Uncle Joe and O. Henry.* In Princeton University Library.

Rollins, Ryder, E. *O. Henry, A Critical and Historical Sketch.* In Princeton University Library.

Zuehl, W. E. *The Work of O. Henry.* In Princeton University Library.

# Index